The Promise and Reality of European Security Cooperation

States, Interests, and Institutions

Edited by Mary M. McKenzie
and Peter H. Loedel

Foreword by Ernst-Otto Czempiel

Westport, Connecticut
London

Library of Congress Cataloging-in-Publication Data

The promise and reality of European security cooperation : states, interests, and institutions / edited by Mary M. McKenzie and Peter H. Loedel ; foreword by Ernst-Otto Czempiel.
p. cm.
Includes bibliographical references and index.
ISBN 0–275–95949–X (alk. paper)
1. Europe—Foreign relations—1989– . 2. Europe—Military policy. 3. Security, International. 4. European cooperation. I. McKenzie, Mary M., 1961– . II. Loedel, Peter H., 1965– .
JZ1570.P76 1998
327.1′72′09409049—dc21 97–33705

British Library Cataloguing in Publication Data is available.

Library of Congress Catalog Card Number: 97–33705
ISBN: 0–275–95949–X

First published in 1998

Praeger Publishers, 88 Post Road West, Westport, CT 06881
An imprint of Greenwood Publishing Group, Inc.

Printed in the United States of America

The paper used in this book complies with the Permanent Paper Standard issued by the National Information Standards Organization (Z39.48–1984).

10 9 8 7 6 5 4 3 2 1

Dedicated with deepest affection to the memories
of Wolfram F. and Lani Hanrieder

Contents

Foreword

ERNST-OTTO CZEMPIEL

Of all the burning problems in our world, reordering Europe is the most important one. The old continent had been at the center of the East-West conflict. Its fate today is the center of everybody's attention. Whether the world of the twenty-first century will be marked by cooperation or by confrontation will be decided in Europe. Of course, the Asia-Pacific region is no less important. But Europe offers such a concentration of population and power, of wealth and wisdom, of ingenuity and innovation that for a long time to come it will rank far above all other regions of the world.

Europe's future is also crucial for the foreign policy of the United States. During the cold war, western Europe was the most important ally of the United States; the European Community is the second pillar of the Atlantic Community. At stake now is the integration of central and eastern Europe into the orbit of the western part of the continent. The reordering of this part of the continent will require, as well, a rethinking of the relationship with Russia and the Commonwealth of Independent States (CIS). As a matter of fact, the Eurasian continent waits for a new order.

Not very much has been done in this regard since 1989–1990. The rubble of the East-West conflict still can be seen, and a new comprehensive order is not in the making; NATO and the European Union (EU) will expand eastward, ordering the European space as far as Warsaw, but not as far as Vladivostok. The European Union will deepen, but nobody knows precisely what that means or for whom. The United States keeps its engagement in expanding NATO, but it is doubtful whether a military alliance, even a changed one, can bring order to a political environment in which danger does not derive from military threats but from social unrest, ethnic cleavages, and national policies of states. A new political order must be invented in order to prevent the renaissance of the old European system. The greatest danger for Europe's future is the possible regression to its past.

It is easy to demand a new political order; it is very difficult to conceptualize it. In foreign policy there is no guidebook, no blueprint for the organization of the international state system that would produce meaningful stability and an enduring peace. Traditionally, states after war have prepared themselves for the next one. The first exception to this rule, the United Nations, survived only for three years, to be submerged for four decades. After 1989–1990, the idea of a "new world order" popped up again, accenting once more the United Nations. But it seems that the second try is not faring much better than the first one. For the western powers, NATO seems to be more important than the United Nations. The European affiliate of the United Nations, the Organization for Security and Cooperation in Europe (OSCE), was forgotten shortly after it had been revitalized in 1990. Europe and the world tumble into the future without systematic reflection and meaningful new concepts.

As a consequence, old concepts are being reanimated. In Germany, the "return to normality" has become the official slogan. Of course, Europeans and Americans alike condemn the old notions of balance of power, spheres of influence, and power politics. In practical terms, however, they follow exactly those prescriptions because of the absence of others. Is Europe doomed to inherit its past as its present?

There are alternatives. Political science shows how to escape the temptations and seductions of European *Realpolitik.* For decades, political science has studied the strategies of international politics and has assembled vast amounts of systematic wisdom. Particularly in the United States, there has been much learned about the causes of war and the possibilities for peace. Scholars know very well how "zones of peace" can be established, how violence can be avoided and order created in an international system. Ironically, this knowledge does not enter the realm of practical politics.

There is, also, in Europe a great divide between politics and political science. Scholars confine themselves to the famous ivory tower of academics and universities. Politicians claim a monopoly of political wisdom since politics is their business. The revolving door between politics and political science is open only for persons, not for programs and policy prescriptions.

There have been, and there still are, some scholars who hope to change the nature of this nonrelationship. They seek to protect their scholarly integrity, independence, and neutrality, but they feel obliged to let policymakers and the public share their insights and benefit from their analyses. They translate the results of their scientific research into a language comprehensible to politicians and a broad segment of society. These scholars transgress the boundaries between politics and political science, and they try to fill the great divide.

One of these scholars was Wolfram F. Hanrieder, Professor at the University of California at Santa Barbara. Born a German and grown up an American, he constantly walked the frontiers between the United States and the Federal Republic. Working as a scholar, but wishing to contribute to the American-German friendship, Hanrieder published numerous works on many aspects of the transatlantic relationship. His most important—and last—book, *Germany, America, Europe: Forty Years of German Foreign Policy*, documents his endeavor to analyze, and to explain, how the issue of security is being dealt with in the decisionmaking processes of the Atlantic Alliance.

Written by his friends and former students, this book leads on where Wolfram Hanrieder was forced to leave off. The editors and authors are well-known political scientists, and their book is devoted to a subject dear to Wolfram Hanrieder and crucial for world politics: European security cooperation. It is a scholarly book and utilizes the most current theories and hypotheses in the field to scrutinize the developing European order; it looks into the old school of realism and the new one of institutionalism to find out which is more capable of explaining what is occurring. It submits that the political reality is more complex than a single theory can claim. States follow what they understand to be their national interest. But they do so in an environment marked by levels of interaction and communication, and institutions and cooperation that clearly differentiate it from the environment of earlier centuries that gave birth to the seemingly iron concept of *Realpolitik.*

Reading this book will facilitate the understanding of what is going on in Europe. The book is valuable for students and politicians alike. By thoroughly analyzing the structures and processes at work in European security, the book offers many deep insights into the problems of the developing "security architecture" in Europe. This volume will be of great value for political scientists, but it could be useful for politicians, diplomats, and publicists as well.

The authors and editors of the volume see themselves as intellectual heirs of Wolfram Hanrieder, and correctly so. Many of Hanrieder's findings have found their way into this book. The intricate relationship between domestic and foreign policies, for instance, colors all contributions; Hanrieder's concept of compatibility (with the external environment) and consensus (with the domestic society) is used as a key to more thorough description and deeper understanding of the decisionmaking processes in Europe. The authors develop these concepts further, elaborate on them, and refine them. They add what has been discovered recently and what is being discussed in the field.

The intention to honor Wolfram F. Hanrieder has thus stimulated a very modern and extremely interesting book that is as timely as it is profound. Because of its professionality, it will enrich the scholarly debate; it could also enlighten the public discussion. The volume does not bridge the two realms and remains on the bank of political science. However, it should be read by the decisionmakers in the United States and in Europe. They could learn what security means under present conditions, and they could be encouraged to look for modern solutions to security, not to fall prey to the old ones. The volume offers political science at its best, and thus the best advice politics can get.

Abbreviations

ACVS	Armored Combat Vehicles
ATTU	Atlantic to the Urals
CDE	Conference on Disarmament in Europe
CEE	Central and Eastern Europe
CFE	Conventional Armed Forces in Europe (Treaty)
CFE-IA	Supplemental Agreement on Conventional Armed Forces in Europe (limiting personnel)
CFSP	Common Foreign and Security Policy
CIS	Commonwealth of Independent States
CJTFs	Combined Joint Task Forces
CPC	Conflict Prevent Center
CSBMs	Confidence- and Security-Building Measures
CSCE	Conference on Security and Cooperation in Europe
CSO	Committee of Senior Officials
CWC	Chemical Weapons Convention
EAPC	Euro-Atlantic Partnership Council
EC	European Community
EMU	European Monetary Union

EPC	European Political Cooperation
ESDI	European Security and Defense Identity
EU	European Union
EUROFOR	European (land) Force
EUROMARFOR	European Maritime Force
FAWEU	Forces Answerable to WEU
FRG	Federal Republic of Germany
FSC	Forum for Security Cooperation
FSU	Former Soviet Union
GATT	General Agreement on Tariffs and Trade
HCNM	High Commissioner on National Minorities (OSCE)
IFOR	Implementation Force (Dayton Accords)
IGC	Intergovernmental Conference (EU)
IMF	International Monetary Fund
INF	Intermediate-range Nuclear Forces
MAD	Mutual Assured Destruction
MBFR	Mutual and Balanced Force Reduction (talks)
NAC	North Atlantic Council
NACC	North Atlantic Cooperation Council
NATO	North Atlantic Treaty Organization
NNA	Neutral and Nonaligned
NPT	Non-Proliferation Treaty
ODIHR	Office for Democratic Institutions and Human Rights (OSCE)
OECD	Organization for Economic Cooperation and Development
OEEC	Organization for European Economic Cooperation
OOV	Object of Verification
OSCE	Organization for Security and Cooperation in Europe (formerly CSCE)
PEST	Pan-European Security Treaty
PfP	Partnership for Peace
SFOR	Stabilization Force (follow on to IFOR)
START	Strategic Arms Reduction Treaty
TEU	Treaty on European Union
TLE	Treaty Limited Equipment

U.N.	United Nations
UNHCR	U.N. High Commissioner for Refugees
UNPROFOR	U.N. Protection Force
VD90	Vienna Document 1990
VD92	Vienna Document 1992
VD94	Vienna Document 1994
WEAO	Western European Armaments Organization
WEU	Western European Union
WTO	Warsaw Treaty Organization
WTO	World Trade Organization

1

Introduction: States and Institutions in European Security

MARY M. MCKENZIE AND PETER H. LOEDEL

The end of the cold war brought with it high hopes for fundamental change in the shape and nature of European security. Perhaps best symbolized by the 1990 Paris summit of the Conference on Security and Cooperation in Europe (the CSCE, now the OSCE), many analysts and leaders believed that a European order that had been characterized by conflicting interests and bipolarity could give way to a more cooperative security framework based on common interests and truly "interlocking" institutions. The blueprints for such an order variously included the creation of a regional collective security system based in part on the CSCE; an enlivened pace for the integration and enlargement of the European Union (EU) and its proposed defense arm, the Western European Union (WEU); a radically altered or even diminished role for NATO; a more significant role for the European pillar in the transatlantic security context; and increased efforts at arms control.

Despite these high hopes, the European security environment remains characterized by a striking mix of continuity and change—the continuity of national interest amidst a changing institutional context and a shifting security landscape. New conflicts, old tensions, and geopolitical uncertainties have muted the calls for a new security "architecture" that would include all of Europe.[1] Although some change has been made, the hopes for an invigorated institutional security framework for Europe remain unfulfilled. National interests, institutional inertia, and new sources of threat have combined to foster only incremental adjustments in the overall structure of European security. It is in this context that we are interested in explaining the forces shaping European security cooperation in the post-cold-war era.

To set the stage for the individual contributions that follow, this chapter explores two general themes of the book: one, the role of states and the concept of national interest; and two, the role of institutions and cooperative security in the processes of European security cooperation. We posit these two sets of concepts as antipodes of state behavior. National interest suggests a state-centered approach whereby states act on interests resulting from the distribution of power. Acting in the national interest may require unilateral action. On the other hand, cooperative security suggests an institution-centered approach in which national interests are replaced by collective interests. States depend on cooperation with other states to meet security needs, fostering the institutionalization of security cooperation and multilateral processes of conflict resolution. These themes will be addressed more fully in each author's case study of European security cooperation.

For our purposes here, we first argue that states conceptualize their own understanding of security and seek to provide a level of security commensurate with their perceived national interest. Second, each state's definition of security is not determined in an institutional vacuum. Rather, a broader definition of security often must incorporate existing and possibly new institutional arrangements. As a result, an analysis of European security cooperation involves the integration of both state-level and institution-level concerns.

With this focus, the following chapters enter a lively debate within the field of international relations and address one central theoretical question for understanding security cooperation: how is European security cooperation shaped? Are traditional conceptions of state power and national interest adequate to explain post-cold-war developments in European security institutions? In other words, does the theoretical tradition embodied in realism hold? Or, as neoliberal institutionalists would suggest, are institutions having an independent effect on interstate cooperation in the security realm, acting as a constraint on behavior and helping to define interests in the same way as the distribution of power does?[2] Insofar as they have done this, do they represent a move toward truly collective interests, a security community among European states?

Theoretically, then, as this emphasis on "national interest" and "states" and on such concepts as "cooperative security" and "institutions" suggests, we allow for a broad range of focal points and approaches in the following chapters in order to present a wide array of interpretations that focus on the role of states and institutions. National interest and cooperative security offer two very different explanations for security cooperation in Europe, and this is what we seek to address. If we are to construct a security framework for Europe for the 1990s and beyond, understanding the dynamic between national interest and cooperative security within the institutional framework of European security is necessary.

So, too, is understanding the role of the political processes within states. Just as the system of European security has been undergoing change, so have the domestic political arenas of European states. National security and conceptions of national interest as articulated in the domestic arena cannot be divorced from the constraints and influences of the international and institutional arena within which European security policy takes place. A state's conception of interest will be grounded not only in the norms of the state system but also in the norms and politics of its society. This is why the authors are concerned with the connection between domestic and international affairs, a linkage Wolfram F. Hanrieder viewed as crucial to understanding states' foreign policies.[3]

In sum, the primary objective of this volume is to assess the challenges of rebuilding European security institutions and to analyze the processes of security cooperation in the context of the changing security environment in Europe. As they have sought to address the challenges of the Balkans, the transitioning nature of European integration and the transatlantic relationship, and the changed security environment of central and eastern Europe and Russia, security institutions have undertaken reforms that have reflected aspects of both national interest and the increased pressures of security interdependence.[4] Although security interdependence—where states are dependent for their security on cooperation with other states—was recognized by some authors in the realm of cold-war nuclear politics,[5] we are interested to see whether it is more viable now with the emergence of new types of threats. We seek to determine if and when new or existing structures and processes of European security cooperation will emerge and how they will be shaped to meet new challenges. There have been numerous volumes concerned with the changes in European security, but few have addressed the dynamic interplay between state interests, institutional restructuring, and a changing security environment as this work does.[6]

This chapter applies these concepts and issues to the European arena, the concern of this book. First, the chapter sketches the broad contours of the changes in the European security environment. The next section elaborates our focus on states and national interest by introducing the countries included in this volume. Third, the chapter turns to the role of European security institutions in fostering cooperation by presenting the Organization for Security and Cooperation in Europe (OSCE), the North Atlantic Treaty Organization (NATO), and the Western European Union (WEU). This introduction concludes by outlining the individual essays in the book.

THE CHANGING NATURE OF EUROPEAN SECURITY

With the demise of the cold war, the collapse of the Berlin Wall, the disintegration of the Soviet Union, and renewed ethnic conflict at its center, Europe is faced with new challenges that have led some analysts to predict a reversion "back to the future."[7] The adversarial relationship of the cold war led to a concentration of western security efforts on military power, based on a traditional notion of collective defense aimed at the Soviet Union and its allies. The strategy of containment was devised and implemented to protect the vital interests of the transatlantic community from the Soviet threat. Wolfram F. Hanrieder insightfully argued that postwar U.S. policy was actually based on double containment: the containment of the Soviet Union at arm's length, the containment of Germany with an embrace.[8] For over forty years, this was a stable system.[9] However, bipolarity no longer characterizes Europe's place in the global system, and containment of the Soviet Union has lost its logic. New and difficult choices face the leaders of Europe and the transatlantic community as they rethink the shape that European security should take and the strategies upon which it should be based.[10]

What characterizes the European security order in the post-cold-war era? The most notable and obvious change to the European security order is the end of bipolarity, requiring a fundamental rethinking of the relationship between East and West. The effects of this change were felt early in the decade as the Warsaw Treaty Organization dissolved in 1992, leaving NATO without an adversary and as the only defense organization in Europe. The end of bipolarity has highlighted directly the dynamic interplay of national interest and institutions, as the mission of containing the Soviet threat has dissipated. Although the processes of NATO and EU enlargement are meant to project stability in the emerging European landscape, the prospects are growing that they will instead create new lines of demarcation. A residual "us versus them" mentality conflicts with the institutional goal of projecting stability through integration. There is a contradiction between the institutional forces and motivations behind enlargement and the continued distinctions made based on national-level considerations about who "fits" these institutions.

The end of bipolarity has not only affected the relationship between former adversaries, but it has also required a reorientation among allies within existing institutions. An asymmetrical dependency[11] is being transformed with potentially significant consequences for the international system as a whole. Does the post-cold-war era reflect a "unipolar moment"?[12] Or are we instead witnessing a rebirth of a multipolar system in which Europe (some would argue, Germany alone) is one of the magnetic poles? Can the European allies "go it alone" in the security sphere? The answers to these questions are central for the transatlantic relationship and continued American engagement in Europe (and elsewhere). Again, the dynamic interplay between national interest and European security interdependence will determine the outcome of the debate over the emerging international structure.

Intra-European relations have also been affected by the end of the cold war, especially by the unification of Germany in 1990. After all, as Hanrieder's notion of "double containment" suggested, containment had a European function. The processes of German unification led to a renewed push toward European political union. The Maastricht Treaty envisaged a sort of united states of Europe with a common European currency (the euro) and the eventual inclusion of a purely European defense and security component under the umbrella of the Western European Union. Germany and its allies shared the priority of preventing the renationalization of German security policy. At the same time, these institutions are expanding, pushing Europe's division eastward. The role of Germany as an economic giant but political dwarf may be changing, but Germany's reliance on economic diplomacy promises to remain at the forefront of its foreign and security policy. Among Germany's allies, the critical role of France is central to the new security order in Europe. France has searched for a new role within both existing European and transatlantic institutional structures and within newer multilateral and institutional frameworks in Europe. At the same time, French leaders continue to emphasize traditional Gaullist tendencies toward security policy independence and cast a wary eye toward their powerful neighbor. Of particular importance to European security will thus be the relations of these two nations to each other and within the institutional framework of Europe.

Not to be neglected, the relations among the former Warsaw Pact states are also currently characterized by the contradictory forces of national interest and European institutional developments. First, among the Visegrad states of central Europe, there have been attempts to create real cooperation. This has taken the form of the Visegrad Treaty for economic and political cooperation as well as plans for a Central European Free Trade Area. Second, the demise of the Brezhnev doctrine lifted the lid on centrifugal pressures and has resulted in the collapse of the structures of the WTO and the rebirth of ethnic conflict in many parts of Europe and central Asia. Although many of these states have sought to redefine their national interests with their newly found sovereignty, they are at the same time pounding the doors for integration into the institutions of the West, from the World Trade Organization to the Organization for Economic Cooperation and Development (OECD) to the Council of Europe to NATO and the European Union.

In their search for economic stability and security, the states of central Europe have expressed a renewed interest in pan-European security structures and the promise of collective security.[13] This is not only because of the security that inclusiveness might perpetuate, but also because of the nature of new security threats and the perceived ability of collective security to deal with them. An increased emphasis on conflict prevention and crisis management in Europe reinforces a security conception grounded in concerns for individual rights, economic stability, and democracy.

However, one event explains the diminished hope for the success of anything resembling a collective security system in Europe: war in the former Yugoslavia. Not only was the United Nations (the global collective security organization) unable to ameliorate the conflict; but the Europeans, too, were unable to construct a successful European security policy. Further, the lack of commitment of the United States in the conflict until summer 1995 betrayed a lack of interest in Europe, which some regarded as worrisome for the long-term transatlantic relationship. Collective security in Europe would require cooperation and speedy mobilization of resources during or immediately following an act of aggression, something the international community was not predisposed to pursue in the former Yugoslavia. In short, collective security foundered on national interest. Many scholars remain unconvinced and unimpressed with NATO's role in providing a lasting security arrangement for the former states of Yugoslavia, as the foundations laid in the Dayton Peace Accords are viewed as less than sturdy. Despite the end of the cold war, security in Europe remains an elusive quest for some states and an unfulfilled promise for others. Economic instability, slow advances toward democratic reform, ethnic conflict, and huge numbers of displaced persons are among the new sources of insecurity in Europe.

In this environment, state policies and European security institutions are being molded to accommodate new and changing circumstances. One scholar has noted that the problems facing analysts and policymakers today match those of the immediate postwar period, when the European system was created from the rubble of World War II. Similar tradeoffs must now be made among foreign policy objectives, between foreign affairs and domestic affairs, and between nonmilitary and military policy instruments.[14] Moreover, the cold-war emphasis on a militarized conception of security blinded scholars to other definitions and dimensions of security, including economic competition, immigration, democracy, and human rights. In the post-cold-war era, these are emerging as *national* security concerns, as state leaders redefine the very notion of security in an environment in which the goal of security is increasingly just one of many public policy goals competing for attention and resources. The goal of national security is undeniable and should not be factored out of any understanding of European security cooperation or the use or reformulation of security institutions. The debate about the meaning of security and the transformation of the international system thus are interrelated and are integral to analyzing the institutional preferences of states.[15]

Our objective, of course, is to understand how such state-level concerns for, and definitions of, security and national interest compete with the norms of security cooperation reflected in European security institutions. The nations of Europe are, in some way, all interested in European security, although they may disagree as to what exactly it is, what it should look like, and how it might come to be assured. Nonetheless, the goal of European security, encompassing territorial integrity, economic and political stability, and perhaps even the protection of human rights and some mix of existing or future European or transatlantic institutions—including the European Union, NATO, the OSCE—is shared by all participants. How these institutions are molded to provide the coordination of military means, diplomacy, information exchange, and economic statecraft is a key to understanding the future of European security cooperation, as is an understanding of norms and expectations promulgated by these institutions. The nature of security in Europe today reveals powerful continuities of institutional action and the assertive role of national-level state interests among the discontinuities of the changing security environment. How these powerful forces interact will determine the outcome of European security cooperation.

THE ROLE OF STATES

The cold-war paradigm of security rested on the prerogatives of national interest in a bipolar conflict. The relevance of the precepts of realism and *Realpolitik* can hardly be questioned in this context. The adversaries of the cold war sought to one-up each other in the battle of armaments as states became overridingly preoccupied with the premise of military security. Under the cold-war paradigm, states were engaged in a long-term struggle for survival. While military alliances and collective defense provided some modicum of structure to the international system, for realists, the United States and the Soviet Union were largely self-reliant when it came to their particular security needs. Not surprisingly, deterrence theory, military statecraft, and arms control became the topic of much scholarly attention and focused on these two countries and their struggle for control over the European and global arenas. Some European scholars and politicians did not share this view, but the basic proposition that the United States and the Soviet Union dictated security issues in Europe remained the dominant realist mode of analysis in both countries.

One could contend, as institutionalists do, that the end of the cold war should put an end to the overreliance on the militarized notions of national security as well as the emphasis placed on the nation-state and the concept of national interest. Many scholars believe realism—with its basis in these ideas—failed to predict the end of the cold war; as a result, the focus on realist concepts and definitions should be relegated to the theoretical dustbin.[16] However, the contributors to this study are not entirely convinced of the merits of discarding some of the underlying foundations of realism's focus upon the state and national interest that have informed international relations theory. In fact, the end of the cold war may have heightened the role of states and their understandings and conceptualizations of national interest, especially as the presupposed basis for their security cooperation—the cold war—has disappeared. States will be central actors in devising a new security architecture for Europe, even if security has taken on a broader meaning and value for many of these states. European security cooperation and the institutions providing the structure for such cooperation will be shaped in large part by the interests and actions of states. To deny otherwise would be analytically reckless and misleading.

Arguably, the United States and Russia remain the key states in determining the outcome of the debate over European security: the United States as the only power with a global reach; Russia because of its ability to threaten its neighbors and to thwart attempts at institutional change. European security cooperation may, in fact, ultimately be determined by the actions of these two actors. Regardless of the outcome of reforms in European or transatlantic institutions, the interests of Russia and the United States—based on the interplay of domestic and international politics—will be crucial to any and all security debates in Europe. These two actors must be emphasized in any account of the developments of European security cooperation. In sum, size and power still matter.

When looking at the complex issue of state interests and European security cooperation, a central question is the American commitment to Europe. Although perennially questioned, this commitment is once again central to discussions of European security, almost as though the cold war commitment of the United States was the historical exception rather than the historical rule. This, however, takes too narrow a view of the relationship.[17] Nonetheless, the current leadership in the United States has taken as one of its lessons of the George Bush presidency that more attention should be focused at home and less abroad. Although more recent foreign policy initiatives of the Clinton presidency have been deemed successes and suggest that his lack of Euro-enthusiasm has been reversed,[18] the undercurrent of pulling back is reflected in the fact that the United States has downsized its military deployment in Europe to 100,000 (from 300,000), and has emphasized that its continued commitment in Yugoslavia will remain limited in duration. The deployment of the Implementation Force (IFOR) and the Stabilization Force (SFOR) in Bosnia and the recent decisions taken to strengthen NATO may have put the concerns about the U.S. commitment temporarily to rest, but the United States arguably has had the most difficulty of the states under consideration in redefining security in Europe beyond a collective defense paradigm, where such a paradigm is linked to a restrictive definition of national interest.

For many scholars and policymakers, the realization that stability in Europe is impossible without Russian stability suggests a leading role for Russia in constructing the new European security architecture. The uncertainty and unease surrounding Russia's 1996 presidential election and the questionable health of President Boris Yeltsin have highlighted Russia's centrality as well as the importance of the success of domestic reform in Russia for European security. Russia retains a negative influence over European security developments—the power to make things *not* happen. Its instability and its remaining nuclear capability make Russia a state to contend with. For their part, Russian leaders are concerned by the West's policy preferences of enlarging western institutions to Russian borders, while excluding it from these processes. Russia's preferred institution, the OSCE, in which it is included as an equal partner, is relegated to a secondary security role by other—western—states.

Of course, the Europeans together and separately are in a position to be more assertive about defining their own security interests. Unified Germany is now able to participate in multilateral military missions under the umbrella of international security organizations. This is, in effect, a recognition of the legitimacy of national interests, a concept the Federal Republic had shied away from during the cold war. "National interest" is no longer a dirty word in the German vocabulary.[19] However, it is also important to recognize that during the cold war, and in its wake, Germany receives its international legitimacy—some would say its very identity—from its active participation in these international institutions and therefore views the role these institutions can play in central and eastern Europe as crucial to Europe's stability.[20] Despite outward signs of reluctance, France is making its way back into NATO after the bluster and poor diplomacy of on-and-off-again nuclear testing, defining its preferences more in terms of inclusion over exclusion, and also recognizing that NATO is increasingly the only game in town. You will have more influence if you are involved than if you are sitting on the sidelines, it seems to be realizing.[21]

Together the Europeans have made efforts to build a defense and security arm of their own, which may or may not become a European pillar of the alliance. The aptly titled Intergovernmental Conference (IGC) of 1996–1997 showed an inability to overcome the original hesitation of many member states to empower the EU as a supranational body in the foreign and security policy realms. In this very real sense, security cooperation is different than economic, monetary, legal, and social policy. Despite the functionalist quality of some of the debates and negotiations surrounding the IGC, the *Realpolitik* of state action and national interests has prevailed in the security arena. Again, to discount this possibility would be irresponsible to any comprehensive analysis of the changing nature of European security cooperation.

From this very brief sketch, it can be seen that the states involved in shaping European security efforts define the nature of security and their interests in Europe and European security institutions differently. This was obvious in the inability of these allies to agree on a policy in Bosnia before American engagement in summer 1995. If these factors dominate in shaping the European security order, then the realization of collective or even more cooperative security interests and policy will remain elusive. This means that security institutions will remain purely intergovernmental in structure, leaving nothing to the vagaries of an indeterminate notion of institutionalism.

THE ROLE OF INSTITUTIONS

From the above analysis, it is evident that states are shaping European security and its institutions based on their own national or vital interests.[22]

What is not clear is whether and how institutions shape state interests and definitions of security, or how they impact state preferences. Can we specify the conditions under which institutions have an impact on state priorities and European security cooperation? Can institutional reform and change in European security lead to the redefinition of security interests on the part of states, whereby multilateralism might be seen as an integral component of security policy? In short, can and do institutions matter?

A brief word is in order about what we mean by institutions. Although most of our cases involve international organizations, our definition is broader than this would suggest. International institutions are defined here as persistent and connected sets of rules, both formal and informal, that prescribe behavioral roles, constrain activity, and shape the expectations of participating actors. This is similar to the textbook definition of regimes utilized in regime theory, but we seek to emphasize the way in which the treaty-based rules of such institutions shape European security cooperation. Of particular interest in the security realm is whether and how institutions gain the "institutional power" that legitimizes the decisions taken within them.[23] The question of these chapters, then, is not whether institutions in and of themselves promote peaceful behavior (a focus of much of the institutionalist literature), but whether they are forcing states to redefine security interests and compelling security cooperation. By looking at the changes that have been made to accommodate the post-cold-war era, we can judge if these institutions have increased interstate cooperation in the security realm, and whether this cooperation is based on a conception of security that transcends the national level. We might find that this depends on the role each institution is playing in the emerging security order in Europe. An interesting phenomenon has occurred that might be described as "institutional competition," whereby these organizations are creating a division of labor and staking out their own turf, instead of constructing a web of interlocking institutions.[24] Is security interdependence relevant in some areas, but not in others? Why are some institutions "more equal" than others?

In short, we conceptualize institutions in terms of both dependent and independent variables. In looking at them as dependent variables, we are interested in explaining why and how states would construct and support institutions. Under what conditions do states benefit from cooperation provided by institutions, and can we expect states to construct and support such institutions when they do benefit? Is there a difference in how states approach this question in terms of economic and security issues? As independent variables, international institutions are themselves shaping the security interests of states, and we are interested in explaining how they foster European security cooperation. Do the rules and norms of various European and transatlantic security institutions guide the actions of states? If the international structure is shifting so rapidly, why do institutions persist and why do they continue to provide a forum for cooperation in European security? Again, our purpose is to analyze the dynamic interplay of state interest and institutional engagement.

As a brief introduction to European security institutions, a few generalizations about the reform and potential roles of the OSCE, NATO, and the WEU follow. As noted above, the first institutional signpost to a new European "architecture" was the 1990 Paris summit of the Conference on Security and Cooperation in Europe. Renamed in January 1995 to the Organization for Security and Cooperation in Europe (OSCE), this organization has undergone significant institutional change. With the end of the cold war, the CSCE was seen by many as the logical institutional home for collective security in Europe because of its pan-European scope and its broad conception of security. Many leaders, especially in the Soviet Union (and later Russia), but also in the Federal Republic of Germany, lay special emphasis on building the capacities of the CSCE in the traditional security realm (from the highly proscribed arms control role during the cold war).

Although there was some early discussion of equipping the CSCE with its own peacekeeping forces, by 1992 this had given way to a relationship with the United Nations (as a regional arrangement of the global organization) and a reliance for peacekeeping forces on WEU, NATO, or even CIS troops, although the modalities of such arrangements were far from clear. There would be no independent military capabilities for the OSCE. Its "market gap" is seen instead in the interrelated arenas of conflict prevention and the protection of human rights. The tasks and missions of the OSCE have underlined its role in these "pre-"military (or "soft") functions, as is shown in its many missions to parts of Asia and its role in Bosnia.[25]

One might argue that the OSCE is based on a recognition of security interdependence among states. The OSCE continues to play an important role in arms control and confidence- and security-building measures. The successful conclusion and implementation of such measures aim to enhance the OSCE's role in preventive diplomacy and strengthen member states' commitments to the norm of renunciation of force. In other words, these regimes are meant to shape interstate behavior among members. The OSCE had its first success in this realm in 1986, and work on CSBMs continues as a focus of the Forum for Security Cooperation (FSC), created in 1992.

NATO's role has also undergone dramatic change as it has been compelled to redefine its mission in Europe. Although the focus of much attention on NATO in the new security environment has been on its policy of enlargement, its institutional changes have been more comprehensive than this focus suggests. NATO began its changes in 1990 and continues through this writing.

NATO extended the "hand of friendship" to the states of the former Warsaw Treaty Organization (WTO) in London in 1990, but the most fundamental changes in NATO's strategy and relationship with the East occurred at the summits of 1991 (Rome) and 1994 (Brussels). The two most important results of the Rome summit were the adoption of the New Strategic Concept, guiding military contingencies in post-cold-war NATO, and the creation of the North Atlantic Cooperation Council (NACC) with the Declaration on Peace and Cooperation. The 1991 Strategic Concept claimed to recognize a "radically different" strategic environment.[26] Although the heart of NATO remains its commitment to collective defense in the face of an armed attack on one or more of its members, elements of change were also unveiled in the Strategic Concept, including steps away from forward defense and flexible response (nuclear weapons became weapons of last resort), and toward smaller forces with increased flexibility, which would include the development of rapid reaction forces. Its involvement in the former Yugoslavia opened yet another new chapter and encroaches further on the OSCE's domain of conflict prevention and nation building.

Arguably, NATO's changes reflect a broadened definition of security. Not only does this definition include political and military aspects of security, but it also has a multidimensional risk conception, including economic instability, proliferation of weapons of mass destruction, terrorism, and the supply of critical resources. In fact, now "it is difficult to distinguish NATO's enlarged mandate from the overall approach of the Conference on Security and Cooperation in Europe."[27]

Structurally, NATO began to create mechanisms for the integration of the states of central and eastern Europe and the former Soviet Union and to develop a more operational European pillar within the alliance. With the task of containing the Soviet Union gone, the North Atlantic Cooperation Council (NACC) and the Partnership for Peace Program (PfP) were created to accommodate the desires of the former Warsaw Pact states to join the alliance, although many believe that their purpose was actually to delay such admittance and again to usurp the OSCE's role. However, at its summit in Madrid in 1997, NATO issued its first invitations to new members and created the Euro-Atlantic Partnership Council (EAPC) to enhance cooperation with all partner states.

An independent European pillar was given new shape with NATO's concept of Combined Joint Task Forces (CJTFs). CJTFs are meant to widen "the role of Europe in the alliance"[28] and were conceptualized in 1994 and agreed to at NATO's summer 1996 meetings. CJTFs allow NATO (as an organization) to opt out of a mission while allowing its resources and technology to be used by the WEU. The stated goal of this program is to foster the defense identity of the Europeans without duplication of effort, under the motto of "separable but not separate" forces. Although many at first believed this meant that the WEU would have carte blanche over these resources, in fact, the North Atlantic Council will decide on any mission. This program has developed slowly, but its goal is to allow the eventual integration of even non-NATO states into operations under the command of CJTFs.[29]

The precise role of the Western European Union under CJTFs, however, remains unclear. The WEU, created in 1955, lay dormant until the mid-1980s, when it was rejuvenated by the French, German, and British governments. The 1987 Hague "Platform on European Security Interests" espoused a dual role for the WEU: to provide Europe's security identity and to serve as the bridge between NATO and the European Community.[30] In the Maastricht Treaty, the WEU was given a central role in creating the defense identity of the European Union, including the "eventual framing of a common defense policy." In the Declaration accompanying Maastricht, WEU members outlined the three areas with which WEU needed to be concerned: relations with the European Union; relations with NATO; and building up its own operational capabilities.[31] At the same time, WEU members pledged to work toward developing a European security identity that was "compatible" with the common defense provided by the Atlantic Alliance.[32] Although the WEU's treaty expires in 1998, no real progress was made at the 1996-1997 IGC toward delineating the relationship of the WEU to the EU or toward the development of a common European defense.

Although the WEU already had been active in missions involving global security concerns in the late 1980s (in the first Gulf conflict), the most significant signpost to a new WEU military role came in summer 1992, at a meeting that resulted in "the Petersberg tasks." Meeting in Germany, WEU members agreed that the WEU could go out of area (unlike NATO at the time) in order to meet the new challenges to European security. These included humanitarian and rescue operations, and peacekeeping and crisis management missions. (This made the WEU a more difficult fit for the Federal Republic of Germany, due to its lingering constitutional hesitations.) Like NATO, the WEU now participates in humanitarian or peacekeeping missions under the auspices of the United Nations or the OSCE—operations that are also seen as the most likely candidates for CJTFs.[33] Some are concerned that a division of labor between NATO and the WEU may be emerging, whereby NATO would be responsible for tasks falling under collective defense obligations, and the WEU would be prepared to undertake the "Petersberg" missions with the benefits of NATO resources, if necessary.[34] This concern was substantiated by the outcome of the EU's Intergovernmental Conference.

These changes reflect a mixture of continuity and change underlying the roles of these institutions. But has the way security is conceived in Europe and among the member states also been transformed? Do these developments represent steps toward a security community where the norm of consultation becomes more relevant for the future of NATO than the norm of collective defense?[35] Do they reflect a growing interdependence in the security realm? Or can we explain developments in European security simply by looking at the interests and policy priorities of the most interested and powerful states? The chapters that follow will more thoroughly address the implications of these changes and what they portend for the future shape of European security.

THE DESIGN OF THE BOOK

One of the primary objectives of this project, then, is to assess the challenges of rebuilding European security institutions in the context of a changing European security environment in the 1990s. Without an overly intrusive theoretical framework, the contributions address the balance between sovereign state interests and institutional influence in defining and meeting the challenges of European security cooperation. The following chapters do not share a conviction on the feasibility of particular security institutions or arrangements in Europe, nor do the authors all agree on the conceptual utility of national interest or cooperative security. However, the authors share a recognition that states *and* institutions are currently shaping European security policy and have a desire to ascertain what matters and when.

The chapters that follow apply these ideas and concepts to individual states and institutions in European security. In chapter 2, Steve D. Boilard begins the section on state interests by focusing on the continuing significance of double containment for an American policy that has lost its coherence. Sabine Huebner-Monien addresses the importance of interest and identity formation in understanding Russian policies toward European security institutions in chapter 3. In chapter 4, Peter H. Loedel analyzes Germany's changing role in European security institutions and suggests that a broader conceptualization of security may provide the basis for a more secure European framework. Robert Ladrech closes the section on individual states with an examination of French policy toward European security institutions under the Gaullist leadership of Jacques Chirac. The volume turns to institutions of European security in chapter 6, in which Mary M. McKenzie addresses the hesitant construction of the European pillar. In chapter 7, Richard E. Rupp and McKenzie explain the unique pan-European and mediating role of the OSCE. Graeme P. Auton attempts in chapter 8 to elaborate the vast linkages that exist among regimes and institutions in European security with a special eye toward the arms control realm. In chapter 9, Rupp applies the concepts of national interest and institutionalism to the Balkan conflict. He illustrates the difficulties facing European security cooperation under the full-scale assault of military conflict, power politics, and divergent interests. Finally, in chapter 10, Loedel and McKenzie summarize the findings of these studies, attempting to answer what matters and when in determining the shape of European security cooperation.

This book is dedicated with deepest affection to the memories of Wolfram and Lani Hanrieder.

NOTES

1. See Ronald Asmus, "The Rise—or Fall?—of Multilateralism: America's New Foreign Policy and What it Means for Europe," in *European Security and International Institutions after the Cold War,* ed. Marco Carnovale (New York: St. Martin's Press, 1995), 153–176.

2. See Thomas Risse-Kappen, *Cooperation among Democracies: The European Influence on U.S. Foreign Policy* (Princeton: Princeton University Press, 1995).

3. Wolfram F. Hanrieder, *Germany, America, Europe: Forty Years of German Foreign Policy* (New Haven: Yale University Press, 1989); also idem, "Compatibility and Consensus: A Proposal for the Conceptual Linkage of External and Internal Dimensions of Foreign Policy," *American Political Science Review* 61, no. 4 (1967): 971–982.

4. See Gene Lyons on the tensions between interest and security interdependence in the U.N. context in "International Organizations and National Interests," *International Social Sciences Journal,* no. 144 (June 1995): 261–276.

5. See "Epilogue" in Wolfram Hanrieder's *Germany, America, Europe.*

6. A few of the key studies on European security are Christoph Bertram, *Europe in the Balance: Securing the Peace Won in the Cold War* (Washington, DC: Carnegie Endowment for International Peace, 1995); Beverly Crawford, ed.,

The Future of European Security (Berkeley: U.C. Center for German and European Studies, 1992); James Sperling and Emil Kirchner, *Recasting the European Order: Security Architectures and Economic Cooperation* (Manchester: Manchester University Press, 1997); Catherine McArdle Kelleher, *The Future of European Security: An Interim Assessment* (Washington, DC: The Brookings Institution, 1995); Jonathan Dean, *Ending Europe's Wars: The Continuing Search for Peace and Security* (New York: Twentieth Century Fund, 1994).

7. John Mearsheimer, "Back to the Future: Instability in Europe after the Cold War," *International Security* 15, no. 1 (Summer 1990): 5–56.

8. Wolfram F. Hanrieder, *Germany, America, Europe*, 6.

9. See John Lewis Gaddis, "Looking Back: The Long Peace," *The Wilson Quarterly* 13, no.1 (Winter 1989).

10. Gary Geipel discusses the necessity of choice in the German case in "Germany and the Burden of Choice," *Current History* 94, no. 595 (November 1995): 375–380.

11. Thomas Risse-Kappen, *Cooperation among Democracies.*

12. Charles Krauthammer, "The Unipolar Moment," Foreign Affairs 70, no. 1 (1991).

13. The central contributions to the collective security debate include Charles A. Kupchan and Clifford Kupchan, "Concerts, Collective Security, and the Future of Europe," *International Security* 16, no. 1 (Summer 1991): 114–161; Richard K. Betts, "Systems for Peace or Causes of War? Collective Security, Arms Control, and the New Europe," *International Security* 17, no.1 (Summer 1992): 5–43; Thomas Weiss, ed., *Collective Security in a Changing World* (Boulder, CO: Lynne Rienner Publishers, 1993).

14. David Baldwin, "Security Studies and the End of the Cold War," *World Politics* 48 (October 1995): 117–141.

15. On the need for distinguishing between national and vital interests and a discussion about what this means for interstate cooperation, see Marco Carnovale, "Vital and National Security Interests after the End of the Cold War," in *European Security and International Institutions after the Cold War*, ed. Marco Carnovale, 1–18.

16. Central contributions to this debate include Robert Jervis, "The Future of World Politics: Will It Resemble the Past?" *International Security* 16, no. 3 (Winter 1991); John Lewis Gaddis, "International Relations Theory and the End of the Cold War," *International Security* 17, no. 3 (Winter 1992); Charles W. Kegley, "The Neoidealist Moment in International Studies? Realist Myths and the New International Realities," *International Studies Quarterly* 37, no. 2 (June 1993): 131–146; Richard Ned Lebow, "The Long Peace, the End of the Cold War, and the Failure of Realism," *International Organization* 48, no. 2 (Spring 1994): 249–277.

17. Miles Kahler and Werner Feld, *Europe & America: A Return to History* (New York: Council on Foreign Relations Press, 1996).

18. Ronald Asmus, "The Rise—or Fall?—of Multilateralism."

19. On these developments and how they reflect a changing conception of Germany's role, see Mary M. McKenzie, "Changing Conceptions of Normality in the Post-Cold-War Era: Germany, Europe and Foreign Policy Change," *German Politics and Society* (Summer 1996).

20. See William E. Paterson and Simon Bulmer, "Germany in the European Union: Gentle Giant or Emergent Leader?" *International Affairs* 72, no. 1 (January 1996).

21. On the recognition of this dilemma in the French context, see Steven Philip Kramer, *Does France Still Count? The French Role in the New Europe* (Westport, CT: Praeger, published with the Center for Strategic and International Studies, 1994); and Thomas Risse-Kappen, *Cooperation among Democracies*, pp. 225ff.

22. Ernst Haas, *When Knowledge Is Power: Three Models of Change in International Organizations* (Berkeley: University of California Press, 1990).

23. Michael C. Williams, "The Institutions of 'Security'" (paper prepared for the annual meeting of the International Studies Association, San Diego, CA, 16–20, April 1996).

24. Ibid.

25. Alexander Moens and Christopher Anstis, "Failures of the First Round," in *Disconcerted Europe: The Search for a New Security Architecture*, ed. Alexander Moens and Christopher Anstis (Boulder, CO: Westview Press, 1994).

26. See Michael Legge, "The Making of NATO's New Strategy," *NATO Review* 39, no. 6 (December 1991): 9–14. The unchanged fundamentals are "the purely defensive purpose of the alliance; the indivisibility of Alliance security; the collective nature of Allied defense; and the crucial importance of the transatlantic link." Indeed, some argue that the Strategic Concept and the new NATO are not at all new. See Alexander Moens, "The Formative Years of the New NATO: Diplomacy from London to Rome," in *Disconcerted Europe,* ed. Moens and Anstis, 24–47.

27. See Werner Bouwens et al., "The OSCE and the Changing Role of NATO and the European Union," *NATO Review* 41, no. 3 (June 1994): 21–25.

28. "Europe to Widen Its Role in NATO," *Los Angeles Times*, 4 June 1996, A1; see also Charles Barry, "NATO's Combined Joint Task Forces in Theory and Practice," *Survival* 38, no. 1 (Spring 1996): 81–97.

29. See the "Ministerial Meeting of the North Atlantic Council Held at NATO Headquarters, Brussels, on 1 December 1994," Press Communiqué M-NAC-2(94) 116.

30. For the text of the Platform, see Alfred Jean Cahen, *The Western European Union and NATO* (London: Brassey's, 1989). On the history of the WEU, see also Clive Archer, *Organizing Europe: The Institutions of Integration* (London: Edward Arnold, 1994), ch. 10.

31. For the WEU's assessment of its progress in these areas, see "WEU Contribution to the European Union Intergovernmental Conference of 1996," Press and Information Service of the WEU, 14 November 1995.

32. See Clive Archer, *Organizing Europe*, 248.

33. On these developments, see Willem van Eekelen, "Die Position der WEU in der Europäischen Sicherheitspolitik," 3 December 1993, mimeo.

34. See Nicole Gnesotto, "Common European Defense and Transatlantic Relations," *Survival* 38, no. 1 (Spring 1996): 19–31; see also Jose Cutileiro, "WEU's Operational Development and Its Relationship to NATO," *NATO Review* 43, no. 2 (February 1995), web edition.

35. See Thomas Risse-Kappen, *Cooperation among Democracies.*

2

From Double Containment to Double Vision: The Fragmentation of America's Europe Policy in the Post-Cold-War Era

STEVE D. BOILARD

For much of this century, the European political order has depended on the United States. Notwithstanding polite diplomatic fictions about collective security, and despite the repeated efforts of the Soviets and sometimes the French, Washington's troops, nuclear weapons, intelligence-gathering networks, and diplomatic efforts have been the sine qua non of European security and stability. What began in 1917 as an "expedition" and returned in 1941 as a "final assault on tyranny" in the mid-1940s became an open-ended American commitment to European stability and west European security. As years and then decades passed, the Atlantic Alliance became a fixture, indeed the centerpiece, of American foreign policy. Turning the Monroe Doctrine on its head, America became a European power.[1]

America's commitment to this new transatlantic alliance was cemented with the North Atlantic Treaty in 1949. Then, almost exactly forty years later, the primary threat against which NATO was founded evaporated. Some saw the collapse of communism in eastern Europe in the fall of 1989 as more damaging to NATO's long-term prospects than, say, a victory of communism in western Europe. The president of the United States himself proclaimed the end of the cold war and the advent of a new era in which the bipolar imperative and the doctrine of containment would not pertain. In fall 1990, President George Bush envisioned the possibility of a new world order, "freer from the threat of terror, stronger in the pursuit of justice, and more secure in the quest for peace, an era in which the nations of the world, East and West, North and South, can prosper and live in harmony."[2]

Although this vision has not yet come to pass, the new world order, such as it is, represents the fulfillment of virtually all of the goals that had been articulated in connection with America's containment policy in Europe: the "rollback" of Soviet influence in eastern Europe, the "liberation" of the east European peoples, the unification of Germany "under a democratic federal state within the framework of a European association,"[3] and "the break-up or the gradual mellowing of Soviet power."[4] Of course the extent to which each of these events, and the particulars surrounding them, is attributable to the intentional policies and actions of Washington is open to debate. But the fact is that, unlike so many of America's domestic and foreign policies, its containment policy was finally abandoned because its explicit goals were achieved. How might this bear upon America's future role in European security institutions?

DOUBLE VISION

Wolfram Hanrieder was fond of the saying that when God wants to punish, he gives us what we ask. The undeniable western triumphs that collectively constitute the end of the cold war have not ushered in Bush's new world order. More precisely, they have not created a world order, or even a European order, that Washington considers entirely suited to America's interests. President Bill Clinton was faced with this reality shortly after taking office in January 1993. While the Clinton administration came up with labels to replace containment ("enlargement") and to reject isolationism ("engagement"), Washington has been slow to devise a security policy concerning Europe. Some degree of transitional turbulence is inevitable, of course, as the conclusion of the cold war, and particularly the demise of bipolarity, suddenly and fundamentally altered the international balance of power and the geopolitical face of Europe. And yet America's post-cold-war Europe policy suffers from a more visceral condition: the inability to define the country's fundamental interests vis-à-vis Europe. Instead, America's policymakers and public alike stumble about in search of meaning, alternately embracing and rejecting military, economic, ideological, and moralistic definitions of security and interests. The resultant policy develops segmentally and discordantly, responding to the perceived issue of the moment and changing public moods. It has neither long-term vision nor internal consistency. It is, in a word, incoherent. And this may be even more damaging than American isolationism to European security.

America's Europe policy in the 1990s thus stands in sharp contrast to that in any other decade since World War II. Although the four decades of the cold war experienced their own fluctuations and inconsistencies, American policy through most of this period was grounded in a basic commitment to the principles of containing Soviet power and protecting America's sphere of influence in western Europe. Together, these goals fell under the general rubric of containment. But it was not merely the Soviet Union that was being contained; America simultaneously sought to circumscribe the expansion of postwar German power. There resulted a cohesive, mutually reinforcing foreign policy doctrine that Wolfram Hanrieder termed "double containment." For Hanrieder, double containment's elegance came from its utilization of the very same set of institutions (primarily NATO, but also GATT, the OEEC, and even the EC) to lock out the Soviets and lock in the West Germans. In Hanrieder's words, double containment provided for "the containment of the Soviet Union at arm's length, and of West Germany with an embrace."[5] The doctrine helped to preserve peace on the Continent for almost half a century.

The unanticipated collapse of the Soviet sphere of influence in eastern Europe in 1989, and the demise of the Soviet Union itself in 1991, fundamentally altered the two primary targets of double containment. The Federal Republic of Germany absorbed the German Democratic Republic, and the Soviet Union disintegrated into its fifteen constituent republics. In subsequent years, the security institutions of Europe have been rapidly changing in an effort to accommodate the new geopolitical landscape. It is no secret that Germany and Russia remain the two Continental powers most critical to the creation of a stable European order. Yet how these two newly transformed countries, with their respective geopolitical appetites and their histories of global conquest, are to be integrated into the new European order is still not clear. Until the European equivalent of Bush's new world order arrives, might America's good offices still be required in Europe?

Alas, the United States has not been able to articulate, let alone act upon, a coherent strategy to replace double containment. Instead, one sees evidence of what might be termed "double vision," whereby Washington simultaneously holds two different visions of Europe. One vision bears a resemblance to Europe at the time of the Monroe Doctrine: a continent conflicted by petty rivalries, diplomatic intrigue, regional military clashes, and other home-grown problems neither of consequence to America's interests nor worth the expenditure of America's treasure and blood. The competing vision sees Europe as it was in the early twentieth century: a geostrategically imbalanced collection of states whose nationalistic and ethnic rivalries threaten to ignite regional conflicts and Continental wars that could harm America's trade and security interests. This second vision also occasionally takes on a somewhat paternalistic cast, portraying Europeans as unable to conduct their affairs without the benevolent leadership of the United States.

The two visions of Europe are not easily reconciled, but this seems to trouble neither American public opinion nor the policymakers in Washington. Instead, there emerges from these two visions an attitude that seems to demand for America a leadership role in Europe, while simultaneously seeking to extract the country from the international responsibilities that go with such a role. This double vision thus promotes an untenable combination of engagement- and isolation-oriented policy choices. Following this prescription is likely to be salubrious for neither America nor Europe.

THE RELEVANCE OF THE UNITED STATES TO EUROPEAN SECURITY

Despite the unprecedented economic integration and military collaboration achieved by western Europe during the cold war, and despite the pan-European cooperation that has been developing since the lifting of the Iron Curtain, Europe is currently unable to provide for its own stability and security. There are three primary reasons for this.

First, Russia remains a very real and powerful threat to Europe. Although frequently viewed as history's victim in Europe's wars, Russia has a tradition of foreign intrigue, a broad glacis along Europe's eastern flank, an enormous, if poorly managed, nuclear arsenal, and a tenuous political environment. To be sure, Soviet President Mikhail Gorbachev and his successor, Russian President Boris Yeltsin, have worked to integrate Russia with Europe. Gorbachev sought a European political order that corresponded with his vision of a "common European home," and now Yeltsin calls for a "politically, economically and spiritually unified architecture for our continent, which must not isolate countries or groups of countries or separate them according to the criteria of friend or enemy."[6] But post-cold-war developments in Europe, particularly the former Warsaw Pact states' efforts to join NATO and the mounting social and economic dislocations among the Russian population, give rise to fears of Russian revanchism. The electoral successes of Communist and nationalist parties in Russia, the Russian parliament's unwillingness to ratify the START II Treaty, its insistence on renegotiating the CFE Treaty, and its statements about "countering" NATO expansion give some substance to concerns about Russia's relationship with Europe.

Considering the country's size, arms, political instability, and history, Russian power must be balanced. The Continent's next largest power, Germany, has forsworn nuclear weapons and thus is limited in its ability to serve a balancing role. France and Britain possess their own national nuclear forces, but these are inadequate to serve as a deterrent to, say, Russian adventurism in the Balkans or east central Europe. Although France has suggested that its *force de frappe* might eventually be "Europeanized," extending to Germany and perhaps beyond, this has encountered resistance from various quarters—not least the German Left—and in any event appears to be more a symbolic goal than a significant augmentation of nuclear strength.[7] Meanwhile, the incorporation of the east central European states into NATO, discussed at the May 1997 Madrid Summit, will not begin for several years at the earliest, and even then there are questions about extending Article V guarantees east of Germany. Despite the end of the cold war and the demise of bipolarity, therefore, only America can balance Russian power.

The second reason for Europe's inability to provide a self-contained European security arrangement stems from long-standing political obstacles. Despite over four decades of western European economic integration, European powers remain divided on numerous defense, political, and strategic matters. Efforts to create a European Security and Defense Identity (ESDI), though at times energetic, have produced little in the way of concrete results. The favorite locus for an ESDI traditionally has been the Western European Union (WEU), virtually stillborn in 1948 but periodically subject to resuscitation efforts to make it either a potential defense arm of the EU/EC or a "European pillar" of NATO. In the wake of the cold war's demise, the WEU issued its 1992 Petersberg Declaration, committing itself to peacekeeping and humanitarian aid on the Continent. But with neither a clear European consensus on the specific role and structure of Forces Answerable to the WEU (FAWEU), nor a firm commitment of NATO assets for WEU-led operations, the WEU remains a nebulous and subaltern entity.

Meanwhile, European efforts to pursue a Common Foreign and Security Policy (CFSP) within the EU have foundered on the same "deepening versus widening" debate that has plagued other objectives of the 1991 Maastricht Treaty. The ability of individual member states to veto CFSP initiatives is especially problematic. And the most recent candidate for giving substance to an ESDI—the concept of Combined Joint Task Forces (CJTFs) made up of European NATO (and perhaps some non-NATO) troops operating outside of direct U.S. command—is clearly subordinate, not an alternative, to NATO.[8] At best, the CJTF concept appears headed toward the role of "contingency operations," and not the actual defense of European NATO members.

Giving military expression to an ESDI thus hangs up largely on Europe's inability to develop a consensus on the particulars of its security arrangements. The irony is that the same phenomenon that seemingly provided the opportunity for western Europe to take more leadership in its own security—the end of the cold war's logic of bipolarity—has also reduced the ability of the western European countries to work together, instead allowing the reemergence of regional disputes and a reassertion of distinct national interests. Without the focusing power of the Soviet threat, which was infinitely starker than the current Russian threat, national interpretations of European security interests are drifting apart. The concept of a cohesive European defense "identity" thus becomes defined too broadly to provide a meaningful underpinning for a self-contained European defense posture.

What is lacking in the post-cold-war European security environment, therefore, is European leadership. And for the moment at least, only the United States can provide a substitute. Not only has Washington remained the dominant voice in NATO, but it has also provided decisive leadership in addressing post-cold-war European conflicts—notably in former Yugoslavia. This leadership did not materialize without hesitation, of course. During the Bush and early Clinton administrations, Washington accepted Europe's contention that the civil war in Bosnia was a European problem. But after it became evident that Europe could not or would not sufficiently address this problem (and, significantly, after the United Nations demonstrated its own impotence in the region), the United States, through NATO, provided the first effective response to the genocide and war in the Balkans. Then, at Dayton, the United States was able to broker a reasonably effective, if imperfect, political settlement among the warring factions. In 1997, Europe again demonstrated its inability to coordinate a military response to regional unrest—this time in Albania. Meanwhile, American leadership continues in such matters as NATO expansion, developing a NATO-Russia charter, and creating a Central European Nuclear Weapon Free Zone.

For the foreseeable future, American leadership is simply indispensable on the Continent. In the words of former British Prime Minister Margaret Thatcher, the post-cold-war European order can be stable only if

> the Atlantic Alliance remains, in essence, America as the dominant power surrounded by allies which, in their own long-term interest, generally follow its lead. Such are the realities of population, resources, technology, and capital that if America remains the dominant

partner in a united West, then the West can continue to be the dominant power in the world as a whole.[9]

The third primary reason that Europe cannot provide for its own security hinges on economics. For a variety of reasons, the peoples and governments of Europe are unwilling to take on the full expense of self-security, even if it were politically and militarily feasible. Although America has sought to redirect some of the costs of European security back to Europe through the principle of "burden sharing," European security remains significantly subsidized by the United States. Despite optimistic proclamations at Maastricht about the implementation of a CFSP, the EU as an entity and its individual members have displayed an unwillingness to back up the concept with funding.

Indeed, individual governments are working to reduce, not expand, their defense budgets. Britain has cut its defense spending by about a fifth since 1990, and one could expect to see these cuts deepened under the Labour government. Germany cut its combined postunification forces from 670,000 troops to 340,000, and its defense budget has been the target of the country's subsequent austerity program. France, Italy, and Spain have also worked to cut defense spending. Most west European countries now spend between 1.5 and 3 percent of their GDPs on defense.[10] Meanwhile, due to its infrastructure and defense budget, the United States remains by far the world leader in weapons technology, intelligence-gathering capabilities, and various other aspects of military security.[11]

It is not simply a matter of burden sharing across the Atlantic; the various countries of the EU continue to fight over the apportionment of financial costs, military contributions, defense contracts, and decisionmaking responsibilities. The introduction of these interstate political issues into Europe's defense procurement can result in inferior weapons systems being purchased at above-market prices.[12] And the widening of the EU will only exacerbate these difficulties. All this bodes poorly for Europe's ability to create an adequate, self-contained regional defense posture.

In summary, America provides the nuclear umbrella, the diplomatic leadership, and the financial underwriting for European security. Some Europeans have long resented the second of these. Now many Americans are questioning the other two.

AND THE RELEVANCE OF EUROPEAN SECURITY TO THE UNITED STATES

Although Americans predictably challenge their country's involvement in most regional crises, be it Bosnia or Somalia or Haiti, America's commitment to Europe, at least *western* Europe, is almost never challenged. The experience of War II and America's international coming of age during the cold war have lent to the transatlantic relationship an almost organic quality that is wholly revisionist in its ignoring of the Monroe Doctrine and the bitter battles over whether Europe was worth the trouble in 1917, 1941, and even 1945–1946. Instead, Americans are viscerally linked to Europe, considering it to be either America's sphere of influence or the home of fellow westerners.

Yet the sense of fraternity and paternalism that undergirds Americans' attitudes toward the Europeans dissipates as one moves eastward across the Continent. By the time Sarajevo is reached, Americans, while expressing dismay about the inhumanity of ethnic cleansing, question whether American interests can be served in peacemaking there. The issue of American interests in eastern Europe deserves frank and honest discussion. But, particularly after the cold war, so does the issue of American interests in western Europe.

Questioning America's interests in western Europe is almost heretical, given the centrality of the region to America's postwar foreign policy. But an honest evaluation of the transatlantic alliance in the new world order requires a fresh examination of how America's interests are defined. America's Europe policy during the cold war was founded upon a vaguely defined, tactically shifting amalgam of military, economic, and ideological interests, all somehow figuring into an umbrella concept called national security. Expressions of each set of interests are well represented in the warp and woof of the cold war. In the early postwar years, before the advent of Mutual Assured Destruction (MAD), the balance of power in Europe was critical to preventing the Soviet Union from acquiring the means to overwhelm the United States—hence, the Truman Doctrine. America's launching of the Marshall Plan, its sponsorship of the Bretton Woods Monetary System, and its support for the OEEC/OECD derived in large part from U.S. economic interests. And frequently suffusing all of this was Washington's claim to be supporting freedom and democracy—a slippery mission fraught with ambiguity.

How do these three bases of American interests in Europe fare in the post-cold-war era? Given the collapse of Soviet power and influence, it would be a stretch to say that Russia poses a credible threat to American territory. But clearly the domination of Europe by any country—most probably Russia or Germany— would threaten America's ability to project power in critical parts of the globe. America, like Britain before it, has considered a united Continent to be virulent to the global balance of power, and it is the fear of such a global imbalance, more than a concern for the Europeans themselves, that is likely to resonate with Americans. If the United States worried about "fortress Europe" when the European Community was perceived (prematurely, as it turned out) to be on the verge of full economic integration in the 1980s, imagine the reaction to a Continent under the hegemony (economic, political, or otherwise) of Berlin or Moscow. Again, this writer does not consider such outcomes to be looming on the horizon. But this is precisely because of the continuing effects of America's double-containment policy. That is, the institutional arrangements that the United States used to "contain" Germany continue to serve that purpose—at least so long as Washington is willing to support them.

Economically, Europe remains critical to the U.S. economy. America's economic links to western Europe were expanded and strengthened throughout the cold war, as transatlantic trade and financial structures were "pressed into the service of containment," as Wolfram Hanrieder used to say. That legacy has survived the demise of the cold war. Today, Europe is second only to Asia in the ranking of America's trade partners. And transatlantic investment is greater even than Sino-American investment. American corporations in Europe generate earnings in the tens of billions of dollars each year. In addition, several million Americans are employed by European businesses that have located subsidiaries in the United States. If the sentiment of a transatlantic "community of fate" still pertains in the post-cold-war era, it is in significant part due to interdependent economic interests.

The third traditional basis of American interests—ideology—may, like economics, be considered a vital component of the country's security interests. This was illustrated somewhat ambiguously in George Kennan's "X" article, and elaborated in his subsequent writings.[13] Every American president from Harry Truman onward has cast America's European interests in terms of the protection of western or American ideological principles such as democracy, freedom, and self-determination. President Ronald Reagan was only dressing up the concept in famously melodramatic terms when he described America's foreign policy as a stand against Moscow's "evil empire."

The first post-cold-war president, Bill Clinton, continues the theme of America's ideological interests in Europe, although without the apocalyptic language of American good against Soviet evil. Instead, the language of America's ideological interests has taken on a more universalistic cast, famously articulated in Francis Fukuyama's (frequently misinterpreted) thesis that the amalgam of values known as "western liberalism" has essentially been "universalized . . . in the realm of ideas or consciousness," but "is as yet incomplete in the real or material world."[14] The promotion of western liberal ideology is thus no longer a life-and-death battle with the evil empire, but rather a mop-up operation as "the end of history" nears.

In place of those ideological battles that have largely been won, Clinton and others have followed in the tradition of Reagan by founding American foreign policy upon not only national interests but also human interests, frequently invoking the language of "human rights." The notion of expanding the definition of America's interests to encompass human rights is not entirely new, of course; the "crimes against humanity" with which America and its allies charged Hitler's Germany and Hirohito's Japan occurred half a century before America made a commitment to halting the ethnic cleansing in former Yugoslavia. The atrocities in Bosnia, as execrable as they are, are but a pale shadow of the Holocaust. But America's involvement in Bosnia could hardly be justified by a narrow definition of American interests, while its war against Hitler could. Thus, America's post-cold-war intervention in Bosnia (like its interventions outside of Europe, such as in Somalia) must be linked to America's interests through values and morals. This need not entirely exclude the realist motive of increasing power; to the extent that American "soft power," as Joseph Nye has called it,[15] depends on a reputation for defending universal concepts of morality, promoting human rights may be within a narrowly drawn American national interest.

America's interests thus can be seen to be threatened by three potential crises in European politics: the military threat of Russian revanchism, the economic threat of German hegemony, and the ideological challenge of eastern European civil war and chaos. Presumably America's Europe policy, whatever else it does, should be aimed at preventing these potentialities. It is in this way that American and European interests intersect. But the simple intersecting of interests does not guarantee a convergence of policies. While their interests may intersect at some points, they may conflict at others. Moreover, each country's foreign policy must take into account a range of domestic and international political considerations.

THE ENGAGEMENT VISION AND THE ISOLATIONIST IMPULSE

Multilateral security institutions are created to promote shared interests. America is central to the premier European security institution—NATO—as well as to the recently upgraded Organization for Security and Cooperation in Europe (OSCE). More ad hoc security missions such as the U.N.-authorized Implementation Force (IFOR) and the subsequent Stabilization Force (SFOR) would be unthinkable without America's participation and leadership. The questions for this study are how Washington's foreign policy toward Europe might be constrained by those institutional arrangements, and how the institutions themselves continue to be shaped by American foreign policy. Given America's disproportionate weight within these institutions, it is evident that American foreign policy enjoys a much greater autonomy than, say, Germany's or even Britain's. As regards European security, the shape and efficacy of the institutions will overwhelmingly depend upon America's emerging policies and commitments.

As a rule, American foreign policy, perhaps to its credit, is not developed by academics. It is circumscribed by political realities, including, increasingly, the exigencies of the public mood. And America's isolationist impulse, arising from a lingering sense of Manifest Destiny and nurtured by the populist appeals of figures such as Pat Buchanan, is perhaps the largest obstacle to an engaged American foreign policy in the post-cold-war era.

The Clinton administration nevertheless has tried to build support for the strengthening of the Atlantic Alliance. As discussed above, the Clinton administration has continually expressed a firm commitment to European security. The administration's first secretary of state, Warren Christopher, repeatedly spoke of the need to "shape a world conducive to American interests and consistent with American values," which included building "a new European security architecture." He emphasized that "deep political, military, economic, and cultural ties make Europe's security and prosperity essential to ours."[16] These themes were carried into Clinton's second term; in his first State of the Union speech after his January 1997 inauguration, the president committed the United States to ensuring an "undivided and democratic Europe," explaining that "when Europe is stable, prosperous, and at peace, America is more secure."[17]

This engagement vision recognizes that Europe matters to America. And it understands that Europe is too politically fragmented to provide sufficiently for its own security and stability. These matters are understood adequately within the beltway to ensure Washington's continued leadership of NATO, its heading of military missions such as IFOR and SFOR, its brokering of political resolutions to regional crises such as Bosnia, and its sponsorship of arms control treaties with Russia.[18]

Beyond this, however, a large segment of American public opinion is unfavorably disposed toward increasing economic commitments, the permanent stationing of additional troops, and especially the incurring of human casualties. These proscriptions are driven by an isolationist impulse that views Europe more as a quagmire than a sphere of influence; that views Europeans more as a congeries of quarreling ethnonational peoples than as fellow members of a western "civilization"; that sustains the dismissive side of America's double vision concerning Europe.

The isolationist view therefore discounts the necessity of American engagement for defending whatever military, economic, and especially ideological interests the country might possess. This view is founded upon various combinations of three rationales. First, if America were to abandon the transatlantic alliance, Europe would be forced to stop free-riding on American strength and finally address its own security. This could be called the "tough love" rationale. Second, Europe has sufficiently democratized to prevent the appearance of twenty-first-century Hitlers and Stalins. Call this the "end of history" rationale. Third, military threats from Europe—indeed, from anywhere abroad—are inconsequential due to the collapse of the Soviet Union and the preponderance of America's nuclear might. This could be dubbed the "surfeit" argument.

Such wishful thinking incurs a good measure of risk. Particularly worrisome is whether MAD still pertains in the post-cold-war world—a matter with grave implications for America's nuclear deterrent. Indeed, it is Russian instability, political collapse, and civil war, more than, say, a resurrection of Moscow's empire, that most concerns Washington's Atlanticists. This helps explain why the *Bulletin of the Atomic Scientists'* symbolic "doomsday clock," even after the passing of the cold war, still indicates an uneasy fourteen minutes to nuclear Armageddon.

But American isolationism has no patience for the finer points of deterrence theory; it is enough that America's nuclear weapons make an attack on its shores unthinkable. Europe's relevance to American security is thus discounted. A recent article in *The Atlantic Monthly* argued that "the demise of the Soviet Union has shattered any rational basis for extensive U.S. involvement in European security affairs and has undermined shared interests that made possible U.S.-European security cooperation outside the North Atlantic region during the Cold War."[19]

The political wisdom in Washington is that public opinion cannot be ignored. Although American public opinion on international matters is neither well informed nor cohesive, in the post-cold-war era it has been studiously heeded by Washington.[20] This is the irony: that while the Clinton administration has largely accepted its responsibility to lead the Atlantic Alliance, it has wavered in its leadership of American public opinion. Part of this is congenital; after President George Bush presided over the endgame of the cold war, the 1992 presidential elections served as a referendum on America's international commitments in the new era. If campaign themes are an accurate indication of the public mood, the "new world order" did not capture the imagination of the voters. Instead, it was "the economy, stupid." When President Bill Clinton's handling of American affairs came up for a plebiscite in fall 1996, Americans renewed his mandate. But unlike 1992, it should be emphasized that 1996 did not offer a choice between foreign policy and domestic policy emphases. Indeed, candidate Bob Dole's campaign virtually ignored foreign policy. Clinton seems to have succeeded in sustaining America's international leadership position while simultaneously placating the public's demand that American resources, and particularly American lives, not be squandered abroad.

But at what cost? With regard to Europe, America has scaled back its troop presence by about two-thirds since 1991. Congress has made the continued presence of the remaining troops dependent on the Europeans' willingness to increase their share of the costs. One budget amendment was introduced that would have withdrawn all U.S. troops from Europe by 2000 if the Europeans did not accept financial responsibility for America's defense of Europe. Although the amendment was defeated, Congress has required that Europe cover 37.5 percent of nonsalary costs by the end of fiscal 1998. While such a figure represents only a small increase in Europe's share, these efforts to force costs on Europe imply that stationing American troops in Europe is a service to Europeans, and not a contribution to shared interests. Similarly, the president was able to commit U.S. troops to Bosnia only after ensuring that they would not be placed in unduly dangerous situations, and after promising (somewhat disingenuously, as it turns out) that they would be withdrawn within a year.

Washington's Europe policy therefore seeks to retain America's leadership position while scaling back its economic commitments and minimizing personnel risks. Following this prescription results in awkward diplomatic stances and inconsistent policies as Washington responds to emerging post-cold-war issues such as NATO expansion, arms reduction, the applicability of nuclear first-use doctrine, and the definition of NATO's peacekeeping role. America's double vision vis-à-vis Europe is even more dangerous as it concerns European crises such as that in Bosnia, a possible widening of unrest elsewhere in eastern Europe, or the projection of Russian power in the "near abroad." In all of these contexts, America's double vision concerning Europe threatens to sacrifice the interests of Europe and the United States alike.

LORD ISMAY REDUX

America's continued contribution to European security hinges on its participation in NATO—an institution that only a few years ago pundits on both sides of the Atlantic had presumed to be an anachronism. Today, most of Europe belongs either to NATO or to the Partnership for Peace; eastern European and former Soviet states are applying for membership to NATO proper; the Russians have made NATO expansion and a NATO-Russia "charter" their highest-profile foreign policy priorities; and France and Spain are considering integration of their forces into NATO's military command structure. Far from an obsolete relic of the cold war, NATO has become one of the most popular clubs in Europe.

Yet what of the future? Could NATO indeed become a pan-European security institution? Although many Americans now are more circumspect about the desirability of dismantling the organization, and although Secretary of State Albright has become an ardent supporter of NATO expansion, the U.S. Congress is reassessing Washington's economic and military obligations to NATO (as well as the United Nations). Some Europeans, meanwhile, continue to place hope in supplemental, and perhaps one day supplanting, organizations.

An honest evaluation of America's enduring interests in Europe, articulated frankly and unapologetically by the political leadership, would do much toward correcting the country's double vision. And a clarity of purpose—what George Bush called "the vision thing"—would provide the best antidote to the contradictions in Washington's Europe policy. It might also help illuminate the future role and constitution of NATO.

Some years ago Lord Ismay postulated NATO's purpose as maintaining the proper geometry of three major powers in Europe: Russians out, Americans in, and Germans down. Even the turbulence occasioned by the cold war's demise has not yet entirely vitiated the logic of double containment.

NOTES

1. For an elaboration of this concept, see Richard Holbrooke, "America, a European Power," *Foreign Affairs* 74, no. 2 (1995): 38–51.

2. George Bush, "Toward a New World Order," *US Department of State Dispatch* 1, no. 3 (1990): 91.

3. U.S. Senate Committee on Foreign Relations, "Statement by the Allied High Commission on the Establishment of the 'German Democratic Republic,' October 10, 1949," *Document on Germany, 1944–1970* (Washington, DC: U.S. Government Printing Office, 1971), 173.

4. “X” [George Kennan], “The Sources of Soviet Conduct,” *Foreign Affairs* 25, no. 4 (1947): 576.

5. Wolfram F. Hanrieder, *Germany, America, Europe: Forty Years of German Foreign Policy* (New Haven: Yale University Press, 1989), 6.

6. Cited in John Laughland, “The Philosophy of ‘Europe,’ ” *The National Interest* 39 (1995): 58.

7. See Mark Hibbs, “Tomorrow, A Eurobomb?” *Bulletin of the Atomic Scientists* 52, no. 1 (1996): 16–23.

8. For details on the CJTF concept, see Charles Barry, “NATO’s Combined Joint Task Forces in Theory and Practice,” *Survival* 38, no. 1 (1996): 81–97.

9. Margaret Thatcher, “Why America Must Remain Number One,” *National Review* 47, no. 14 (1995): 26.

10. In the Reagan era the United States was devoting about 6.5 percent of its GDP to defense. This has dropped significantly since the end of the cold war.

11. For a particularly forceful argument about America’s advantages in military technology, see “The Future of Warfare,” *The Economist* (8 March 1997): 21–24.

12. See Craig Covault, “European Politics Burden Weapons Procurements,” *Aviation Week and Space Technology* 142, no. 11 (1995): 57–61.

13. X [George F. Kennan], “The Sources of Soviet Conduct,” *Foreign Affairs* 25, no. 4 (1947): 566–576. Kennan subsequently clarified that he had meant for containment to counter the politico-ideological, rather than the military, threat emanating from the Soviet Union. See, *inter alia*, George F. Kennan, *Memoirs 1925–1950* (Boston: Little, Brown, 1967) and “Interview with George F. Kennan,” *Foreign Policy* 7 (Summer 1972): 5–21.

14. Francis Fukuyama, “The End of History?” *The National Interest* 16 (1989): 4.

15. Joseph S. Nye, “The Changing Nature of World Power,” *Political Science Quarterly* 105, no. 2 (1990): 181.

16. Warren Christopher, “Principles and Opportunities for American Foreign Policy,” *U.S. Department of State Dispatch* 6, no. 4 (1995): 41–45.

17. Telecast of State of the Union address, February 4, 1997.

18. For a powerful statement of America’s leadership role, see Bill Clinton, “The Vital Tradition of American Leadership in the World,” *U.S. Department of State Bulletin* 1, no. 3 (1995): 157–160.

19. Alan Tonelson and Robin Gaster, “Our Interests in Europe,” *The Atlantic Monthly* 276, no. 2 (1995): 28; see also Ted Galen Carpenter, *Beyond NATO: Staying Out of Europe’s Wars* (Washington, DC: CATO Institute, 1994).

20. On the increasing salience of public opinion on foreign policymaking, see Michael Clough, “Grass Roots Policymaking: Say Good-Bye to the ‘Wise Men,’ ” *Foreign Affairs* 73, no. 1 (1994): 2–7.

3

Russia and European Security: The Case against NATO's Eastward Expansion

SABINE HUEBNER-MONIEN

INTRODUCTION

With the end of the cold war, the collapse of the Warsaw Pact, and the dissolution of the Soviet Union, the frame of reference for Moscow's foreign policy has changed dramatically. More than five years after Soviet disintegration, Russian leaders are still struggling to create a foreign and security policy that reflects Russia's specific geopolitical position and resulting national interests. This process is an especially difficult one in a domestic context characterized by political crises, ethnic conflict, and uncertainties resulting from the simultaneous transition toward democracy and a free market economy. Russian foreign policy elites, still adapting to the loss of superpower status and new geopolitical realities, are confronted with the need to define a new Russian identity and to identify Russia's security needs in the post-cold-war world.

This difficulty has become particularly apparent in the debate concerning new security arrangements in Europe. The situation in the early nineties was characterized by NATO's attempts to institutionalize consultation and cooperation with both the central and eastern European and the Soviet successor states on the one hand, and an increasingly assertive Russian foreign policy on the other. While NATO's Partnership for Peace program (PfP) was debated hotly in Russia, Moscow was content that major decisions concerning NATO's enlargement were repeatedly postponed. However, in 1995 it became clear that the Western Alliance was moving ahead with the admission of new members despite Russia's condemnation of those plans. With both Boris Yeltsin and Bill Clinton reelected in 1996, the issue acquired new saliency in early 1997, and attention subsequently focused on an agreement that would specify Russia's future relationship with NATO.

This chapter examines Russian foreign policy priorities concerning post-cold-war security arrangements in Europe, particularly Moscow's reactions to NATO's plans to admit former members of the Warsaw Pact. NATO's plans to expand eastward developed at a time when Russia was trying to establish its new place in the world and in the emerging security order in Europe. Consequently, the policies of the Western Alliance—still seen as hostile in Moscow—were a major external determinant of Russia's conception of its security interests. After an initial pro-western period, growing frustrations with western policies were translated into a new Russian foreign policy consensus, emphasizing Russia's Eurasian position and great-power status. This new consensus in turn shaped Moscow's reactions to NATO initiatives and its attempts to affect changes in European security arrangements that would meet Russian security needs.

This analysis starts by briefly discussing the role of national identity and national interests in Russian foreign policy. Second, it analyzes the reasons for the evident shift from an early pro-western to a more assertive foreign policy approach with respect to European security arrangements. The third section examines Russian reactions to NATO's programs aimed at expanding consultation and cooperation with central and east European and Soviet successor states, focusing particularly on the Partnership for Peace program launched in 1994. Finally, this chapter assesses Russian reactions to NATO's plans to admit several central and east European states, showing that a new Russian foreign policy approach allows for the acceptance of NATO's plans, if the West is willing to make concessions to Moscow and to acknowledge Russia's great-power status.

THE ROLE OF NATIONAL IDENTITY AND NATIONAL INTERESTS

Western and Russian leaders frequently make reference to the "national interest" in an attempt to defend their foreign policy initiatives. However, with the bipolar confrontation over, the new and more complex international system has made it more problematic to determine just what a country's national interest is. The lively discussion in the international relations literature of the concept as both a tool of political analysis and of political action has found it to be ambiguous. However, "national interest" can legitimately be considered one of the "large concepts" that, as Wolfram Hanrieder said, "attain their prominence from sustained diplomatic use, not by virtue of the theoretical invitation or analytic manipulation." The ambiguity of these concepts may result from the fact that they "are not theoretical but political abstracts, imposed on diplomatic parlance and the public debate by the makers and not the observers of historical events."[1]

The concept of the national interest did not officially play a role in Soviet foreign policy, which was guided instead by Marxist-Leninist ideology. It was only in the late 1980s that Mikhail Gorbachev and his foreign minister, Eduard Shevardnadze, introduced the concept in an attempt to differentiate their "new thinking" from the foreign policy of the Brezhnev era. With their insistence that Soviet policy be guided by national interests, Gorbachev and Shevardnadze sought to free Soviet foreign policy from the dictates of Communist doctrine while at the same time attempting to gain domestic support for their reformist policies by couching them in the language of nationalism.[2]

The concept acquired new significance following the disintegration of the Soviet Union when Russia and the other successor states were required not only to define their national interests but, even more fundamentally, to define their national identity.[3] This was particularly difficult in Russia, since Russians found it hard to accept that the former Soviet republics had become independent states. This view held especially true with regard to Ukraine, which is considered the historic birthplace of Russian civilization, and the Ukrainians, together with the Belorussians, are viewed as part of a larger Slavic nation. Thus, Russians feel that losing Ukraine "is tantamount to losing an important part of Russian history and consequently, identity."[4] Given their historic ties, Moscow's relations with the states of the so-called near abroad will continue to play a central role for Russia's definition of its national identity and interests. A second important aspect in the determination of security interests is Moscow's interpretation of Russia's geographical and geopolitical position. In the Russian leadership's shift from a pro-western foreign policy to a Eurasian perspective, we find support for the thesis that definitions of state or national interests "are typically based on culturally rooted perceptions of geographical position and the implications of that position for national security."[5]

Early post-cold-war foreign policy was characterized by Russian efforts to break with the Communist past and to establish a new identity as a western state. The Yeltsin administration stressed universal human values and insisted that Russia was going to become a member of the western family of nations or, as then-Foreign Minister Andrei Kozyrev called it, the "civilized world." With the bipolar confrontation over, Moscow insisted that it wanted to build a "strategic partnership" with the West, and it set political integration and economic integration into the West as Russian foreign policy priorities. Motivated also by the dire condition of the Russian economy, Russian foreign policymakers attempted to achieve integration into western institutions such as the General Agreement on Tariffs and Trade (GATT) and the International Monetary Fund (IMF); they were more cooperative in the U.N. Security Council; and they even briefly considered membership in NATO. By the same token, European security was to be achieved in cooperation with the West and with western institutions, such as the CSCE (now OSCE), the EU, and NATO.

By early 1993, however, Russian foreign policy had shifted to an approach that represented a geopolitical conception of Russian interests and defined Russian security needs as distinct from those of the West. This was in direct contrast to the pro-western or "Atlanticist" perspective that had stressed, as Saikal and Maley put it, "the importance of social and institutional factors in determining the quality of interstate relations, and downplayed the significance of geography and primordial culture,"[6] and that had neglected the question of a specific Russian national identity. Yeltsin and his ministers, now subscribing to a new "Eurasianist" perspective, attempted to delineate Moscow's sphere of influence. Foreign policymakers in Moscow sought to regain influence in the states of the near abroad and adopted a more interventionist policy. At the same time, Russian officials revised their policies toward western security institutions. They unanimously rejected NATO's plans to admit central and eastern European states and insisted that the OSCE (then the CSCE), a nonmilitary body including all European states and Russia as full members,[7] was better suited to deal with European security problems than NATO, still seen in Moscow as an anti-Russian defense alliance. The Yeltsin administration clearly favored a collective security system based on the OSCE over a NATO-centered security system and insisted that the fifty-five-member organization play a coordinating role for European security issues. Thus, the new definition of Russian identity, the focus on Russian uniqueness and on its special security needs, which had replaced the initial eagerness to be integrated into western institutions, clearly made Russian cooperation with the West more difficult.

NEW RUSSIAN ASSERTIVENESS

Domestic opposition to the pro-western policies of Yeltsin and Kozyrev had increased throughout 1992 and 1993. When it became clear that political concessions to the West were not resulting in the levels of financial aid that had been expected in Moscow, support for the westernist approach, which had never been high, started to dwindle. The continuing economic downturn added to the population's disenchantment with the reformist course, and it became increasingly popular to blame the West for Russian difficulties. Frustration with western policies, however, was not limited to the public at large. Among the political elite, it resulted from a "sense of entitlement."[8] Members of Russian leadership circles had expected to be rewarded with a welcome into the community of "civilized nations" once they had renounced Communist ideology and military doctrine. When this reward did not materialize, they became increasingly critical of the West and western policies.

In the controversial domestic debate that ensued, Russian economic problems, the civil conflicts in the Russian Federation, the situation in the near abroad, and the fate of ethnic Russians in the Commonwealth of Independent States (CIS) and the Baltic states emerged as central issues.[9] The westernists continually lost ground to those seeking to rebuild the Russian empire and to revive Russia's superpower role. Even moderate critics such as Alexei Arbatov, director of the Center for Geopolitical and Military Forecasts in Moscow, argued that Russian foreign policy after independence had "too easily made concessions to the West" and that Russian foreign policymakers needed to be "much more assertive regarding Russia's own interests and priorities."[10] Criticizing Yeltsin's and Kozyrev's willingness to accept western proposals on arms reductions and western designs for a new European security architecture, opponents of the reformist policies stressed the great power role Russia should play in international affairs. Communists and nationalists argued that by virtue of its size, population, location, as well as its military and particularly nuclear capabilities, Russia was still a great power and needed to be treated as such. A focus on Russian national interests, they insisted, would remedy the flaws of early reformist and western-oriented foreign policy.

A new foreign policy consensus emerged in early 1993, based on a different conception of Russia's geopolitical position, national identity, and resulting national interests and foreign policy priorities. The thinking of those who have been variously labeled the "moderate liberals," "centrists," or "Eurasianists" starts with the assumption that Russia's specific location should determine its foreign policy. Eurasianists argue that Russia cannot and should not become fully integrated into the West since it is part of both Europe and Asia. Consequently, Moscow needs to prioritize relations with the states of the CIS and the protection of the interests of the Russian diaspora over relations with the West. Unlike more extremist foreign policy positions, however, this approach is not hostile to the West. Eurasianists consider cooperation with the United States and western Europe desirable on a range of issues but stress that Russia must define its specific national and security interests independent of western preferences. In other words, good relations with the West do not entail "automatic acceptance of all positions and proposals of current Western governments."[11]

By early 1993, Yeltsin had adapted his foreign policy to the new political mood in Russia and subscribed to a more nationalist approach. Changes in foreign policy encompassed strengthened ties with the CIS on the one hand and a reassessment of western attempts to reorganize the European security system on the other. With respect to its relations with CIS states, Russian leaders claimed that Russia had special rights and responsibilities in other Soviet successor states since it needed to protect the human rights of the twenty-five million Russians living outside the Russian Federation. Yeltsin and Kozyrev attempted to gain legitimacy from both the OSCE and the United Nations for what they described as their "peacekeeping role" in the near abroad, arguing that "Russia's special role and responsibility in the former Soviet Union must be borne in mind by its Western partners and given support."[12]

The new consensus in Russian foreign policy also extended to opposition to the eastward expansion of NATO. As "part and parcel of the shift away from Atlanticism,"[13] Russian foreign policymakers made it clear that the admission to NATO of former members of the Warsaw Pact stood in direct opposition to Russia's security interests. This view was shared not only by Yeltsin and Kozyrev but endorsed as well by Prime Minister Viktor Chernomyrdin and then-Defense Minister Pavel Grachev. The only major detour from this course came in August 1993 when Yeltsin, visiting Warsaw, declared that it was the decision of the Polish leaders alone whether or not Poland would join NATO—Russia would not keep them from doing so. Walesa and Yeltsin signed a statement according to which the decision to join NATO "taken by a sovereign Poland in the interests of overall European integration does not go against the interests of other states, including the interests of Russia."[14] However, Yeltsin's statement as well as the joint declaration were later described as improvisation, and a campaign was implemented to retract them.[15]

In late 1993, Russian foreign policy was informed also by a domestic crisis in Moscow, in which the confrontation between Yeltsin's government and the Russian parliament culminated in the shelling of the Russian White House by presidential troops. Yeltsin, recognizing the importance of the support of conservative circles, reaffirmed his opposition to NATO expansion. A study of the Russian Foreign Intelligence Service published in November 1993—in keeping with the new consensus—characterized NATO as the "biggest military grouping in the world that possesses an enormous offensive potential" and described the Western Alliance as an organization wedded "to the stereotypes of bloc thinking."[16] The authors made it clear that Moscow would accept NATO expansion only under two conditions: First, that not only the central and eastern European states would be integrated, but that Russia would be admitted as well; and second, that NATO would undergo a transformation from a system of collective defense that had been directed at the Soviet threat to a system of collective security ensuring security for all of Europe.[17]

The parliamentary elections of December 1993 confirmed the growing support of the Russian public for more conservative and even nationalist positions in domestic and foreign policies. Yegor Gaidar's reform-oriented party, "Choice of Russia," which had been expected to win the elections easily, received less than 15 percent of the votes. Vladimir Zhirinovsky's ultranationalist Liberal Democratic Party and the Communist Party received a total of 38 percent.[18] Given the election results and his own need to garner domestic support, Yeltsin moved to the right of the Russian political spectrum, all but abandoning his earlier pro-western foreign policy.

THE PARTNERSHIP FOR PEACE PROGRAM

The Russian leadership had been confronted early on with western attempts to establish new forms of post-cold-war security cooperation. After the demise of the Warsaw Pact in mid-1991, central and eastern European states, no longer part of the Soviet empire, quickly indicated their interest in joining NATO. In response to their arguments that the security vacuum that had emerged in Europe needed to be filled by the Western Alliance, NATO established the North Atlantic Cooperation Council (NACC) as a forum for consultation and cooperation. Activities within the framework of the NACC were limited to consultations on political and security-related issues, work on defense budgets and defense conversion, as well as programs in scientific and environmental affairs.[19] Its inaugural meeting was held on December 20, 1991—the very day that marked the end of the Soviet Union. After the disintegration of the Soviet Union, participation in the NACC was extended to the Soviet successor states, including Russia. All former members of the Warsaw Pact, including Albania, and all Soviet successor states eventually became members. While the NACC clearly failed to meet the demands of the central and east European states for enhanced security, it served the needs of both Russia and the Alliance to postpone discussions regarding NATO enlargement.

In subsequent years, Russian diplomacy concerning NATO expansion attempted, as MacFarlane put it, "to marry the concepts of special interest and international cooperation."[20] On the one hand, Russian politicians—in accordance with the Eurasian foreign policy perspective—sought recognition of a special status for their country. On the other hand, Russian leaders continued discussions with the Western Alliance about NATO's plans to strengthen its ties with the states of central and eastern Europe and the former Soviet Union, all the while making it very clear that Moscow preferred a new collective security system under the auspices of the OSCE to any arrangement building on NATO.

Despite Russian objections, however, NATO—after grappling with the issue of enlargement throughout 1993—offered a new program that went beyond the consultation offered by the NACC. The Partnership for Peace program, (PfP) launched at NATO's summit meeting in Brussels in January 1994, represented the next initiative by the West to establish a new framework for security cooperation in Europe. Official NATO statements were enthusiastic. The new program was hailed as an initiative to move NATO into the post-cold-war era and as a "strategy for projecting stability into Central Europe."[21] PfP was meant to go "beyond dialogue and cooperation to forge a real partnership,"[22] and, in the words of General George A. Joulwan, Supreme Allied Commander Europe, to extend "the hand of friendship to the new democracies of Central and Eastern Europe and beyond."[23] Partnership for Peace offered participating states "the possibility of strengthening their relations with NATO in accordance with their own individual interests and capabilities"[24] and involved practical programs of military cooperation and joint peacekeeping actions. While the program fell short of extending security guarantees to the partners joining the program, it contained a "hint of solidarity in the event of a threat."[25] The framework document specifies that "NATO will consult with any active participant in the Partnership if that partner perceives a direct threat to its territorial integrity, political independence, or security."[26] Besides the former members of the Warsaw Pact, a number of Soviet successor states demonstrated their interest in the new partnership: the Baltic states and Ukraine were among the first to join the program, much to Russia's dismay.

It became clear early on that PfP was confronted with differing expectations. The West had sought to respond to the continued pressure of the central and eastern European states without antagonizing or isolating Russia. Central and eastern European states hoped to obtain security guarantees and admission to the Western Alliance, while Russia vigorously opposed full membership for the former members of the Warsaw Pact and sought to use the new program to start a process of overhauling the entire European security order.[27] To meet these contradictory demands, the partnership program had to be sufficiently ambiguous to be interpreted in different ways. Whereas NATO hopefuls viewed their participation as an interim step toward full NATO membership, Russian officials clearly preferred the program—open to all European states—over admitting any central and east European states as full members of the Western Alliance.

By spring 1994, a lively and controversial debate about PfP had unfolded in Russia. Some commentators favored the new program, even claiming the partnership concept originally had been a Russian idea introduced to the West by Yeltsin, who had pointed out Russian intentions "to establish full-scale cooperation with the bloc in specific areas, not to join the bloc."[28] Critics pointed to the hostile nature of the Western Alliance arguing that NATO's goal after the end of the cold war was still the containment of Russia. They contended that the Western Alliance aimed at "weakening Moscow's military-political position" and at "bringing its foreign and military policy under the West's control."[29]

Official Russian criticism focused on the equal treatment of all NATO partners and on the role of the OSCE. Concerning the first point, Russian diplomats complained that being treated as simply another NATO partner was not in the Russian interest. That sentiment was illustrated by the argument that even the fourteen countries that already had joined PfP combined did not "have the same significance as Russia when it comes to changing geopolitics and geostrategy."[30] Russian officials pressed for a special bilateral agreement between NATO and Russia and again asserted Russia's great power role, arguing that Russia could join PfP only if its special status were recognized. On the second point, Yeltsin and Kozyrev insisted that PfP was to be considered subordinate to a much-needed new European collective security system and stressed that both NATO and the European security system had to undergo far-reaching transformations. They demanded an enhanced role for the OSCE in coordinating security policies in Europe. In May 1994, then-Russian Defense Minister Pavel Grachev proposed to NATO defense ministers the creation of a mechanism for consultation on matters of international and European security, a mechanism that in turn would be a step toward "the formation of a future collective security system in Europe under the aegis of the CSCE."[31]

After repeated postponements of the signing of the partnership document and after continued hesitancy on the part of Russian leaders, Kozyrev on 22 June 1994, finally put his signature on the basic framework document. The official NATO statement that was issued after the meeting recognized a Russian role in Europe but made no special concessions to Moscow.[32] Defending the Russian decision to join the program, Kozyrev emphasized that Russia viewed "the establishment of a system of collective security and stability in Europe"[33] as the main goal of cooperation within the framework of the PfP. While Kozyrev saw benefits arising from cooperation in the military realm, especially in joint peacekeeping operations, preventing the spread of weapons of mass destruction, and in defense conversion programs, he insisted again that Russia preferred a new European system of collective security based on CSCE over any extended role for NATO. He expressed the hope that "the dynamic development of the partnership, as well as cooperation within the CSCE and the NACC framework, will make less pressing the issue which is widely discussed today, i.e. the eastward expansion of the NATO zone."[34] Moreover, Kozyrev reaffirmed Russia's great power status arguing that it should "be clear that a genuine partnership is an equal partnership. Our relations should be deprived of even the slightest hints of paternalism." Instead western relations with Russia should be characterized by "close cooperation based on respect for the interests of the other side."[35]

The Russian leadership's motivation for joining PfP obviously resulted from the fact that Russia risked being isolated if it were to remain outside the program. Moreover, Russian diplomats apparently believed that an attempt to obstruct or at least delay and limit NATO expansion from the inside would be more successful than trying to influence NATO policies from the outside. The Yeltsin administration wanted to make sure that the partnership program would not become a step toward the full integration of the central and eastern European or Soviet successor states into NATO and thus used the chance of getting through PfP "some access to NATO councils and hence an entry point to lobby for policies favored in Moscow."[36]

NATO'S "STUDY ON ENLARGEMENT" AND DETERIORATING NATO-RUSSIAN RELATIONS

The Partnership for Peace program did not, as the Russians had hoped, put an end to the debate over NATO's objective to admit new members. On the contrary, the Western Alliance moved ahead with its plans. In December 1994, NATO's foreign ministers initiated a study to examine more closely the admission of new members to the Western Alliance. Attempting to assuage Russian apprehensions about being excluded from new security arrangements, NATO declared that "enlargement, when it takes place, will be part of a broad European security architecture based on true cooperation throughout the whole of Europe. It will threaten no one and will enhance security and stability for all of Europe."[37]

The Russians, however, remained unconvinced. When it became clear that the Western Alliance was no longer discussing the "if" but the "how" and "when" of admitting new members despite continued Russian opposition, relations with the West deteriorated. Foreign policymakers in Moscow, who had hoped that the issue of expansion had been put to rest at least temporarily, now accused NATO of replacing cooperation in PfP with a policy of rapid enlargement. In December 1994, at the OSCE's summit meeting in Budapest, Yeltsin suggested making the OSCE the basis for a new European security system. When he failed to win approval for the Russian proposal, Yeltsin warned that Europe, "which has not had time to rid itself of the legacy of the cold war, runs the risk of plunging into a cold peace."[38] He appeared irritated that Russia's difficulties resulting from its domestic transition were perceived as a potential threat to European security, and he criticized the West for losing faith in Russia's ability to establish a stable democracy.

In early 1995, Russian opposition to the expansion of the Western Alliance was almost universal. In fact, asserting that the admission of central and east European or even Soviet successor states was not in Russia's national interest was one of the few policy issues on which there existed a national consensus. It united Russian political parties ranging from Zhirinovsky's ultranationalist LDP to Grigory Yavlinsky's liberal Yabloko bloc. Vladimir Lukin, former ambassador to Washington and chairman of the Duma's Committee on International Affairs, expressed the new consensus when he stated that an "advance by a very powerful military force" toward a "very weak and vulnerable" Russian army was clearly unacceptable to Moscow.[39]

Throughout the year, the reaction of Russian diplomats to NATO's continuing plans to move ahead with the admission of new members centered on the issue of Russia's participation in new European security arrangements and the need for a collective security system. Contemplating the effects of the Alliance's eastward expansion, the Yeltsin government reiterated that Russia must not be isolated. Vladislav Chernov, member of the Russian Ministry of Foreign Affairs, argued that Russia faced a choice between two equally unacceptable options: either be ousted from the European security system or be a satellite of western institutions. Rejecting pro-western policies, he stressed that "those in Russia who are concerned about her national identity and world power role" believed that policies aimed at joining western institutions "will lead to national humiliation."[40]

Reiterating that European security should be assured by a system of collective security, Russian officials argued that NATO had to undergo reform parallel with expansion, and that its doctrine as well as its nuclear posture needed to be revised. Kozyrev, in an article aimed at an American audience, emphasized that the Western Alliance "established during the Cold War and acting without the participation of Russia" should be transformed into "a new institution with the goal of maintaining security and stability in close cooperation with Russia."[41] He called for a transitional period in which NATO should evolve into a "pan-European security organization and a joint instrument for the efficient response to new common challenges, such as ethnic conflicts, terrorism, proliferation of weapons of mass destruction, and drug trafficking."[42]

A study published in May 1995 by the Council on Foreign and Defense Policy, a nonpartisan organization including politicians from various parties, business people, scholars, and journalists, analyzed the consequences of NATO expansion for Russian security. The study outlined what was considered the consensus among liberals and centrists at the time, making it clear that even those groups in favor of cooperation with the West were strictly against NATO admitting new members. Discussing Russia's interests in Europe, the report emphasized that Moscow was "vitally interested . . . in full-fledged participation in a common European system of collective security." The document cautioned that NATO enlargement might "initiate a security process in which there will be no place for a full-scale participation of Russia," and argued that "an effective and reliable security system in Europe is unimaginable without both NATO and Russia partaking in it."[43] The study warned that integrating the central and east European states into NATO would deepen the feeling of injustice in Russia, revive old fears, and compel Moscow to create a system of collective security and defense in the framework of the CIS. In a similar vein, the Yeltsin government and Russian scholars started to warn the West in 1995 that Russia would have to buttress its own sphere of influence to counterbalance NATO's expansion to the East. Alexei Arbatov cautioned that NATO's eastward extension to the borders of the former Soviet Union or, worse, to Russia's borders would "undermine the prospects of genuine post-Cold War European security." NATO expansion would create a "new security watershed in Europe" that would in turn "encourage Russia's increased pressure to fortify its own security space by extending its strategic domain over Ukraine, Belarus and other European post-Soviet states."[44]

The issue of NATO expansion obtained new saliency after NATO's "Study on Enlargement" had been presented to the twenty-six NATO partners who had gathered in Brussels in September 1995. The study once again emphasized that "enlargement will contribute to enhanced stability and security for all countries in the Euro-Atlantic area."[45] It stated that "enlargement will occur through a gradual, deliberate, and transparent process, encompassing dialogue with all interested parties." Furthermore, it specified that "there is no fixed or rigid list of criteria for inviting new member states to join the Alliance," and made it clear that "no country outside the Alliance should be given a veto or droit de regard over the process and decisions."[46] To alleviate Moscow's objections to NATO expansion, the document emphasized that enlargement "will occur as one element of the broader evolution of European cooperation and security currently underway" and will be "only one important element of a broad European security architecture that transcends and renders obsolete the idea of 'dividing lines' in Europe."[47] Regarding NATO's relations with Russia, the study noted that "Russia has an important contribution to make to European stability and security," and described the progress that had been made in 1994 and 1995 toward developing a "cooperative NATO-Russia relationship aimed at enhancing mutual confidence and openness." The study also specified that the development of a special NATO-Russia relationship beyond the Partnership for Peace program—which had been another Russian demand—"should take place in rough parallel with NATO's own enlargement."[48] The document did not, however, ameliorate Russian apprehensions about NATO expansion, and Russian leaders continued to be very outspoken in their opposition.

At the time the NATO study was published, Ukraine announced that it wanted to enhance its relationship with NATO. Ukrainian leaders wanted to extend their cooperation with the Western Alliance beyond PfP. Russian suspicions with respect to Soviet successor states thus were not completely unfounded. The three Baltic states and Ukraine have turned out to be very active participants in PfP and have taken part in several joint exercises. Whereas the leaders of Estonia, Latvia, and Lithuania made it very clear that their goal was entry into the Western Alliance, Ukrainian officials, fully aware that such aspirations would provoke Moscow, maintained that they had no intention of applying for full NATO membership.[49]

The issue of NATO extension continued to inform Russian relations with the West throughout 1996. While NATO foreign ministers had decided that the next phase of the enlargement process would "consist of intensified, individual dialogue with interested Partners,"[50] there was also an agreement that no major decisions were going to be taken until after the presidential elections in both Russia and the United States. While the exchange of the all too well known arguments for and against NATO enlargement continued, minor shifts indicated that a compromise was becoming increasingly possible.

At the beginning of 1996, prospects for a solution to the controversy still seemed dim. The replacement in January of Kozyrev by the head of Russia's Foreign Intelligence Service, Yevgeni Primakov, pointed to a more conservative foreign policy approach, confirming the mood that had been indicated by the outcome of the December 1995 parliamentary elections.[51] Primakov, who was endorsed by Communist leader Gennadiy Zyuganov as well as by the ultranationalist Zhirinovsky, defended his reputation as a staunch nationalist by insisting that "in spite of the present difficulties, Russia was and remains a great power."[52] He emphasized, once again, that Russia should cooperate with the West when appropriate while at the same time pursuing its legitimate interests within the CIS. The new foreign minister promised to fight the inclusion of central and eastern European states or even the Soviet successor states into the Western Alliance and argued that "it is vitally important for Russia to fend off developments that could bring NATO's military infrastructure closer to our border."[53]

However, Primakov's statements, while still in line with the Russian anti-NATO rhetoric, indicated that an agreement between Russia and the West was achievable. Realizing that Moscow would be unable to prevent NATO enlargement in the long run, Russian foreign policymakers now attempted to influence the terms and scope of expansion and to attain a number of concessions. The focus shifted from general opposition to NATO's expansion to opposing NATO's "infrastructure" being moved up to Russian borders. This theme was reiterated in the Russian presidential election campaign in spring 1996, during which all presidential candidates were united in their more or less vigorous opposition to NATO extension. While an expanded NATO continued to be viewed as a security threat in Moscow, opposition now was directed particularly against the deployment of NATO troops and nuclear weapons in new member states. At the OSCE summit in Lisbon in December 1996, Chernomyrdin emphasized Russian opposition to plans to move NATO's infrastructure closer to Russia. The Russian prime minister presented a message from Yeltsin, who was still recovering from major heart surgery, in which the president reiterated his warning of a "cold peace" and a new division of Europe. Chernomyrdin cautioned, as Kozyrev had done before, against a new security watershed in Europe, arguing that new demarcation lines would damage the international political climate.[54]

In late 1996, attention turned to the issue of a NATO-Russia charter that would define Russia's special relationship with the Alliance and delineate future NATO-Russia cooperation. Yeltsin, who had been reelected on July 3, insisted that a treaty be concluded before any new members were admitted to the Western Alliance, while Western diplomats wanted it to be worked out parallel to NATO's enlargement. Disregarding the objections of Russian Defense Minister Igor Rodionov, who had replaced Pavel Grachev in July,[55] NATO defense ministers emphasized in September that NATO would move ahead with its plans, with or without an agreement on the charter. However, when it became increasingly clear that Moscow was going to accept the admission of a few central and eastern European states into NATO, the West obviously felt that it had to offer something in return and finally granted Russia's request for a coordinating role for the OSCE in the new security system. The United States made it clear, however, that this new role did not imply a subordination of NATO or the WEU to the OSCE, but rather the creation of a network of complementary institutions. The central statement of the declaration of Lisbon issued at the end of the OSCE summit underscored that the fifty-four OSCE member states would participate equally in the new and yet to be established "security architecture for the twenty-first century."[56]

To assuage Moscow's apprehensions about the NATO infrastructure moving closer to the Russian heartland, and to ease Moscow's acceptance of new NATO members, NATO foreign ministers agreed that there would be no deployment of nuclear weapons on the territory of new members, and NATO defense ministers pledged that no NATO troops would be stationed permanently on the territory of the admitted central and east European states. The Western Alliance also renewed its offer of a special charter with Russia that would formulate "common principles" for European security, list several fields of cooperation, and define a new body that would bring together Russia and NATO governments.[57] In mid-January 1997, NATO General Secretary Javier Solana started negotiations with Moscow on the NATO-Russia agreement, which he hoped would be signed before the July 1997 NATO summit at which Poland, Hungary, and the Czech Republic were to be nominated for full NATO membership.

Concerning the future relationship of Russia to NATO, Solana and Primakov agreed that Russia would have permanent representation at NATO's headquarters in Brussels and that foreign policy decisionmakers and experts were going to meet regularly in a new NATO-Russia Council to discuss a broad range of topics, including peacekeeping, defense, arms control, nuclear safety, nonproliferation, emergency relief, and crisis management. While the two diplomats were successful in negotiating the text of the NATO-Russia charter, disagreement persisted about its status. Whereas the Russians demanded a legally binding treaty, i.e., a treaty ratified by the parliaments of all member states and the Russian Duma, the Alliance proposed a document that would have political weight only.

In mid-February, several Western diplomats, including German Foreign Minister Klaus Kinkel and Italian Foreign Minister Lamberto Dini and the new U.S. secretary of state, Madeleine Albright, traveled to Moscow to continue discussions about the NATO-Russia charter and to attempt to assuage Russian opposition to NATO enlargement. In her talks with Chernomyrdin, Primakov, and Yeltsin, Albright sounded a conciliatory note and stated that "NATO no longer has an enemy in the East."[58] Russian officials, however, were less exuberant and demanded that Russia have a say equal to those of any NATO member in matters affecting Russia's vital interests. What Russian diplomats in effect sought was a veto over NATO decisions, especially over those concerning the stationing of NATO troops and nuclear weapons and over the admission of new members, particularly those of former Soviet republics. With respect to NATO infrastructure, the Yeltsin administration demanded that NATO guarantee that military equipment or troops would never be stationed on the territory of new member states, while NATO would only commit itself not to station troops and equipment under present and foreseeable circumstances. Concerning NATO's eastward extension, Russia sought a NATO commitment to abandon any further enlargement after the first round and specifically wanted NATO to rule out the admission of CIS or Baltic states as members.[59]

During the weeks preceding the Clinton-Yeltsin summit in mid-March 1997 in Helsinki, Russian officials continued to demonstrate their hostility toward NATO enlargement and to speculate publicly on Russian countermeasures. With the summit approaching, however, it became clear that much of the aggressive Russian anti-NATO rhetoric was intended to get the best bargain possible in return for accepting the inevitable. Clearly, the Yeltsin government did not want to lose its chance to obtain Western concessions in return for its toleration of NATO extension.[60]

At the summit meeting on March 20–21, 1997, discussions no longer focused on the issue of NATO expansion per se. The two presidents continued to disagree on the issue—Clinton viewing NATO expansion as the basis for an undivided and secure Europe and Yeltsin seeing it as creating a new dividing line and threatening Russian national security—and then moved on to discussing the NATO-Russia charter. The agreement, called the "Founding Act on Mutual Relations, Cooperation, and Security between NATO and the Russian Federation," provides for consultation, cooperation, and joint action in various fields and creates the Russia-NATO Permanent Joint Council as the "principal venue of consultation between NATO and Russia in times of crisis or for any other situation affecting peace and stability."[61] Clinton described the agreement as giving the Russians "a voice but not a veto" in the Western Alliance. The charter was characterized in a joint communiqué as "an enduring commitment at the highest political level" and effectively paved the way for NATO's eastward expansion.[62]

Yeltsin and Clinton resolved disagreements concerning strategic arms control and agreed to accelerate cutbacks. To make the outcome of the Russian-American negotiations more palatable to the Russians, Clinton announced that the United States would support Russia's admission to the major international economic institutions, including the WTO and the OECD. Moreover, he promised that the Russians would be integrated into the G-7 group of leading industrial nations, and that the summit in June 1997 would be called the "Summit of Eight." He also agreed to "accelerate negotiations" to revise the treaty on Conventional Forces in Europe (CFE).[63]

Yeltsin welcomed Washington's willingness to help integrate Russia economically, but he still faced the problem of explaining the outcome of the summit meeting at home. While the Russian president sought to use the summit meeting to demonstrate to his domestic constituency that he is taken seriously by the United States and still has a say in European security issues, it was apparent that none of the Russian demands concerning NATO expansion had been met, a fact that was not lost on Yeltsin's opponents. Communist leader Gennadiy Zyuganov condemned Yeltsin for selling out Russian national interests and described the outcome of the summit negotiations as "Russia's Versailles."[64] The Russian press noted that Moscow obviously had to give in again: Much as Gorbachev and Shevardnadze had to accept German unification within NATO, Yeltsin and Primakov today have to accept NATO expansion on western terms.[65]

CONCLUSION

Ever since the admission to NATO of central and east European states has been considered by the West, Russia has vigorously opposed it. Despite several rounds of negotiations and the redefinition of Russia's relations with

NATO, both the Russian government and the Russian opposition have criticized NATO's plans and will most likely continue to condemn further enlargement of the Western Alliance. Russian sensibilities concerning NATO's plans to admit former members of the Russian-led Warsaw Pact are easily understandable given the traditional strategic importance of east European states for Moscow.[66] At a more fundamental level, however, the opposition of the Russian leadership to NATO's eastward expansion has a lot to do with Moscow's continued efforts to determine its national identity and interests and to find its place in the post-cold-war world.

The harsh reactions of Moscow's leadership to the prospect of NATO's admitting several central and east European states indicate that NATO enlargement, as Sergei Karaganov, deputy director of the European Institute in Moscow and one of the leading figures of the Council on Foreign and Defense Policy, has noted, "is a psychological question as much as a strategic one."[67] Confronted with NATO approaching its borders when it was becoming increasingly clear that the transition to a prosperous and powerful democracy was going to be neither quick nor easy, Moscow found it difficult to accept what it considered to be a strengthening of the Western Alliance. For many Russians, the eastward extension of the major rival military alliance of the Soviet Union for more than forty years is an emotionally charged subject. Russian politicians and the Russian population at large fear that Moscow is losing its clout with western powers and its leverage in international affairs. In recent years, arguments have become popular that "the West has repeatedly cheated and insulted Russia," and that NATO expansion "will add the crowning touch to Russia's humiliation."[68] While Moscow eventually accepted NATO's admission of the Visegrad countries, NATO membership of Soviet successor states remains an altogether different issue. Western moves toward integrating Ukraine most likely will continue to be regarded "as a catastrophe of epochal proportions."[69]

Given NATO's policies and Moscow's needs, what then are the options for Russian policy? First, the Yeltsin administration can continue its present course, which combines harsh anti-NATO rhetoric with grudging acceptance of its enlargement. So far, cooperation with the West has been possible despite the more assertive tone of Russian foreign policy and the focus on Russia's Eurasian identity. Cooperating with NATO rather than remaining outside the Western Alliance would allow Russian diplomats to influence NATO policies from the inside, and to try and help shape the future of the organization as a friend rather than a foe. It would also allow Moscow to accept what the West has to offer in return for Russian tolerance of the admission of new members into NATO. Clearly, the Russian economy—after decades of isolation from the West and several years of stagnating reforms—would benefit from the integration of the country into major international economic institutions. Moreover, if the opposition of the Yeltsin administration to NATO expansion is based on Russian fears of being isolated and cut off from the West, the western offers announced at the Helsinki summit and embodied in the May 1997 "Founding Act" could go a long way toward calming those fears.

The second option for Russian foreign policy toward NATO expansion would be a more conservative and nationalist stance, with the Yeltsin government heeding the advice of Communists and ultranationalist forces. There are still many "unreformed generals, . . . KGB-style intelligence officers, . . . [and] red directors of national industry"[70] who have their own reasons for opposing NATO enlargement, and who attack what they consider Yeltsin's foreign policy weaknesses. While even a more conservative Russian foreign policy would have to accept NATO expansion since it lacks the means of preventing it, cooperation with the West would become more difficult. A foreign policy approach that is much more conservative than that based on the Eurasianist consensus would involve an attempt to regain superpower status and moves to reintegrate the CIS states, if necessary by force, and to look to the Middle East and Far East for future allies. Such a policy approach would probably mean the end of arms control negotiations, and could ultimately involve a new arms race with the West, which in turn would lead to the economic collapse of the country.

So far, the Yeltsin government has clearly opted for the first alternative. The Russian president has made it very clear that Russia has two main goals: First, it wants to participate in European affairs and to be integrated into the West. In the words of Alexei Pushkov, director of foreign affairs at the Russian Public Television, Russia believes that "it has every right to comprehensive inclusion in modern Europe—economically, politically, and with regard to its security dimensions as well."[71] Second, Moscow seeks recognition as an equal partner, which makes a special relationship with NATO all the more important. In this context, the West should not underestimate Russia's concern with its status in world affairs. Moscow has always struggled to be acknowledged in the international arena. In the 1970s, it strove to be recognized as a superpower commensurate to the United States, a longstanding aspiration that reflected, as Hanrieder noted, "a deep seated Soviet need for self-assurance and international recognition of Soviet achievements."[72] What was true about the Soviet Union then can also be applied to Russia today. Its conduct in foreign affairs cannot be understood "without recognizing this mix of self-doubt and self-assertiveness, the grudging recognition of Western economic and technological superiority"[73] that made up the Soviet political personality in the past and makes up the Russian political personality today. Thus, what is required is at least a token recognition of Russia's special status as a great power and the acknowledgment of specific Russian interests and security needs by the West.

Finally, Russia today seems to realize that an expanded NATO does not have to entail a diminished Russia. While Moscow cannot stop NATO expansion, it might accept that a bigger NATO, which is busy bringing the military of the new members up to NATO standards and divvying up the costs of enlargement, and which is willing to negotiate a special relationship with Russia, actually represents less of a threat than in the past.

NOTES

1. Wolfram F. Hanrieder, *Germany, America, Europe: Forty Years of German Foreign Policy* (New Haven: Yale University Press, 1989), x.

2. For a detailed discussion, see Stephen Sestanovich, "Inventing the Soviet National Interest," *The National Interest* (Summer 1990): 3–16.

3. For a theoretical discussion of the concept of "national identity," see Jonathan Valdez, "The Near Abroad, the West, and National Identity in Russian Foreign Policy," in *The Making of Foreign Policy in Russia and the New States of Eurasia*, ed. Added Dawisha and Karen Dawisha (Armonk, NY: M. E. Sharpe, 1995), 84-109; esp. 85–88.

4. Roman Solchanyk, "Ukraine, The (Former) Center, Russia, and 'Russia,' " *Studies in Comparative Communism* 25, no. 1 (March 1992): 31–45, 32.

5. S. Neil MacFarlane, "Russian Conceptions of Europe," *Post-Soviet Affairs* 10, no. 3 (1994): 234–269, 248.

6. Amin Saikal and William Maley, "From Soviet to Russian Foreign Policy," in *Russia in Search of Its Future*, ed. Amin Saikal and William Maley (Cambridge: Cambridge University Press, 1995).

7. It was not until January 1996 that Russia was admitted to the Council of Europe. See *Facts on File* 56, no. 2878 (1 February 1996): 55.

8. Angela Stent and Lilia Shevtsova, "Russia's Election: No Turning Back," *Foreign Policy* no. 103 (Summer 1996): 92–109, 102.

9. For an examination of the whole spectrum of Russian foreign policy conceptions, see e.g., Alexei Arbatov, "Russia's Foreign Policy Alternatives," *International Security* 18, no. 2 (Fall 1993): 5–43; S. Neil MacFarlane, "Russian Conceptions of Europe," 234–269; Olga Alexandrova, "Divergenzen im russischen aussenpolitischen Denken," *Aussenpolitik* 44, no. 4 (1993): 363–372; Gebhardt Weiss, "Die Russische Föderation zwischen imperialer Versuchung und legitimer Interessenpolitik," *Aus Politik und Zeitgeschichte* B 46/95 (10 November 1995): 13–25.

10. Alexei Arbatov, "Russia's Foreign Policy Alternatives," 5.

11. Ibid., 11.

12. Andrei Kozyrev, "The Lagging Partnership," *Foreign Affairs* 73, no. 3 (May/June 1994): 59–61, 69.

13. Hannes Adomeit, "Russia as a 'Great Power' in World Affairs: Images and Reality," *International Affairs* 71, no. 1 (January 1995): 35–68, 49.

14. ITAR-TASS, 25 August 1993, quoted in Michael Mihalka, "Squaring the Circle," *RFE/RL Research Reports* 3, no. 12 (25 March 1994): 1–9, 2.

15. Suzanne Crow, "Russian Views on an Eastward Expansion of NATO," *RFE/RL Research Reports* 2, no. 41 (15 October 1993): 21–24.

16. Quoted in Hannes Adomeit, "Russia as a 'Great Power' in World Affairs," 49.

17. Yevgeni Primakov, quoted in Gerhard Wettig, "Die Rolle der NATO aus Moskauer Sicht," *Aussenpolitik* 45, no. 2 (1994): 123–133, 127–128.

18. The LDP received 24 percent, and the CP almost 14 percent of the vote. For a detailed discussion of the parliamentary elections of December 1993 and December 1995, see Beat Kernen, "The Russian Parliamentary Elections of 1993: A Quasi-Historical Interpretation in Light of the 1995 Elections," *East European Quarterly* 30, no. 2 (Summer 1996): 235–250.

19. See NATO, *NATO at a Glance* (Brussels, 1996), 27–30.

20. S. Neil MacFarlane, "Russian Conceptions of Europe," 257.

21. See e.g., the article by the permanent U.S. representative on the North Atlantic Council, Robert Hunter, "Enlargement: Part of a Strategy for Projecting Stability into Central Europe," *NATO Review* (May 1995): 3–8.

22. Partnership for Peace: Invitation and Framework Document reprinted in *NATO Review* (February 1994): 28–30, 28.

23. General George A. Joulwan, "NATO's Military Contribution to Partnership for Peace: The Progress and the Challenge," *NATO Review* (March 1995): 3–6, 3.

24. NATO, *Basic Fact Sheet*, no. 9 (March 1996). NATO publications are available on the internet and can be accessed at [HTTP://WWW.NATO.INT].

25. Nick Williams, "Partnership for Peace: Permanent Fixture or Declining Asset?" *Survival* 38, no. 1 (Spring 1996): 98–110, 103.

26. Partnership for Peace: Framework Document, NATO Press Communiqué, M-1 (94) 2, 10 January 1994.

27. Williams notes correctly that PfP was never judged on its own terms and considered by many as a program with little intrinsic value: "Its importance could only be judged in relation to enlargement and the extent to which it hastened or delayed the admission of new members to NATO." Nick Williams, "Partnership for Peace," 99.

28. *Nezavisimaya Gazeta*, 8 December 1993, 4.

29. *Nezavisimaya Gazeta*, 23 February 1994, 4.

30. *Nezavisimaya Gazeta*, 20 April 1994, 4.

31. *Pravda*, 27 May 1994, 3.

32. "Both the Alliance and Russia have important contributions to make to European stability and security," *NATO Review* (August 1994): 4.

33. Andrei Kozyrev, "Russia and NATO: A Partnership for a United and Peaceful Europe," *NATO Review* (August 1994): 3–6.

34. Ibid., 6.

35. Ibid., 3.

36. Peter Shearman, "Russian Policy toward Western Europe: The German Axis," in *Russian Foreign Policy since 1990*, ed. Peter Shearman (Boulder, CO: Westview Press, 1995), 93–109, 102.

37. NATO, *Basic Fact Sheet*, no. 13 (Brussels, March 1996).

38. *Rossiiskaya Gazeta*, 7 December 1994, 1; see also Lara Cantuti, "U.S., Russia Open New Dialogue on Strains over NATO Expansion," *Arms Control Today* (January/February 1995): 25.

39. *Nezavisimaya Gazeta*, 14 March 1995, 1–2.

40. Vladislav Chernov, "View from Russia. The Expansion of NATO and the Future of the CFE Treaty," *Comparative Strategy* 14 (1995): 87–90, 88.

41. Andrei Kozyrev, "Partnership or Cold Peace?" *Foreign Policy* no. 99 (Summer 1995): 3–14, 13.

42. Ibid.

43. "View from Russia. Russia and NATO: Theses of the Council of Foreign and Defense Policy," *Comparative Strategy* 15, no. 1 (1996): 91–102, 94.

44. Alexei Arbatov, "NATO and Russia," *Security Dialogue* 26, no. 2 (1995): 135–146, 142.

45. NATO, *Study on Enlargement* (Brussels, September 1995), 1.

46. Ibid., 4.

47. Ibid., 5.

48. Ibid., 9.

49. See F. Stephen Larrabee, "Ukraine's Balancing Act," *Survival* 38, no. 2 (Summer 1996): 143–165.

50. NATO, *Basic Fact Sheet,* no. 13 (March 1996).

51. In the December 1995 parliamentary elections, the Communist party won 22 percent of the popular vote and 40 percent of the Duma seats; the LDP with 11 percent gained only less than half of the votes of the 1993 elections; and the reformist group Yabloko again received about 7 percent. Gaidar's "Democratic Choice of Russia," with less than 5 percent, failed to gain representation in the new Duma. For an analysis of both elections see Beat Kernen, "The Russian Parliamentary Elections of 1993," 235–250.

52. *Los Angeles Times*, 13 January 1996, A10.

53. Ibid.

54. *Süddeutsche Zeitung*, 3 December 1996, 2.

55. Ibid., 30 June 1996, 8.

56. Ibid., 4 December 1996, 7.

57. See *The Economist* (14 December 1996): 31; and *Süddeutsche Zeitung*, 18 December 1996, 2.

58. *Süddeutsche Zeitung*, 22/23 February 1997, 2.

59. *The Economist* 342, no. 8008 (15 March 1997): 15–16; see also *International Herald Tribune*, 21 March 1997, 12.

60. Ukrainian leaders were at the same time pursuing their own agenda. After NATO had signaled in December 1996 its willingness to establish "a strong, stable, and enhanced partnership with Ukraine, whose independence and territorial integrity are important factors for overall European stability," Ukrainian Foreign Minister Hennadiy Udovenko started negotiations "toward the formalization of the NATO-Ukrainian relationship" (NATO Press Communiqué, M-NAC(DM)-3(96)172). He visited NATO headquarters the very same day the U.S.-Russia summit started in Helsinki. See *NATO Press Release* (97)30, 20 March 1997.

61. "Founding Act on Mutual Relations, Cooperation and Security between NATO and the Russian Federation," 27 May 1997, 5. See also Harvey Sichterman, "The Loud Voice of the NATO-Russian Council," *Transitions* 4, no. 3 (August 1997): 50–55.

62. *International Herald Tribune*, 22/23 March 1997, 1; see also Madeleine Albright, "Why Bigger Is Better," *The Economist* 342, no. 8004 (15 February 1997): 19–20.

63. See *Neue Zürcher Zeitung*, 22/23 March 1997, 3; and *The Economist* 342, no. 8010 (29 March 1997): 32.

64. *Süddeutsche Zeitung*, 24 March 1997, 9.

65. *Izvestiya*, 22 March 1997, 3.

66. For a discussion of the changing relationship of Moscow to its former satellite states, see Mike Bowker, "Russian Policy toward Central and Eastern Europe," in *Russian Foreign Policy since 1990*, ed. Peter Shearman (Boulder, CO: Westview Press, 1995), 71–92.

67. Karaganov as cited in Anatol Lieven, "Russia's Opposition to NATO Expansion," *The World Today* (October 1995): 196–199; esp. 198.

68. Ibid., 196.

69. Ibid., 198.

70. Andrei Kozyrev, "NATO Is Not Our Enemy," *Newsweek* 129, no. 6 (10 February 1997): 31.

71. Alexei K. Pushkov, "Don't Isolate Us. A Russian View of NATO Expansion," *The National Interest,* no. 47 (Spring 1997): 58–62, 59.

72. Wolfram Hanrieder, *Germany, America, Europe*, 201.

73. Ibid.

4

Searching for Security: Redefining Germany's Security Interests

PETER H. LOEDEL

> Mindless pursuit of established policies can sometimes be the worst way to maintain a desirable stability.
>
> —*A. W. Deporte*

> As a Liberal, I certainly don't aim to militarize our foreign policy, but as a realist, I know there are situations where violence and aggression can only be stopped by force.
>
> —*German Foreign Minister Klaus Kinkel*

INTRODUCTION

Ah, Schönes Deutschland! Wonderful Germany! A recent book by Thorsten Becker[1] alludes to the present state of Germany—to a people who are just beginning to realize that their country no longer resembles a huge, affluent, secure pleasure island. For Germany, Becker implies, the pleasure cruise is now over, and difficult choices will have to be made. Superlatively staging the peculiarities of a reunited Germany that is at odds with itself, Becker wrote a parody in which Germany has redivided after a failed try at reunification. His book is perfect for a country learning to come to grips with its new-found unity, a historic event that has placed long-established traditions, relationships, and beliefs under strict scrutiny. While economic problems certainly dominate many of the discussions and debates surrounding the long-lost pleasure island "Germany," the proper German relationship to the security architecture of Europe also faces an intense review both within Germany and among its neighbors. This chapter is an account of the efforts to define a new German role in European security cooperation.

What might be the role of Germany in the altered European geostrategic landscape? One answer is offered by Germany's foreign minister, Klaus Kinkel. Kinkel suggests that German foreign policy remains an ongoing effort to balance the continuities of German foreign policy with the striking changes confronting policymakers. On the one hand, Germany seeks to continue its traditional multilateral and demilitarized security policy with its emphasis on enmeshment and entanglement in multiple European and international institutions. In other words, the established foreign policy consensus fostered through coalition politics will continue. On the other hand, Germany is currently redefining and reevaluating its traditional policy to reflect the post-cold-war changes in the European security landscape. In this vein, a search for "normality" in German security policy is under way, a policy that may include a stronger assertion of German national interest and the use of force under certain prescribed situations.[2]

Despite the best efforts and good intentions of the German balancing act, German security policy can nevertheless be characterized at times by puzzlement and confusion. The central argument of this chapter is that Germany's post-cold-war security policy remains unclear and beset by distorted reasoning. This distorted reasoning, a "psychosis," finds German security policy caught between more traditional collective defense notions of NATO, a more assertive national-interest-based policy, and a more fully integrated European security identity. Indeed, torn between competing interest-based pressures and institutional constraints, difficult and complex choices face the Germans. They cannot be all things to all people—whether to the United States and the Atlantic Alliance, to their European partners, or to Russia. These many faces of German security policy thus confront Europe with a fundamental problem as it seeks to redefine European security cooperation in the post-cold-war era. In what direction will German security policy finally proceed?

A major theme of this chapter is that Germany's leadership role in European security affairs must be intensified. Ultimately, the German question is a European question. In other words, Europe's security is weak as long as Germany's security needs are not met. When Germany's security needs are fulfilled, Europe's security is that much more stable. The creation of a viable framework for European security cooperation demands German clarity on security policy. Germany must reaffirm its interest in a common European security framework while reassuring its European partners of its commitment to European integration. A core set of three principles—political cooperation, economic integration, and strategic calculation—should be more tightly interwoven to form the foundation of Germany's future role in Europe. This is why Germany's leadership role as a committed European partner as well as a critical link to central and eastern Europe (CEE) and Russia necessitates that Germany facilitate the creation of a European security order built on the EU and the Western European Union (WEU). Germany cannot rely solely upon NATO to serve European or German security interests.

The chapter is divided into four parts. First, with Germany as a focal point, I examine briefly the history of security developments in Europe since the end of the cold war. This period of European security cooperation is best characterized by "institutional competition." Second, I look at the existing strands of German security policy, including the German-U.S. transatlantic partnership, the role of NATO, and German-Russian bilateralism. Third, I evaluate such policies within the context of the analytical framework of this volume. In other words, is German security policy driven by interests or institutions? Finally, I redefine German security in terms of the political, the economic, and the strategic.

CREATING A EUROPEAN SECURITY FRAMEWORK: INSTITUTIONAL COMPETITION

During the period 1990 to 1997, the United States and the Europeans have struggled over the definition of a future European security framework; this struggle has centered on what role institutions would play in the provision of security in a new Europe. Which entity—NATO, the WEU, the OSCE, or some combination thereof—could best keep the peace in Europe in this new post-cold-war era? None of these security institutions has emerged unscathed or with its credibility entirely untarnished by the developments in the Balkans. Each institution revealed weaknesses inherent in its decisionmaking structure as well as functional operation. Further, states had differing conceptions of the proper role, usage, and functions of the institutions. For NATO, it was the requirement of U.S. leadership—which was not always forthcoming—that led to periods of waffling over how NATO forces would be deployed. For the EU, it was the failure of institutional decisionmaking and institutional mechanisms for implementing a true Common Foreign and Security Policy (CFSP) that spelled disaster. Moreover, interstate differences between French, British, and German leadership over a CFSP weakened any claim to a united European security policy. For the OSCE, it was the lack of a clear agenda among its members that has led to an ill-defined course for the future. The end result has been European security cooperation beset by institutional competition and, more tragically, policy inertia on the ground.

Admittedly, it would be difficult to think that a quick construction of a new European security regime would be possible. Yet, compounding this difficulty, the Germans, Europeans, and the United States decided to pursue multiple institutional and interest-based avenues of European security cooperation. Indeed, no security regime could realistically function in the confusion over the Balkans. For example, early on in the conflict, German expressions of support for an independent Croatia and Slovenia and pressure on EU partners to support such a plan led some commentators to conclude that a recently reunified Germany was dangerously wielding power in pursuit of national interest. For their part, the French reasserted old ties to the region, and Russia expressed concern for their Slavic allies, the Serbs. In the later stages of the conflict, acceptance by the United States and most Europeans of Croatia's military drive for control of the Krajina—which restored a semblance of balance of power in the region—came on the tacit recognition of the *Realpolitik* of Balkan politics. Furthermore, Serb aggression toward U.N. safe havens led to a reinvigorated U.S.-led NATO response, culminating in the Dayton Accords, which starkly revealed the necessity of major power involvement for stability in the region. In each case, conceptualizations of power and state interests defined the course and outcome of European security policy and hindered the development of a coherent common policy.

At the same time, institutions provided constraints on state policy and provided the context for the development of a "European" response in the Balkans. Despite the difficulties, the Europeans believed that a traditional multilateral and institutional approach to the Balkan crisis could effectively bring it to a conclusion—if certain institutional weaknesses in the CFSP could be quickly sorted through. Furthermore, many Europeans felt that they could employ the mechanisms of the CFSP and the OSCE, along with the United Nations to bridge the "security" gaps and secure peace in the region. U.N. blue helmets and/or OSCE observers would provide buffer zones and safe havens to the various civilian populations, and multilateral institutions could provide for the collective defense of the Bosnians. Moreover, U.N. war tribunals and collective punishment of the Serbs through economic blockades would be enough to bring Serbia to its knees. Even amid the glaring failures, European security cooperation in the Balkans was driven by the institutional context of the United Nations, NATO, the EU, and the OSCE and set the constraints for four years (1991–1995) of individual state and European policy in the region. One can thus argue that a disagreeable mix of interest-based and institutional perspectives guided policy in the Balkans.

The challenge in creating a system of mutually reinforcing institutions in the realm of European security has been compounded by the number of institutions addressing security, confusion as to their respective roles, and the competition for state loyalties in the development of a coordinated European security program. Questions should have been asked (which were not) and then answered (which have not been) prior to the development of the European response in the Balkans. Certainly one of the most commonly asked questions concerning the European security order was, why is it necessary to have so many institutions involved? Further, how does one address the rivalry that inevitably develops among states and institutions? Does it not produce an unnecessary overlapping and unreliable division of responsibility?

The conflict in the former Yugoslavia has shown how difficult it can be for various international institutions and states to function together effectively. While most successful institutions such as the EU or NATO have developed internal mechanisms to minimize potential divisiveness, channeling divergence toward compromise and common purpose, there is no such external mechanism performing this crucial role between institutions. Interests and institutions collided on the stage of European security with neither of the two forces emerging predominant. Similar to a bureaucratic power struggle in which no lines of communication exist between spheres of influence, states and institutions sought to retain autonomy over vested interests and control over their jealously guarded policy arenas. The end result was an inefficient response to the crisis. The same dynamic afflicted the European response to the Albanian crisis. In short, institutional competition and confusion contributed strongly to the failure to create a European security regime and, in the Balkans, to an ineffectual European response.

As a result, seven years after the end of the cold war and the reunification of Germany, a new European security regime that involves more than the old members of NATO and the WEU has failed to emerge. Differing regional and geopolitical interests have led to divisions and disagreements over new programs and policies for European security cooperation. Conflicts have emerged between old allies, between old and "new" institutions, and military confrontation in Europe (the Balkans) has not, one can argue, been definitively settled. A mix of interest-based foreign policy and institutional inertia on the European front has led to a collage of security structures and frameworks—the WEU, NATO, the OSCE, the Eurocorps—none of which may appear at first analysis worthy of fostering European security cooperation.

Caught between all these competing pressures have been the Germans. An intensive internal German debate over a proper role for Germany in any future security regime—the "whether," the "how," and the "under what conditions"—exacerbated the confusion. It is to this "German question" that the chapter now turns.

GERMAN SECURITY POLICY 1990–1997: SECURITY PSYCHOSIS

Traditionally, Germany's foreign and security policy "retained a somewhat tentative, irresolute, and reactive quality, often guided more by a sense of what not to do than by a clear view of what to do."[3] Although Wolfram Hanrieder was describing the period from 1949 to 1989 in German foreign policy, his assertion rings as true today. Through a tentative and irresolute security policy, Germany has contributed centrally to the institutional competition and policy inertia surrounding European security cooperation. The Germans find themselves caught in the middle of competing policy factions in the struggle to define European security cooperation and cannot find a way out. One faction, led not surprisingly by the United States, saw NATO as the sole legitimate arena for security policy in Europe. The French envisioned a more tightly bound European defense identity based on the foundations of the Eurocorps and France's own strategic nuclear sharing with still undefined "partners." The United Kingdom pursued a revamped WEU and NATO—but did not want to see the United States disengage from Europe. The Russians pushed a strong agenda of bilateral Russian-German understandings on security policy, especially with an emphasis on the OSCE.

Each approach apparently retained persuasive and convincing arguments for the Germans for somewhere among these four factions stood German security policy. Robert Art summarized the German position succinctly: "[T]he Germans, by necessity, straddled the fence, trying to please all their allies. Much of the fluidity of the European security struggle before and after unification stemmed from the conscious German decision not to come down unequivocally for any particular institutional design. . . . Germany was receptive to all proposals because it did not want to offend any of its allies."[4] Understandably, Germany sought to reduce apprehension surrounding reunification, and it did not want to alarm its neighbors, which were naturally concerned about Germany's new-found power. At the same time, the unsettled security landscape was magnified by German ambiguity and straddling on security policy. Germany aimed to please each of the competing visions of European security cooperation. The end result of such ambiguity was security psychosis—the multiple faces of German security policy.

To illustrate this security psychosis, let us examine some recent policy pronouncements by Chancellor Helmut Kohl. In an address to the diplomatic corps in Bonn, Kohl argued that "NATO will continue to be the central anchor of European security."[5] Moreover, Kohl stated that "EU enlargement and the opening of NATO are two sides of the same coin. They are the supporting pillars of a pan-European security architecture." The chancellor also suggested that security in Europe would be possible only "in concert with Russia." Adding to the confusion, after a bilateral summit with Russian President Boris Yeltsin in January 1997, Kohl optimistically argued that NATO would never bring its political or military machinery up to Russia's borders. A bilateral German-Russian partnership could anchor a security framework in Europe. Kohl has argued, too, that Ukraine should not fall into a "political-security gray zone"[6] and is central to European stability and security. Or, as Kohl argued repeatedly during the EU Intergovernmental Conference, the WEU should be further integrated into thc process of European integration in order to provide a stronger, self-standing, European security component. Key to the EU-focused security approach is the deepening of the Franco-German alliance. Finally, Kohl has pointed positively toward the OSCE as the foundation of a "common and comprehensive security model for the Europe of the 21st century."[7]

While Foreign Minister Kinkel has often suggested that there are no gray areas in security policy, there would appear indeed to be a great deal of gray within the multiple avenues to security in Europe as suggested by Chancellor Kohl. The questions facing German policymakers are indeed complex. Would Russia act as a partner with Germany in association with NATO, as a member of NATO, or in some other role? In what way will Russia and Ukraine be integrated into the security architecture of Europe? Will the EU and NATO work out a plan for coordination—a "partnership of equals" to use the phrase of Klaus Kinkel? Or will the WEU, with the newly created Combined Joint Task Forces (CJTFs), slowly replace NATO as the primary instrument of enforcing European security—a "separable but not separate" part of NATO? Will the OSCE continue to linger as a leftover from the cold war? Or will it find some role between the EU and NATO? Will the Eurocorps continue to be the linchpin of a Franco-German plan for a "European Defense Identity"? Has the "nuclear sharing" option proposed by France been seriously reviewed? For the lay person and the expert alike, it is hard to disentangle the many "faces" of German security policy.

Gary Geipel has argued that Germany stands at a historical crossroads where the traditional escape routes to moral high ground and political hedging are no longer valid policy options.[8] Moreover, the "burden of choice" facing the Germans demands that the approach thus far taken by the Germans, which has been to deny "the existence of choice, to obscure it in legalism, or simply send mixed signals,"[9] be reevaluated. It is not an easy process of reassessment, for Germany lies at the pivot point between the programs for European security cooperation that stress European institutions (EU), that emphasize both European and transatlantic institutions (the OSCE and NATO), and those that emphasize a more strongly transatlantic orientation (just NATO). Geostrategically, Germany also falls on the pivot point of the European landscape, captured between the competing pulls of East and West and the "middle." To date, it is an uneasy balance, embodied in Bonn's relationships and partnerships with Moscow, Washington, Paris, and Warsaw. Everybody needs the Germans, but for what purpose?[10]

Clearly, Germany lies in a critical position—not only geostrategically but politically as well—and any restructuring of European security cooperation will require the support of the Germans. Bonn has played a supportive role in providing stability in Europe and overcoming the East-West divide during the last fifty years. Germany's policy set the tone of stability in western Europe through the Federal Republic's energetic integration into western structures and institutions. Building on this successful and laudable record, Germany has sought to play a more dynamic role. But as this analysis suggests, it is as yet unclear what that role will entail. Such a role will unlikely be "renationalized," and it is inconceivable to think that the Germans would use military force unilaterally to affect their neighbors for purposes of national interest. Nevertheless, complex underlying transformations in the country's internal and external position must affect Germany's security policy. Germany will have to discard its tendency to seek to please every interest, its tentativeness, and its reactiveness to policy initiatives. Germany cannot indefinitely retain a security policy located somewhere between a transatlantic orientation and an emerging European security identity. A security policy akin to walking a tightrope is no way to span the gaps in European security cooperation.

Moreover, the security policy debate carries over directly into domestic politics. "Foreign policy is domestic policy is foreign policy" conveys a special meaning for the Germans. Specifically, internal consensus on policy and compatibility with external constraints has shaped postwar Germany's foreign policy making.[11] An intensive internal debate on the "whether" and the "how" of German participation in international conflict resolution has added to the ambiguous political zigzag course in German security politics. Certainly the costs of reunification and the political stamina required to see it through have drained the energy from Germany to play any sustained "great power" role in Europe. The ongoing reign of Chancellor Kohl with the liberal Free Democratic Party (FDP) coalition appears firmly poised to continue for the time being the same tired, ambivalent policy. To Germany's neighbors, this may be fine. But as the argument here suggests, the other side of Europe's security gestalt is an unsettling security environment beset by institutional paralysis. Established policies may not in this case be best suited to the development of a balanced internal debate on security policy.

Another area of potential concern among outside observers is the possible domestic policy backlash in German politics. Interminable reassurances and constant bending over backward to Europeans over the fear of German hegemony could produce a more, not a less, nationalistic policy. While less evident in the high levels of politics, an intense intellectual debate over the proper path for German foreign and security policy has emerged—primarily focused on the controversial writings of people associated with the *Neue Rechte* (the "New Right")—including established political scientists such as Hans-Peter Schwartz. The *Neue Rechte* argues that Germany should be recognized as a power in Europe. A distinct antiwestern, anti-U.S., and anti-NATO philosophy underlies some of these ideas. As Jacob Heilbrunn has noted, "the refusal of the Bonn political class to face up to Germany's new position was creating an opening for the new right."[12] Although the impact should not be overestimated, the mere appearance of such a debate in such circles illustrates the complexity and intense emotions involved in defining a new role for Germany. In addition, the perception by Europe that Germany is not cooperating with its neighbors may fuel a defensive isolationism or backlash within Germany. German refusal to participate in European security cooperation would be disastrous. As Art summarized, "Germany could lose both ways: a Germany perceived as too powerful, or a powerful Germany that refused to use its power for the common good. Either could produce destructive domestic results."[13]

Another potential source of isolationism stems from debates within the political Left over Germany's military participation in international missions. While the public in general seems more willing to deploy the German army under a NATO flag in "out-of-area" missions to defend common western interests or to participate in U.N.-sponsored collective security operations, strong opponents of "normalization" among the Social Democratic party (SPD), the Greens, and the Party of Democratic Socialism (PDS) reveal a schism of opinion within Germany over military operations. More radical notions of opposition reject the assumption that Germany should assume a more prominent role in the world or that Germany should think in terms of "national interests." A more moderate form of resistance to normalization envisions Germany pursuing a Swedish or Norwegian notion of normalization, not one based on the role of Great Britain or France.[14] Such a view strikes a strong chord with the German public, which sees a "different" role for German intervention. While some factions within the SPD and the Greens on occasion suggested a stronger German role in Bosnia, for example, there exists no strong consensus among the Left, to say nothing of the public, over what exactly Germany's role—especially a military one—might be and the conditions under which a German role can be defined.

This chapter certainly does not wish to strike an alarmist note, but rather to suggest a concern over possible drift and flux in German security policy. Isolationism and great power politics do not appear on the radar screen of German domestic politics or security policy, yet. However, with an unsettled European security landscape and with no definitive path toward European security cooperation agreed upon, the multiplicity of policy avenues supported by the Germans does raise some concerns. Internationally, Germany prioritizes the transatlantic partnership one day, cements the special bilateral relationship to Russia the next day, and indicates the priority of European political integration with the development of a European defense identity the very next. Domestically, German politicians refer to Germany as "normal," yet "different." Reassuring every interest—both domestic and foreign—merely adds to the disjunction between domestic and foreign policy. While perhaps not delusional, a psychosis does illustrate the gestalt of German security policy—scattered, uninventive, and intellectually deteriorating. From the many faces of German security policy, one vision must emerge ascendant.

In what follows, I suggest that a European prioritization of German security—in other words, redefining German security—would best reconcile the disjunction between foreign and domestic policy and enhance European security cooperation.

THE GERMAN-U.S. TRANSATLANTIC PARTNERSHIP AND NATO

The permanence of the transatlantic alliance and the strengthening of the German-American partnership under President Clinton and Chancellor Kohl suggest that nothing could replace this pillar of European security. The U.S. commitment to Europe and NATO appears strong, and Germany and other European countries acknowledge the importance of the U.S. partnership to European security. Senior American and German foreign policy officials argue correctly that American involvement in Europe has been a necessary component of continental balance for over fifty years. An unstable Europe, so the logic runs, threatens essential U.S. and German interests. Furthermore, other potential security arrangements built around the EU or the OSCE remain merely extras on a stage set and dominated by NATO and U.S. leadership. The future of European security and stability will, according to this logic, be built around adapting and reformulating NATO's guidelines, programs, and doctrines on the back of the U.S.-German partnership.

While this chapter does not discount NATO's importance to today's security environment, it does question the dogged pursuit of a NATO-first policy. Such a role conforms to the prevailing frame of reference and traditional foreign policy consensus in Washington. Unfortunately, this perspective has dominated much of the discussion in the United States and in Europe, stifling the debate on alternative perspectives and approaches to European security. The United States, as Richard Steele has notably commented, is "hobbled by our cold war ways of looking at the world."[15] It is as if U.S. policymakers miss the cold war—the cause to defend and the necessity to lead. Policymakers appear overwhelmingly concerned with the "threat" in Europe. At a time when it is increasingly clear that the United States is committed to expanding NATO and solidifying a NATO-first European security framework, this U.S. policy consensus and perspective must be questioned.

First, Germany cannot and should not take the U.S. commitment to Europe or NATO as a given for the indefinite future. The glue that held the alliance together and focused U.S. attention on Europe for fifty years is largely gone. Domestic political pressures within the U.S., primarily financial, and a reorientation toward other geostrategic regions (Asia and Mexico) wrestle for policymakers' attentions. Second, with all the new dimensions and possible threats to stability in Europe, security for Germans and Europeans in the post-cold-war era should not necessarily mean merely repackaging a familiar product—namely NATO. NATO's actions in Bosnia as well as the disputes between Europeans and the United States over the direction of policy there indicate that no firm model for NATO deployment or operation has evolved.[16] As my earlier analysis over institutional competition demonstrated, NATO's own commitment and cohesion has to be questioned.

Correspondingly, the vagueness of the NATO-first proposals and the failure to clarify what exactly the U.S. role should be, what Europe's role should be, and what Germany's role should be only heighten the need for alternatives to U.S. propositions. Ambiguities riddle the proposals for a continued leadership role of the United States in NATO. Under what conditions would the United States lead? Under what conditions would the United States and Europe act jointly? What specific role is envisioned for Europe? Or for Germany? The failure of such proposals to specify the conditions of U.S. involvement and the German role add uncertainty to the security equation. As noted earlier, ambiguity and waffling are apt characterizations of the Kohl security policy record, to say nothing of President Clinton's foreign policy record. Waffling and ambiguity, however, damage credibility, sabotage reputations, and make commitments less believable.

The debate over NATO enlargement illustrates additional problems. "NATO expansion must strengthen security in the entire region, including nations that are not members" has become the mantra of U.S. policy in Europe.[17] But what exactly is the U.S. interest in expanding NATO? As one scholar has noted, the extension of NATO security guarantees would commit American troops in advance to defend countries, with nuclear weapons if necessary, where no vital American security interest may be involved.[18] Extension for the sake of expansion appears to be part of the overriding U.S. logic, as some U.S. domestic critics have suggested.[19] Does the U.S., or Germany for that matter, seriously want to extend the security and nuclear umbrella to all existing NATO members? Interestingly, as Steele pointingly noted, the British and American empires developed in such a way that each never felt secure, "no matter how much they controlled. The 'frontiers of insecurity' . . . expanded indefinitely."[20] Is that what the United States is doing in Europe? Preventing the emergence of a new hegemon or power in Europe might be an appropriate objective for the United States, but undebated extensions of the security umbrella for ill-defined security interests do not make for a credible U.S. policy. Indeed, the momentum of "expansion" and "empire" still cloud U.S. judgment on this issue.[21]

In addition, the repeated statements of U.S. policymakers concerning the need for the EU and NATO to operate in tandem to form a broad security framework begs the question that has yet to be forcefully asked: How exactly are these two powerful, functionally and politically distinct institutions to operate collectively? During the cold war, the EC and NATO did operate concurrently, albeit in separate functional realms, in order to promote the overriding containment policies. Today, however, it is still unclear from U.S. proposals how these two organizations and institutions would work together and toward what goals. While the Combined Joint Task Forces proposal of the WEU and NATO appears to be the plan for the future, it does not clarify fully the conditions of cooperation. The goal of CJTFs is to create a "militarily more coherent and efficient force that is in a position to operate under the control of the WEU" and thereby establish "a new European security and defense identity within the alliance." But is not the WEU also part of the EU's emerging "defense identity"? Will the EU decide on its own when to use CJTFs? Will the United States veto such action? It is all uncomfortably vague.

Traditionally, the United States has sought to create security dependency in Europe (the focus of which was West Germany), discouraging the Germans from challenging U.S. leadership or even aspiring to more prominent regional or global roles. Such a U.S. orchestration of security policy served Germany's interest during the cold war. Germany remains grateful for the continued interest of the United States in European security. An Atlantic-oriented, free-trading, multilateral, and global Europe with German-U.S. leadership is appropriate. Europeans, however, should be skeptical of a continued security system orchestrated and controlled from Washington. Is double containment of Russia *and* Germany under U.S. domination and NATO leadership still required today? Will a security policy dictated largely by constraints imposed by the United States or NATO serve German interests in the decades to come? Are there no worthy alternatives for the ever-pleasing and programmatic Germans?

Helmut Schmidt's old adage that the FRG "belongs in the West" still holds true, but his assertion that the Atlantic Alliance is the first pillar of German foreign policy and the EU the second should no longer be held as an article of faith. It is hard to find a powerful argument in favor of Germany continuing its military security dependence on the United States. During the cold war, France maintained a strong measure of independence in its security relations with NATO and the United States by retaining a separate nuclear arsenal. Germany, of course, was prevented for moral and political reasons from doing so. The moral arguments against Germany retaining an independent nuclear role remain compelling, and Germany has pledged to keep it so. Yet, the political arguments against Germany developing a cooperative security framework to meet Germany's and Europe's security interests in the coming decades are less compelling than ever. Germany should seek to act more independently of the United States, not necessarily in an antagonistic or overtly competitive sense, but rather to reassure itself and its European partners of its commitment to security and balance in Europe. As Klaus Kinkel recently suggested, "in the long run, it is neither in the American nor the European interest that we have to call our American friends each time something flares up somewhere."[22]

GERMANY AND RUSSIA: PURSUING A EUROPE-FIRST OPTION?

This section begins with a simple premise: stability for Germany in Europe is impossible without Russia. To create stability in Europe, Germany and Europe should not work against Russia; rather, a lasting and equitable security framework—European security cooperation—must include Russia. It is to state the obvious to suggest that Russia's concern with events in Germany and central and eastern European countries has been the source of turmoil and tragedy in Europe for well over a hundred years. Simply put, insecurity in this region has contributed to the major wars of this century. Logically, therefore, CEE and Russia remain the focal point for clarifying a new security structure for Europe. While Russia should not have a veto over any policies and programs involving Germany's security policy, neither should Germany nor the West push Russia into a position where it might feel the need to use a veto.

The issue with Russia is not its military strength but rather its economic and political weakness. Russia is already on the defensive. Ideologically, the Russians have little going for them. Politically, the volatility of the electorate, the weakness of President Yeltsin, and the divided makeup of Russia's parliament suggest continued confusion in domestic and foreign policies. Militarily, the fiasco in Chechnya indicates a military in crisis. Economically, Russia may have at best turned a corner in the transition from a command to a market economy. At worst, the economic situation may be quickly unraveling. Nothing looks certain from the Russian viewpoint, and it must be a little unnerving. In short, Russia's insecurity and instability could very quickly infect the rest of Europe, an infection Germany and Europe should seek to prevent.

Traditionally, Russia's interests in Europe have been to create a western buffer zone or region of stability in central and eastern Europe. This was true in the times of the czar, under Soviet communism, and now under a democratizing Russia. The traditional xenophobia and fear of encirclement from the West will endure if the West and NATO continue to thrust rapidly to the East. NATO expansion merely antagonizes Russia during a period when antagonizing Russia may not be in the West's interest. Again, there is nothing fundamentally wrong at this time with pursuing collaborative plans and policies within the steadying hands of the Partnership for Peace Program (PfP) or a NATO-Russia cooperative council, but Russia will never be satisfied until its traditional foreign policy concerns in the West have been met. Extending NATO to Russia's border will not do this. As Anatol Lieven suggested, NATO expansion "will add the crowning touch to Russia's humiliation."[23] Moreover, "why, with all the hopeful possibilities engendered by the end of the cold war, should East-West relations become centered on the question of who would be allied with whom and, by implication, against whom in some fanciful, totally unforeseeable and most improbable future military conflict?"[24] In short, it is hard to imagine anything more threatening to Russia—politically and military-strategically—than NATO expansion into this buffer zone. Indeed, Russia's strong resistance to NATO's expansion causes some political divisions among European leaders.

Germany has been a central concern of Russian foreign policy because of both its intrinsic importance and its significance for Russian relations with the United States. The primary preoccupation of the Russians has always been to contain Germany, solve the German problem, and prevent Germany from ever again threatening Russia militarily or politically. In doing so, during the cold war, the Soviet Union historically sought to encourage fissures within the Atlantic Alliance. There was more room for Soviet maneuvering in western Europe than for the Russians in today's Europe largely because the primary card they held over the Germans—the potential of German unification—can no longer be played. Nonetheless, the case for creating divisions between the United States and western Europe still makes sense in some circles in Moscow.

Economically, further disputes between Germany and the United States over aid to Russia are likely to occur. The Russians depend heavily on European, primarily German, credits, and the Germans seem unceasingly willing to reschedule debt repayments. The Germans also have been on the forefront in seeking further multilateral international aid for the Russians. The United States on the other hand, has been resistant to increase such aid, causing resentment both in Germany and Russia.[25] For its part, the United States felt some consternation with German activism toward Russia. While such fissures may be superficial, the old Russian desire to create tension and division in Europe remains alive, and Germany's own waffling on what future European security cooperation might entail feeds the mistrust built up between the Russians and the West. It is therefore imperative that Germany and its European partners speak with a united voice toward Russia.

What options exist for German security policy toward Russia and the East? Despite an ambiguous Russian policy that traps Bonn between placating central and eastern European countries and reassuring Russia, Germany's solid integration into EU institutions should allow for a reinvigorated *Ostpolitik* on behalf of Europe. Russia and Germany could pursue a European security framework, building upon existing structures of the EU,[26] although such a view is discounted by some German leaders, including Defense Minister Volker Rühe. Recognizing that instability in the East would be counterproductive to European integration, Chancellor Kohl and Klaus Kinkel have both spoken of a stronger "pan-European" arrangement for Europe based on the EU and the OSCE (especially during the period 1990 to 1991). Strongly supported by Germany, part of this policy has been NATO's Partnership for Peace—a halfway measure between status quo and enlargement. PfP can be seen as an effort to prevent Russian isolationism and reactive nationalism. But PfP does not fully cement security for the Russians, CEE, or the Germans; it delays solidifying a new form of European security cooperation thereby adding to the institutional and policy competition that weakens European security cooperation.

As with its other policies, Germany's bilateral partnership with Russia straddles the divisions within Europe and the transatlantic alliance. Such a policy may be appropriate given the unclear nature of Russian policy today. Nevertheless, Russia's aversion to NATO expansion is clear. A constructive policy aimed at dealing with this reality is thus required. The Europeans, especially the Germans, Russians, and the Poles—each with the most to fear yet with the most to gain from stability in the East—should look to Russian inclusion on European terms into European political, economic, and security structures.[27] Eastward expansion should take the path of inclusion, not selective exclusion. Russia and Germany could return to a relationship of equals—not to squeeze countries in the middle or a return to Rapallo, but to play a constructive economic and political role in Europe.

REDEFINING GERMAN SECURITY: THE POLITICAL ECONOMY OF GERMAN SECURITY

As shown in this chapter, Germany has pursued multiple security options ranging from unilateralism, multilateralism, "superintegrationism," a "Partner in Leadership," and a moral role with no military force.[28] We have seen Germany simultaneously pursue bilateralism with Russia, the transatlantic partnership with the United States and NATO, a new OSCE security architecture, and full political integration in Europe, including the defense component of the CFSP and WEU. Within these multiple options, two larger themes emerge. On the one hand, German security policy still emphasizes the traditional, multilateral, and institutional approach of European security. Germany appears strongly committed to the rule of law and the pacific resolution of conflicts based on institutional principles of security, diplomacy, and economics—all compatible with its half-century commitment to institutionalism. On the other hand, German security policy looks for "normality" and a renewed expression of German national interests. Germany does not, and should not, take security for granted—nor should any other European nation. In terms of the theoretical framework set forth in this volume, Germany therefore calculates its relations to European partners (and they to Germany) in terms of a combination of security concerns, power considerations, and institutional constraints. German security policy thus reflects a mix of interest- and institution-based variables.

Each security track retains a persuasive political and theoretical rationale and, to date, has allowed Germany to avoid antagonizing every interest and institution. Despite such an approach, a more forceful assertion and articulation of German security policy objectives is necessary. This will raise painful and sensitive historical concerns, and such concerns are understandable. Yet, this chapter suggests that the quest for European security cooperation will be made easier if all participants have a clear understanding of German national objectives.[29] While it is always a bit hard to articulate precisely the "national interest," one can argue that there is a discernible set of German national objectives: economic prosperity through European integration and liberalization (*the economics*), political cooperation through a framework of multilateral institutions both regionally and globally (*the politics*), and collective security to safeguard a regional balance in Europe (*the strategic*). These national interests, as Wolfram Hanrieder so eloquently documented in his works, reveal a powerful continuity in German foreign policy.

As a result, there are some who claim that Germany's interests have been, and will continue to be, met in the existing institutional framework. "German foreign policy does not need to be reinvented" would appear to be the dominant frame of reference for many German politicians and U.S. State Department officials. Indeed, free trade and open markets, democratic and prosperous neighbors do not need reinventing. Historically, the strands—*the economics, the politics, and the strategic*—have thus found their fulfillment for the Germans in different institutional arenas. One can argue that this institutional arrangement suited German interests. Moreover, the United States would have it remain that way. According to the United States NATO will continue to serve Germany's security interests; the EU will continue to serve Germany's economic interests; and, Germany can find political expression through its continued involvement in a number of multilateral institutions such as the United Nations, the OSCE, the EU, or the even World Trade Organization.

But German security policy does require some institutional rethinking. Unification has obliged Germany to assume a more exposed role internationally, to examine what role it should play between the East and the West, and to find self-assurance in world affairs. Given the multiple avenues and unclear vision of German security policy, this chapter suggests a renewed emphasis on a definition of German security policy aimed at reducing institutional competition, clarifying Germany's role, and providing a stronger cooperative security framework for Europe. The choice of a definition of security—which is not necessarily new in the minds of the Germans—must be based on domestic consensus and be compatible with the institutional framework that exists in Europe today. Trade-offs between foreign and domestic politics must be recognized as the pursuit of security and necessarily involve calculating political and economic opportunity costs. In an era of limited economic resources and political energy, resources committed to one policy are resources not committed to another policy. As a result, Germany should seek to expend its limited political energy and economic resources on a security goal and institutional framework that would furnish the most political-economic benefits at reduced cost.

As such, security as a goal should be defined more broadly to include economic welfare—which in and of itself can include issues related to the environment, education, immigration, crime, and human rights.[30] The means toward such an end must also be pursued beyond one set of instruments, namely military statecraft. A balance of diplomacy and law, information, economics, and institutions are more relevant than ever before to the pursuit of security for Germany.[31] Neither NATO nor the OSCE fully addresses this balanced definition of security. Instead, the proper instrument of security policy should include the institutional framework of the EU, which does address the larger political-economic-strategic concerns of Germany. Because the EU can provide the informational, military (WEU), economic, institutional, and diplomatic framework for the expression of German security policy, the political-economic-strategic return on resources invested in an EU security option would far exceed the resources spent on reviving NATO or restructuring the OSCE. German power could be pooled efficiently and responsibly in a European system of "associated sovereignty and German semisovereignty."[32]

Given the definition of German security set forth above—what I call the political-economy of German security policy—Germany's European policy would see both the deepening and enlargement of the security and the economic pillars of the EU. The choice for Germany to expand and deepen Europe should not be seen as some diabolic attempt to weaken Germany's ties to the United States. The choice, however, to refocus on Europe is based on a convincing set of considerations.[33] First, all-European confidence building is essential in the post-cold-war period. Second, Europe must develop its own security framework and institutions to deal with potential security and political crises in Europe. Third, Germany should seek to intensify political dialogue surrounding CEE inclusion into the EU. Fourth, Russian isolation must be avoided at all costs. Finally, other than the transitionary PfP policies, NATO still has no clear mandate in the East and therefore is fundamentally unable to carry out essential security functions in that area. These five points are a persuasive package of arguments in favor of Germany's prioritization of Europe in its security policy.

In terms of enlargement, the EU's economic, political, and, ultimately, security framework would first include eastern and central Europe and then, at some future date, Russia. Critical is the promotion of German-Polish reconciliation, which should be first on the agenda of any plan designed to establish an overarching political-economic-security framework for Europe.[34] Even American policymakers see that German-Polish reconciliation "will make a decisive difference to Europe's future whether such security cooperation . . . is undertaken within or without the Euro-atlantic alliance (that is, with or without America's involvement)."[35] Germany and Poland must push this rapprochement under the guise of EU integration, WEU strengthening, and extension. As with German-French rapprochement under the EC, German-Polish (as well as German-Czech) rapprochement should continue as an anchor of the EU's extension eastward. This means a short-term painful opening of economic ties, and trade and agricultural liberalization. It also means openly and honestly exposing occasionally raw historical nerves. Institutionalization rather than words, however, can do more to overcome the long tradition of conflict and animosity between these two countries as well as with the rest of CEE. Germany, the CEE, and Russia should therefore develop mutually supportive security and economic policies within the context of multinational institutions of the EU.

The EU's inability to develop a CFSP to date is the result of the failure to integrate a parallel defense or security arm that matches the ongoing efforts at political and economic integration. In other words, the "deepening" of a European defense identity and the CFSP has stumbled upon institutional-

and interest-based hurdles. This chapter supports the premise and principles of cooperative security and its insistence on an EU-WEU security framework in order to develop the CFSP; deepening European defense and security cooperation must proceed. In such a scenario, the WEU would gradually replace NATO as the primary arm of European security cooperation, helping fortify CFSP. The Europeans thereby would utilize the only credible multilateral, institutional, and European policymaking framework that exists—the EU. By focusing on a general threat of international aggression within Europe rather than on aggression by a specific state (Russia or Germany, for example), European collective security and defense under the EU/WEU has a primary advantage over military coalitions like NATO: it is nondiscriminatory and nonconfrontational except when invoked. Collective security must also be inclusive; hence, nobody in Europe, including Russia, should be excluded.

In many respects, such a Europeanization of the security map has already been developed. The WEU is increasing its importance and range of activities. The fifteen members of the EU agreed that the IGC should flesh out the sketchy commitment of the CFSP to develop a common defense role for the WEU. Specifically, the long-neglected WEU has been given a twin role as the EU's defense arm and the European "pillar" in NATO. In fact, the price for France's partial rapprochement with NATO's military organization was the willingness of the United States to accept a WEU-European defense identity. The CJTF concept would provide the Europeans with the possibility of using the WEU as the primary defense arm of the CFSP. If the relationship with the North Atlantic Council (NAC) could be delinked, the United States and NATO would not have to act. While the United States sees the WEU as a subsidiary of NATO, the Europeans could look to the WEU as establishing the foundation for a future security framework designed and run by Europeans. Germany's security policy would therefore be "Europeanized" within such a framework.

CONCLUSION

The Federal Republic of Germany, at least what we called West Germany up until 1990, was itself a product of the cold war. Both Germany and Europe are becoming something quite different—not just the Federal Republic of Germany or western Europe, but rather Europe, with Germany in the middle. To date, the security psychosis that characterizes German policy has contributed to the relative disorder in European security cooperation. Theoretically and politically, German security policy reveals powerful tendencies toward the forces of both institutionalism and interests. In order to overcome the multiple faces of German security policy, Germany must clarify and prioritize its security policy by reassuring its European partners through its commitment to further integration and extension of the EU's security role. This means rethinking some of the basic logic of NATO. It also means that the WEU and the EU will be more powerfully integrated into one overarching political-economic-strategic framework.

NOTES

Display quotes on page 61 are from the following sources: A. W. Deporte, *Europe between the Superpowers: The Enduring Balance* (New Haven: Yale University Press, 1979), xiv; Klaus Kinkel, "German–U.S. Relations: A Strategic Partnership," *Vital Speeches of the Day* 60 (1994): 489.

1. Thorsten Becker, *Schönes Deutschland* (Berlin: Verlag Volk & Welt, 1996).

2. See Mary M. McKenzie, "Competing Conceptions of Normality in the Post-Cold-War Era: Germany, Europe and Foreign Policy Change," *German Politics and Society* 14, no. 2 (Summer 1996).

3. Wolfram Hanrieder, *Germany, America, Europe: Forty Years of German Foreign Policy* (New Haven: Yale University Press, 1989), 2.

4. Robert Art, "Why Western Europe Needs the United States and NATO," *Political Science Quarterly* 111 (Spring 1996), [http://epn/org/psq/robtart.html]: 6.

5. Kohl is quoted in "Statements and Speeches," *The Week in Germany* 19, no. 15, (4 December 1996).

6. "Kohl in Ukraine: 'Your Success Is Our Success,'" *The Week in Germany*, (6 September 1996).

7. "OSCE Lays Basis for New Security Order," *The Week in Germany* (6 December 1996).

8. Gary Geipel, "Germany and the Burden of Choice," *Current History* (November 1995): 375–380.

9. Ibid., 375.

10. See the commentary and analysis of Nina Grunenberg, "Wir werden gebraucht. Aber wozu?" *Die Zeit* 20 (19 May 1995).

11. Wolfram Hanrieder, "Compatibility and Consensus: A Proposal for the Conceptual Linkage of External and Internal Dimensions of Foreign Policy," *American Political Science Review* 61, no. 4 (1967): 971–982.

12. Jacob Heilbrunn, "Germany's New Right," *Foreign Affairs* 75, no. 6 (1996): 96. Heilbrunn's account has been sharply criticized by German scholars as overly simple and misguided. See the comments of Josef Joffe et. al, "Mr. Heilbrunn's Planet," *Foreign Affairs* 76, no. 2 (1997): 152–161.

13. Robert Art, "Why Western Europe," 13.

14. See the analysis of Philip Gordon, "The Normalization of German Foreign Policy," *Orbis* 38, no. 2 (1994).

15. Richard Steele, *Temptations of a Superpower* (Cambridge, MA: Harvard University Press, 1995), 5.

16. Christoph Bertram, "Bosnien ist kein Modell," *Die Zeit* (27 October 1995).

17. Richard Holbrooke, "America, A European Power," *Foreign Affairs* 74, no. 2 (1995): 45.

18. See, for example, Michael Brown, "The Flawed Logic of NATO Expansion," *Survival: ISS Quarterly* 37, no. 1 (1995).

19. See the comments of Senator Joseph Biden, ranking Democrat on the Foreign Relations Committee, who has questioned whether a public debate over a future role in NATO has been undertaken. Thomas Friedeman, "NATO or Tomato?," *New York Times*, 22 January 1997.

20. Richard Steele, *Temptations of a Superpower*, 50.

21. See also George Kennan, "A Fateful Error," *New York Times,* 5 February 1997.

22. Kinkel quoted in "NATO Plans Component that Will Be All-European," *New York Times*, 4 June 1996.

23. Anatol Lieven, "Russia's Opposition to NATO Expansion," *The World Today* (October 1995): 196.

24. George Kennan, "A Fateful Error."

25. Part of the tension emerged over the pressure the United States exerted on the IMF and Europeans to support the Mexican bailout plan. The Germans initially resisted the plan vigorously.

26. NATO has recognized this premise, of course, suggesting that a "cooperative European security architecture requires the active participation of Russia." See the "Ministerial Meeting of the North Atlantic Council," 1 December 1994, Brussels, Press Communiqué M-NAC-2(94), 116.

27. While the OSCE and EU could be envisioned in this role, I will argue below that the EU is better suited to perform such a function.

28. See Mary M. McKenzie, "Competing Conceptions," for a further review of such options.

29. See Philip Gordon, "Normalization."

30. See the analysis of David Baldwin, "Security Studies and the End of the Cold War," *World Politics* 48 (October 1995): 117–141.

31. See Helga Haftendorn, "The Security Puzzle: Theory Building and Discipline Building in International Security," *International Studies Quarterly* 35 (March 1991), for a review of reforming the field of security studies to include broader definitions of security.

32. Peter Katzenstein, ed., *Tamed Power: Germany in Europe* (Ithaca: Cornell University Press, 1997).

33. See especially Harold Mueller, "German Foreign Policy after Unification," in *The New Germany and the New Europe,* ed. Paul Stares (Washington, DC: Brookings, 1992).

34. See the comments of Helmut Kohl, "Im Bewußtsein der Verantwortung für ein künftiges geeintes Deutschland," *Bulletin* 34, 8 (March 1990).

35. Zbigniew Brzezinski, "A Plan for Europe," *Foreign Affairs* 74, no. 1 (1995): 30.

5

Redefining *Grandeur*: France and European Security after the Cold War

Robert Ladrech

Some six years after the events that brought the cold war to a close, the analyst of European security issues is in a better position to evaluate the implications of this historic watershed for the emergence of a new order. Allowing the "dust to settle" is crucial in this endeavor, for the ending of one order and the construction of a new one are fraught with perceptual dangers, as one is without the definitional "markers" useful in evaluating the medium-to-long-term consequences of state actions. After initial prophesies spanning the euphoric—smooth transitions of eastern economies to capitalist democracies, cooperative new security frameworks—to the gloomy—a return to a past of nationalist security threats among the great powers[1]—we can now more soberly analyze the events and underlying dynamics that have led, in the second half of the 1990s, to modest advances in constructing a new European security order. This chapter analyzes the impact of the changing security framework upon French security strategies and asks to what extent the French search for a new policy has been affected by, and has itself affected, prevailing international institutions.

When addressing French security concerns and policies, one has at the outset a fairly clearly defined postwar policy (post-1958) against which to measure and interpret any subsequent changes. This is, of course, the phenomenon known as "Gaullism." In the first part of this chapter, the Gaullist "consensus" will be briefly sketched in order to demonstrate how well this national strategy has been determined by environmental variables—the cold war—and accepted by political leaders—a cross-party elite consensus. Indeed, as the introduction to the volume suggests, a state's "conception of interest will be grounded not only in the norms of the state system but also in the norms and politics of its society." Thus, any analysis of change in French security policy must be sensitive to changes in the French state and society. Certain consequences of Europeanization impinge upon the policymaking options open to politicians, and in the case of France, the nexus between international institutional development and French economic capability is crucial to understanding present departures from the Gaullist norm in the realm of defense policy.

One particular dimension of the Gaullist model has been a vision and an accompanying rhetoric elaborating France's position in the world. To the extent that change has in fact occurred in the Gaullist foreign policy paradigm, we might expect a new vision to be articulated, or the old one to be repackaged. France occupies a singular position in regard to international institutions, and recent developments in France's policies toward NATO and the European Union's (EU) Common Foreign and Security Policy (CFSP) will be addressed in order to further evaluate the connection between domestic and international affairs and foreign policy change. All of this leads to the following consideration, spelled out more fully in the chapter's conclusion: that the security environment in which international institutions and states exist modifies decisionmakers' perceptions because of "structural constraints."[2] Michael Smith noted that it is "within the structural constraints constituted by power and positions in the international and domestic arenas that state authorities can be creative and attempt to control the costs of various policy options."[3] For many, if not all, states in the European post-cold-war security environment, not only are there fewer discernible structural "markers" or reference points that enable state decisionmakers to evaluate cost options, but in the case of France, there is at the same time a need to redefine a foreign policy orientation that had become over the course of the Fifth Republic part of an elite national security *identity*. It appears that the end of the cold war—and more importantly the dissolution of the "contextual demands and obstacles it represented"[4]—has affected France in a profound manner. The result may be the erosion of the Gaullist model as France becomes more integrated into European security institutions and sheds aspects of its domestic distinctiveness, at least in defense matters. If vision characterized Gaullism, the apparent pragmatism of current French proposals regarding involvement in international institutions may then be seen as a sign of France having "at last become an 'ordinary' European nation, encased in a highly original Community: an unromantic prospect, but a likely fate."[5]

THE GAULLIST CONSENSUS

What constituted the Gaullist model for French national security above all was a foreign policy discourse laying out the precepts of France's role in the world. From these precepts, actual policies, strategies, and relationships were derived. As many analysts of De Gaulle's foreign policy have pointed out, the underlying premise of his view of France can be traced to his analysis of the bipolar dynamics of the cold war, including the alliance systems of the two superpowers. Broadly speaking, the Gaullist model emphasized, in an interconnected fashion, national independence, nuclear autonomy, and the search for *grandeur*.[6] French security policy as it derived from these three precepts is sketched below.

National Independence

French efforts under De Gaulle to resist both American and Soviet hegemony account for the public attempts to distance France from American power by withdrawing from NATO's integrated military command structure in 1966. This policy included a highly critical view of American power within the western bloc and formed the basis of De Gaulle's activities that were designed to balance the two superpowers and were evident in his drive to pursue détente with the Soviet Union in the 1960s. National independence was also a basic principle behind the French push for greater European integration, seen as a means to develop collective European security under French leadership. Despite the fact that French and U.S. interests coincided many times in the 1980s, and Mitterrand publicly supported certain aspects of NATO policy (e.g., stationing of intermediate range missiles in Germany), formal institutional relations nevertheless retained the stance of the 1960s, although "qualified independence" would better describe the French posture from the mid-1970s onward.

Nuclear Autonomy

The development of the independent nuclear deterrent, the *force de frappe*, served both to highlight national independence, to achieve *grandeur* in the exclusive nuclear club, and to emphasize the importance of national defense. Nuclear autonomy does not necessarily imply nuclear *nationalism*, for the refusal to endorse the American-led doctrine of flexible response in the 1960s also could be viewed as an alternative European vision on security. Later developments in French nuclear strategy more clearly opened up possibilities for integrating the French deterrent into purely European policies, as the 1995 Franco-British declaration, with its convergence of views, on nuclear doctrines attested.[7]

Grandeur

Another distinctive aspect of the Gaullist model, the concept of "grandeur" is ambivalent, and probably meant to be so. Essentially, it relates to De Gaulle's notion of the primacy of the nation-state, and in the context of France, to a "certain idea" of its role in the world. According to Philip Cerny, "grandeur" is a symbolic term referring "primarily to the need to create a new and more profound sense of national consciousness, capable of transcending the traditional divisions which have characterized the French polity."[8] Further, grandeur signifies "a certain conception of the general interest, and this, in turn, implies a foreign policy which is not one of aggressive and anachronistic nationalism, but rather a restrained attempt to increase France's role in the world without taking unacceptable risks and without destroying the basis for an interdependence which is as necessary for the survival and development of the national community as is independence." Thus, a simple translation as "greatness" misses the complexity of the term, which conceives of an indissoluble link between domestic and international dynamics. The quest for grandeur then takes account of the international environment, and adjusts tactics according to the external imperatives of the situation. In terms of security policy, national independence and nuclear autonomy are intimately connected with grandeur, and the structure of France's defense, in addition to the nuclear deterrent, again emphasizes national independence, allowing France to assert a *leadership role* in the world. An ambitious international role therefore fulfills De Gaulle's own statement that "France cannot be France without greatness (*grandeur*)."[9]

If the elements of Gaullism appeared somewhat vague on particular points, a political elite consensus nevertheless developed around these principles. Security policy was one of the least divisive policy areas during Socialist President Mitterrand's two co-habitations (1986–1988, 1993–1995) with conservative prime ministers, both of whom came from the neo-Gaullist party RPR (*Rassemblement pour la République*). The issues of

NATO, European integration, and French nuclear strategy had become thoroughly depoliticized. Continuity among De Gaulle's successors on the policies derived from the Gaullist model was a distinguishing characteristic of French security policy, often thought in domestic circles to be a strength of French foreign policy.[10] Until the 1990s, this consensus held, and only with neo-Gaullist President Chirac do we now, in the mid-1990s, see the beginnings of change, though more as reactive behavior than, as De Gaulle would have stressed, bold initiatives worthy of France's grandeur.

In the next section, France's reaction to the end of the cold war will be summarized, focusing on its responses and initiatives to selected events that illustrate the challenges of the new era. In short, from 1990 until 1995, French security policy exhibited a loss of clear direction and a lack of a "vision" of the post-cold-war environment. Instead, "French policies have been characterized by a deliberate tendency to multiply the institutional responses to the new German and European challenges, and to avoid giving a clearcut exclusivity to one particular framework."[11] The Chirac presidency, which began in 1995, appears to have more explicitly "weighted" the European framework, especially regarding the French defense structure, than previous presidencies.

FRENCH RESPONSES TO THE END OF THE OLD ORDER

As many authors have remarked, French reactions to the events of the post-1989 period—the break up of Yugoslavia, the Gulf War, and German unification—displayed a degree of hesitancy, conservatism, and even, according to some, a nostalgia for the old order. The actions of France in the three cases examined here are well documented elsewhere,[12] but it is fair to say that in general, the collapse of the structures of the cold war "all combined to impose on French foreign policy a form of 'aggiornamento.' This effort of adjustment was hesitant, contradictory and remains unachieved."[13]

A few examples of French reactions to post-1989 events will demonstrate the lack of a clear perceptual and strategic map. The Gulf War and the Yugoslav (Bosnia) crisis each imparted lessons based upon a recognition of the restructured terrain in which traditional policy reflexes proved inadequate. Frustration about the efficacy of traditional courses of action eventually led to a reconsideration of the utility of international institutions and revised relations with the United States. In the Gulf War, for instance, France persisted until the "zero hour" in an independent peace initiative derided by some allies as a cynical French attempt to be at the victors' table.[14]

In the end, its military participation came under U.S. command. In the Yugoslav tragedy, France at first proclaimed the need to "go slow" in addressing the unraveling of the Yugoslav federation (taken by many commentators at the time as nostalgia for the status quo) and thus opposed the German drive for recognition of Croatia and Slovenia. France then called for armed intervention that eventually brought French forces into their closest integrated relationship with NATO in decades.

As Stanley Hoffmann has pointed out, the use of international institutions as the means to further French goals should come as no surprise. The experiences of the Gulf War and Yugoslavia especially impressed upon French decisionmakers the limited utility of traditional foreign and defense policy tactics and strategies. In the wake of these events, qualified steps toward the greater use of international institutions ensued, prompting institutional incorporation into French planning. The process toward an embrace of institutions previously kept at arm's length resulted then from a practical need, not an internally generated ideological shift from the tenets of Gaullism. Therefore, the slow and incremental changes noted by most analysts were driven without an overarching programmatic vision. This explains two dimensions of the change. First, since there did not exist a justifying principle to *replace* Gaullism among domestic audiences, the pace of change was slow. Second, the omni-directional nature of the change, institutional in regard to NATO and EU/WEU, and bilateral with the United States and Germany, together with unilateral initiatives again represents the lack of a fundamental vision. Policy shifts announced by President Chirac at the end of February 1996, in a sense an acceleration and consolidation of the direction of the incremental developments noted above, have now been accompanied by the beginnings of a post-Gaullist orientation, suggesting the emergence of a new foreign policy model.[15] For purposes of this analysis, it must be asked to what extent have international institutions shaped or given direction to the French search for a new post-Gaullist perspective, and vice versa?

THE EMERGENCE OF A NEW MODEL?

What evidence is there to support the assertion of a new French security model? This section outlines what appears to be a reformulated approach by France to NATO and to the EU's Common Foreign and Security Policy (CFSP). In both cases, redefining French security needs has meant regarding these international institutions in a new light, as the basis of the Gaullist model—the "structural constraints" of the bipolar cold-war framework—has dissolved. The overarching perspective appears to be a realization that NATO represents less of a "threat" to French independence and that a French-led collective (western) European security agency could be viable, but not in the foreseeable future. At the same time, the autonomy of French defense, a pillar of the Gaullist model, has rapidly given way to the rationalization of the national defense industrial sector.

NATO

Apart from the Bosnian crisis that brought French forces into close tactical relations with the U.S.-led NATO command, reconsideration of NATO's utility to French security needs had been unfolding at least since 1992, despite occasional rhetoric reflecting the Gaullist consensus. Indeed, Janet Bryant commented that by 1994, despite then-Defense Minister Léotard's admonishment that a "cultural revolution" would be required before France rejoined NATO's integrated military command, "the truth is that France *has* been building bridges with NATO over the past few years, and never before has France been so public in her appreciation of NATO and the US."[16]

The details of the French rapprochement with NATO are well documented elsewhere.[17] The key to understanding this "change of heart" by the French lies with a reappraisal of the previously preferred option—an independent European collective security agency, whether that be the WEU or an EU/CFSP/WEU. Here the experiences in Yugoslavia are significant, for France first attempted to rally EU member states to intervene as an exercise in CFSP. The problems and internal contradictions manifested in this episode (which led to U.S.-NATO involvement) signaled the limits of a purely European collective security initiative, or at least the unpreparedness of such an undertaking at that point in time. This, in turn, led to France's reconsideration of the U.S. role within NATO as well as in Europe in general: "France's concerns about U.S. hegemony in Europe continuing by virtue of a new, major NATO role in collective security writ large have also waned. Indeed the underlying French assumption since 1989 that the alliance and U.S. presence will remain overwhelming in spite of the demise of the Cold War now seems doubtful."[18]

Although the "reappraisal" of the United States and NATO was necessarily more complex than this suggests, the key here is that in a search for a viable security logic to replace the one constructed in a completely different international environment, actors once viewed as liabilities may now represent opportunities in the changed environment. French Foreign Minister

Hervé de Charette's announcement in December 1995 that France would henceforth participate fully in NATO's Military Committee is a byproduct of a pragmatic shift that is reevaluating already existing variables—international institutions— and is embedded in the wider search for a new connection between domestic interests and the changed conditions of the post-cold-war framework. In these circumstances, NATO and the United States are viewed as necessary to French interests because the other option(s) have proven inadequate. Grant suggested that France concluded from the Yugoslav episode that

> the US and NATO appeared increasingly necessary not only to maintain Western Europe's collective defence capabilities, but also to meet the challenges of the post-cold-war crises that France initially believed Europe could handle on its own. Thus, Paris began to realize that dealing with Europe's new security needs and establishing France as an important actor on the new security agenda meant more rather than less engagement with the United States and NATO.[19]

The EU and CFSP

At the same time that French estimation of NATO appreciated, the longer term goal of imparting a more autonomous stance for a collective *European* or *European Union* security apparatus appears to have become more attenuated. As Hoffmann and others have argued, a united Europe had been part of the Gaullist orientation involving the projection and leadership of French power and prestige. De Gaulle's certain idea of a united Europe, though, rested much more on intergovernmental cooperation than on a federalist finality.[20] In the post-cold-war era, it would seem logical that the efforts to build this "European pillar" would accelerate. Indeed, in light of German unification, the Maastricht Treaty on Political Union was promoted by France in an attempt to bind Germany ever more tightly to collective decisionmaking. The emphasis in the early 1990s on CFSP represented a renewed and vigorous effort by France, responding to new circumstances, to "capitalize on" the general interest of many, though not all, EU member states in some form of collective security to meet the challenges of both united Germany and a more autonomous European relationship vis-à-vis the United States.

The European policy launched by De Gaulle and later refined under Mitterrand, which sought to satisfy both the German issue and the appropriate posture regarding the United States, has begun to change. This reflects a new pragmatism in reevaluating long-standing policies under the pressure of events. One problematic aspect of promoting European integration as a means by which to achieve certain long-range foreign policy goals has been, paradoxically, the cost to national independence from building an ever more tightly knit international organization. The specific cost resulting from CFSP (not to mention other EU policy areas) has not been overly constraining as the actual treaty provisions essentially represented an enhanced European Political Cooperation (EPC).[21] This reflected the desire by France to advance in an orderly, pragmatic, and incremental fashion, also realizing the domestic difficulties of substituting national autonomy with an as yet unarticulated legitimate supranational replacement. Yet by the time of the 1996–1997 EU Intergovernmental Conference (IGC), with the issue of enhancing CFSP fresh in EU political elites' minds, France was again in a position of having to assert, on the one hand, a leadership role where CFSP's cost would undoubtedly come close to contradicting the Gaullist tenet of national independence. Failure of the IGC, on the other hand, already afflicted by elite and public misgivings about the European Monetary Union (EMU), could precipitate a crisis in the very project of European integration.

Chirac's choices at the IGC negotiations were therefore multifaceted.[22] France could bind Germany ever closer in the Union and thereby forfeit even more French national autonomy. The Yugoslav experience could provide an example of what to avoid in the future, supporting bold advances in the collective decisionmaking of CSFP. Yet the Yugoslav experience could also be interpreted in another fashion. As Frédéric Bozo pointed out, another lesson is that individual member states "must keep an effective veto power so as to prevent ill-advised policies from being collectively adopted by the Community against their own individual will."[23] German recognition of Croatia and Slovenia, followed reluctantly by France and other EU member states, is the precise focus of this perspective. Finally, at the very time that the IGC began in April 1996, French-American and French-NATO relations had reached a historic high point, thereby relativizing the urgent need for an independent European security entity.[24] Consequently, the initial French position at the IGC regarding the enhancement of CFSP was ambiguous. This has been interpreted as "an uncertainty and timidity towards widespread reform of EU institutions which reflect a more general problem. France no longer finds itself able, as effectively as it has in the past, to pursue its national interests via the medium of European integration."[25] Even more, "France appears to have abandoned the goal of playing a leading role in European construction."[26]

Yet by the end of February 1996, and again in the autumn of 1996, France and Germany had proposed an innovation to the EU that dominated negotiations in the first half of 1997: the notion of "flexibility." In the realm of security policy, both countries had come to realize that insisting upon a hard and fast collective decisionmaking procedure based on either unanimity (a non-starter) or majority voting (giving up the national veto by the British was regarded as highly unlikely, if not impossible) meant that negotiations over CFSP could very well end up simply marking out a toothless improvement over Maastricht. Failure to come up with something credible led to a Franco-German plan to employ majority voting, allowing a military (but not a financial) opt-out. In this manner, no single country could hold the rest hostage if a strong majority felt motivated enough to pursue an agreed-upon security exercise. This goes some way in envisioning the CFSP "to be more of an instrument for common action whenever this proves possible on an ad hoc basis, than the single political-military arm of a much fantasized European strategic 'actor.'"[27] In this fashion, France could portray itself as keeping within the vanguard of just about any common EU security initiative, and yet remain outside of what it might regard as a detrimental or ill-advised policy.

French attempts at reconstituting the basis of its European foreign and security policy in the post-cold-war era, as the above discussion demonstrates, has involved interaction with particular international institutions in two ways. The first is as a means to advance French security interests. Redefining the relationship with NATO, and by extension the United States, fits squarely with French re-evaluation of the international environment and a recognition that some of the basic assumptions of the Gaullist model are outmoded. Again, this recognition has been more practical and experiential than a sudden ideological shift. Indeed, the domestic discourse lags behind the policy shifts, but this may be more of a concern to national elites than to the public. Second, as Hoffmann has pointed out, French involvement within these international institutions "also affect[s] the way the French now conceive of their objectives. These are still, in large part, national; but they tend increasingly to be defined in ways that require external participation, support, or consent, and therefore accommodation."[28] I now turn to changes in the Gaullist tenet of autonomy in defense, specifically the maintenance of a comparatively large national defense industrial sector, which is crucial in explaining the adaptation or Europeanization of the French post-cold-war security posture.

CHANGES IN DEFENSE STRUCTURE AND ARMS PROCUREMENT

In February 1994 the French government adopted its first White Paper on defense since 1972. Although the paper did not announce a radical shift in defense concepts (for instance, it rejected reintegration into NATO), it did signal "very clearly indeed the priority given to the European and multinational dimension of defence."[29] The paper underlined the need for "real and extensive cooperation with NATO: France praises the US as the only current military giant and identifies the Alliance/NATO as the 'principal organisation of defence.' "[30] Beyond this movement toward explicit and official reformulation of defense priorities, the paper recommended changes in conventional force posture. Here the lesson of the Gulf War and the French inability to transport sufficient numbers of troops (much less than half of what the British, with a smaller army, were able to undertake) is apparent. Finally, encouragement was given to increase French arms cooperation with European partners "via the future European Armaments Agency, which is supported by France and Germany."[31]

By 1996, a significant shift had taken place that was more than a consolidation of the trends identified over the past few years and that contained a symbolic break with another tenet of the Gaullist model, indeed with French republican military tradition. In late February 1996, President Chirac announced the eventual phasing out of the conscription army. A professional army modeled upon the British system would be developed and the weapons industry would be revamped.[32] In both cases, the tradition of a citizen's army (and all this implies for French republican identity) and defense autonomy were directly challenged; or, as Tiersky has put it, Chirac initiated "cuts into the *gaullien* knot."[33] The uniformed military will shrink in six years by about one-third, and "the Gaullist value of self-sufficiency in all weapons"[34] will be abandoned. These "reforms, said Mr. Chirac, will help build a European defence system and—more immediately important—let France play a fuller part in NATO."[35]

The domestic pressures underlying these changes include the budgetary strain caused by the drive toward monetary union; the inadequacies of the presently configured conventional military, highlighted by the Gulf War; and finally, a recognition that French "objectives may be undermined by a gap between the political will to provide France with the necessary military means and the actual *volume* of credits."[36] The moves toward NATO, the arms industry shake-out, and the reconsideration of the positive role of the United States in Europe are all part of the French adaptation to the new environment. Minus a blueprint of this new post-cold-war framework, and taking into consideration NATO's changing identity (especially in regard to enlargement eastward), the tentative nature of French changes is not surprising. The initiatives announced by Chirac may therefore signal the attainment of a threshold of sorts whereby elite agreement on a new perspective is emerging.

CONCLUSION

The French Gaullist model rested upon several assumptions derived from an understanding of the structural constraints of a bipolar international environment and the dominance of the United States in NATO. Together with De Gaulle's emphasis on French grandeur, French foreign and security policy sought to maintain a distinctive position within this arrangement, all the while proclaiming its desire for its abolishment so as to allow nation-states to recover their "natural" independence. In this context, international institutions were representative of the norms of the system into which the Gaullist model invested so much criticism. The end of the cold war and the subsequent loosening of the cold-war paradigm for *both* France and international institutions, such as NATO and the EU, present an opportunity to reevaluate and thereby reconstruct a new basis of legitimacy for these institutions, allowing them to complement the French search for a new security perspective. In other words, we might say that the experiences of the Gulf War, Yugoslavia, and the disappointments to date with European collective decisionmaking have pushed France to look anew at formerly contested actors precisely at the moment when they have embarked upon a search for a new and legitimate role. Here, too, French perspectives concerning the (re)integration of central and eastern Europe into NATO and/or the EU are tested. Under both Mitterrand and Chirac, French policy has been wary of the rapid membership of these countries into either international institution. In this regard, the role of the Organization for Security and Cooperation in Europe (OSCE) has emerged as a preferred "half-way house" in French eyes. Attempts to demonstrate concern for Russian sensitivities to NATO's eastward expansion also explain this preference for looser institutional arrangements.

Michael Smith noted that states such as France and Germany "have had to respond to calls for an active role in constructing the new European order at the same time as they have been wrestling with domestic challenges and disorder of a more or less violent kind. There is an important potential linkage here in conceptual terms between the limits of state activism and autonomy . . . and the capacity or inclination to contribute to international restructuring."[37] In the case of France, we can see that by 1992, the limits of the old model had become obvious to many political elites. The new basis being established by Chirac for a post-Gaullist model is both a recognition of the limits of state activism and autonomy and an analysis of the most "favourable allocation of the costs."[38] In this regard, the new appreciation of NATO and the United States, and the acceptance of a more limited role for the WEU suggest that France is settling into a new relationship that links state strategies and the international environment, one in which international institutions play a crucial mediating function. The "tighter embrace" of these institutions also reflects the shift to a more explicit European-institutional focus. In perfecting this shift, some international institutions are redefined so that they can now be usefully employed in legitimizing the domestic bases of a changing national security model, the redefinition of which results in a much more interdependent, yet still qualified, relationship with those international institutions. This empirical pragmatism by France seems to reflect very well Hanrieder's observation:

> Governments, in seeking to meet the demands pressed upon them by their electorates, are compelled to turn to external sources in order to meet these demands. But their reluctance to opt either for divergence or for integration places them in an area of ambiguity where coordination appears as the reasonable as well as the necessary course of action.[39]

The post-Gaullist foreign policy model, at once more European as well as institutionally focused, may serve French interests well in the period leading up to both NATO and EU enlargement. A go-it-alone policy in these two areas seems to be a thing of the past, and constructive engagement appears to be the tactic that now accrues greater benefit. This does not mean that the French impulse to chart out a leadership position has vanished, as represented both in calls for a European to be in charge of NATO's Southern Command and Franco-German proposals concerning CFSP at the Intergovernmental Conference. The French government also has been criticized for attempting to restructure its arms industry solely within its domestic context before seeking European partners in order to build a European-based arms industry in competition with that of the United States. This French-first reflex undoubtedly will persist, but the greatest change from the Gaullist model is less in the details and more in the more modest scope of French ambitions. This orientation remains unchanged under Socialist Prime Minister Lionel Jospin, whose left-wing government, elected in June 1997, has continued the scaling back of French ambitions, particularly in the stationing of troops in Africa, a traditional area of French influence. In this respect, one can expect France to remain in the forefront of European integration, but perhaps in a more "ordinary" and predictable manner.

NOTES

1. See John Mearsheimer, "Back to the Future: Instability in Europe after the Cold War," *International Security* 15, no. 1 (Summer 1990): 5–56.

2. See G. John Ikenberry, "The State and Strategies of International Adjustment," *World Politics* 39, no. 1 (1986).

3. Michael Smith, "Beyond the Stable State?: Foreign Policy Challenges and Opportunities in the New Europe," in *European Foreign Policy: The EC and Changing Perspectives in Europe*, ed. W. Carlsnaes and S. Smith (London: SAGE, 1994), 36.

4. Ibid., 36.

5. Stanley Hoffmann, "French Dilemmas and Strategies in the New Europe," in *After the Cold War: International Institutions and State Strategies in Europe, 1989–1991*, ed. R. Keohane, J. Nye, and S. Hoffmann (Cambridge: Harvard University Press, 1993).

6. Other authors include the primacy of the nation-state and a refusal to "submit" to the United States, but I define these three terms broadly enough to incorporate these other added dimensions.

7. See Pascal Boniface, "French Nuclear Strategy and European Deterrence," *Contemporary Security Policy* 17, no. 2 (1996): 227–237.

8. Philip Cerny, *The Politics of Grandeur: Ideological Aspects of De Gaulle's Foreign Policy* (Cambridge: Cambridge University Press, 1980), 4.

9. Charles De Gaulle, *The Complete War Memoirs of Charles De Gaulle* (New York: Simon & Schuster, 1967), 3.

10. Some have seen this consensus in a less flattering light, more as a constraint preventing creative and needed change. See Anand Menon, "The 'Consensus' on Defence Policy and the End of the Cold War: Political Parties and the Limits of Adaptation," in *France: From the Cold War to the New World Order*, ed. Tony Chafer and Brian Jenkins (London: Macmillan, 1996), 155–168.

11. Frédéric Bozo, "French Security Policy and the New European Order," in *Security and Strategy in the New Europe*, ed. C. McInnes (London: Routledge, 1992), 201.

12. See, *inter alia*, Tony Chafer and Brian Jenkins, eds., *France: From the Cold War to the New World Order* (London: Macmillan, 1996); and David S. Yost, *France and the Persian Gulf War: Political-Military Lessons Learned* (Monterey, CA: Naval Postgraduate Institute, 1992).

13. Françoise de La Serre, "France: The Impact of François Mitterrand," in *The Actors in Europe's Foreign Policy*, ed. C. Hill (London: Routledge, 1996), 31.

14. Domestic sources informing this policy are treated by Jolyon Howorth, "France and the Gulf War: From Pre-War Crisis to Post War-Crisis," *Modern & Contemporary France*, no. 46 (1991): 3–16.

15. Although Howorth argues that there really isn't anything new in the emphasis on the European context, the explicitness of the new discourse signals a political and qualitative leap away from the basis of cold-war legitimation of foreign and security policies. See Jolyon Howorth, "France and European Security 1944–94: Re-reading the Gaullist 'Consensus,' " in *France: From the Cold War to the New World Order*, 17–38.

16. Janet Bryant, "Changing Circumstances, Changing Policies? The 1994 Defence White Paper and Beyond," in *France: From the Cold War to the New World Order*, 82.

17. See Anand Menon, "From Independence to Cooperation: France, NATO and European Security," *International Affairs* 71, no. 1 (1995): 19–35; Robert P. Grant, "France's New Relationship with NATO," *Survival* 38, no. 1 (1996): 58–80; and Roger Woodhouse, "France's Relations with NATO 1966–1996," *Modern & Contemporary France* NS4, no. 4 (1996): 483–496.

18. Frédéric Bozo, "France and Security in the New Europe: Between the Gaullist Legacy and the Search for a New Model," in *Remaking the Hexagon: The New France in the New Europe*, ed. Gregory Flynn (Boulder, CO: Westview, 1995), 229.

19. Robert Grant, "France's New Relationship with NATO," 63.

20. Many analysts have noted the discrepancy between French presidential discourse of a federalist hue, but actual policy proposals and behavior revealing an intergovernmental preference. See, e.g., Stanley Hoffmann, "French Dilemmas and Strategies in the New Europe"; and de la Serre, "France," especially pages 19–39.

21. See Françoise de la Serre, "France," 32–35.

22. The agenda of the IGC had already been set and approved at the end of 1995, with the momentum given to CSFP preceding Chirac's election.

23. Frédéric Bozo, "France and Security in the New Europe," 217.

24. The completion of the Combined Joint Task Force (CJTF) concept at the NATO Summit Meeting of June 1996 in Berlin, which would allow in principle for detachable NATO forces to be used by the WEU, has gone far in assuring France of a greater scope for European operational action. "France now seems to be willing to accept US command in major operations, involving the US, in return for European command in smaller-scale operations, i.e. European-led CJTF's, under WEU or EU auspices, when there are no fundamental American interests at stake." Maartje Rutten, "Gaullism or Reality for French Defence Policy?," *CEPS Review* (Brussels: Centre for European Policy Studies) 1 (1996): 21.

25. Anand Menon, "France and the IGC of 1996," *Journal of European Public Policy* 3, no. 2 (1996): 231.

26. Ibid., 249.

27. Frédéric Bozo, "France and Security in the New Europe," 217.

28. Stanley Hoffmann, "French Dilemmas and Strategies in the New Europe," 144.

29. Françoise de la Serre, "France," 36.

30. Janet Bryant, "Changing Circumstances, Changing Policies?," 84.

31. Ibid., 85.

32. The *force de frappe* triad will also be reduced to a two-legged air and naval deterrent. The French arms industry is structured around seven big contractors, compared to Britain's two major contractors, and Italy's and Germany's one each.

33. Ronald Tiersky, "A Likely Story: Chirac, France-NATO, European Security, and American Hegemony," *French Politics and Society* 14, no. 2 (1996): 3.

34. Ibid., 3.

35. "A French Projection," *The Economist*, 2 March 1996, 42.

36. Janet Bryant, "Changing Circumstances, Changing Policies?," 91.

37. Michael Smith, "Beyond the Stable State?," 40.

38. Ibid., 37.

39. Wolfram Hanrieder, "Dissolving International Politics: Reflections on the Nation-State," *American Political Science Review* 72 (1978): 1286.

6

The Construction of the European Pillar: Beyond the Status Quo???

MARY M. MCKENZIE

The role of an independent European defense organization in the European security architecture has long been debated, but the logic of the cold war effectively undercut any evolution in this direction. The end of the cold war, therefore, opened the possibility of intensified European security cooperation and integration, even on a pan-European scale. Indeed, in the 1990s, many leaders in western Europe believed that the time had arrived to build a viable western European defense organization. The demise of the Soviet Union had removed western Europe's adversary. German unification meant that Germany could assume a "normal" role and possibly lead Europe toward fulfilling its promise of being an exporter of security. Finally, it was argued that the United States would lose interest in Europe, thereby necessitating closer European security cooperation.

However, efforts toward intensified security cooperation have languished because of divergent conceptions of purpose. As European security cooperation is redesigned, confusion and hesitancy mark the construction of the European pillar. Is the purpose of European defense to promote European integration, or to provide for collective defense? Should it fortify the Alliance, or break away from it? What threats will the European pillar address? And how should it operate? The answers to these questions are central to determining the role the European pillar will play in post-cold-war

European security cooperation; they are also crucial for locating the European pillar's institutional home. Will it be the European Union (EU), the Western European Union (WEU), or the North Atlantic Treaty Organization (NATO)? An analysis of the European defense pillar requires considering all three institutions and options.

As noted in the introduction to this volume, institutions in European security cooperation must be viewed both as independent and dependent variables, both as actors and as objects of state action. Placing the European pillar in this context, this chapter elaborates the implications of structural and strategic changes for the processes of European security cooperation. What roles are these three institutions developing in security and defense that may be shaping state interests and cooperation? As objects of state action, the chapter examines how the roles and capabilities of these organizations are being molded by member states. What are state priorities for institutional reform in the European pillar, and what conception of security cooperation do these priorities reflect?

The efforts that have been undertaken to construct a European security pillar—or the European Security and Defense Identity (ESDI)—are the subject of this chapter. In order to assess the role of the European pillar, the chapter begins with a brief historical overview of the role of security cooperation in the process of European integration, including the Maastricht Treaty and the EU's 1996–1997 Intergovernmental Conference (IGC). Second, the analysis examines the expanded mandate and operations of the WEU to see how they reflect the vision and viability of a European defense arm. NATO's conception and accommodation of the European pillar are addressed in the third section. Finally, the chapter examines the policy preferences of key states toward the European pillar to evaluate the prospects for greater European security cooperation. The analysis concludes by suggesting that continued disagreements about the purpose of an independent European pillar in a web of interlocking institutions may hinder the emergence of a European defense organization, but may at the same time strengthen the commitment to undertake "new" security missions in a changing European security system. Marked by the push and pull of institutional prerogatives and state interests, the European pillar battles to accommodate a changing security environment by moving beyond the institutional status quo.

THE EUROPEAN PILLAR IN EUROPEAN INTEGRATION

Postwar security cooperation in Europe began with a European initiative. In 1948, Belgium, the Netherlands, Great Britain, Luxemburg, and France joined together under the Brussels Treaty to foster "economic, social and cultural collaboration" and to organize for collective defense. In 1949, NATO was formed to cement the U.S. presence in Europe, displacing the Europeans' efforts. From the outset, the secondary status of a purely European defense organization provided a constant source of debate about Europe's role in its own defense. Continued discord about Europe's role brought about the failure of the European Defense Community (EDC) in 1954, ironically leading to the modification and strengthening of the Brussels Treaty and the formation of the Western European Union the following year.

But the WEU lay dormant until the mid-1980s. Its reliance on NATO for "information and advice" left the WEU without "a clear identity" and perpetuated the institutional dominance of NATO.[1] Until the 1980s, the European pillar was discussed primarily in the context of "burden sharing" within NATO. However, in response to Reagan administration foreign policies, especially those dealing with the disposition and removal of nuclear forces, the perception grew that the United States was not heeding European interests. The vision of a European pillar took on a new vigor, especially on the part of the French and German governments, and European security cooperation was revitalized. In 1987, the WEU staked out an enlivened role in the Hague "Platform on European Security Interests," which identified a dual role for the WEU: to provide Europe's security identity, and to serve as a bridge between NATO and the European Community.[2] The WEU was activated at the end of the 1980s, and member states participated in minesweeping missions in the first Gulf conflict. However, it was not until the end of the cold war and the moves toward European Union, embodied in the Maastricht Treaty, that the WEU became integral to European security cooperation.

The negotiations for the Maastricht Treaty resulted from the transformation of the European security environment. The dramatic changes in the Soviet Union and the diminution of the cold war, fear of U.S. disengagement in Europe, and the desire to keep the German juggernaut contained in the European security space served as the chief motivations for revising the Rome treaties. German leaders, too, viewed reassurance of its commitment to the European Union as a primary function of Maastricht. As members of the European Union moved toward deeper integration, many felt it was time to include European security and defense in the process in order to prevent the "renationalization" of European foreign policies. Thus, the strengthening of the European defense pillar was central to Maastricht.

In the Maastricht Treaty, the European Union equipped itself with a Common Foreign and Security Policy (CFSP) that eventually was to lead to a common defense policy under the umbrella of the WEU. This would occur gradually, and the progress and prospects of both components—foreign and security policy—would be the subject of the 1996–1997 IGC. The language surrounding the specific foreign and security provisions of Maastricht shows, however, that EU members were not united on how deep security and defense union should be. The CFSP was designed to include any issue related to foreign and security policy, which might include weapons proliferation and economic sanctions. The important exception to the CFSP's scope was the realm of pure defense, defined narrowly as military deployments. This area would be reserved for the Western European Union and in the transatlantic realm, for NATO. The dichotomy between foreign and defense policy is cemented into current institutional structures, but it is difficult to maintain in reality. It also is one particularly vibrant aspect of the debate over the future of the second pillar in Europe, as it points to different missions and perhaps to different institutional homes.

The CFSP commits EU members to seek common positions and to abide by them once reached; this may indeed be "a step down the road of a common policy."[3] The CFSP also provides explicit tools for states to carry out these mandates: common positions, joint actions, and "requests" to the WEU to elaborate and implement decisions in the field of defense. Like the European Political Cooperation (EPC) which preceded it, the CFSP lies outside Community mechanisms; therefore, its decisions are based on unanimity. Common positions, the simplest sounding of these tools, has in fact been complicated by the difficulty of distinguishing between security and other EU policies, such as foreign economic policy. Joint action goes beyond making policy to committing to the joint implementation of it.[4] To date, there have been eight such actions, including election-monitoring missions, export controls, diplomatic involvement in the Stability Pact and Non-Proliferation Treaty negotiations, active participation in humanitarian aid provision, the administration of the city of Mostar in Bosnia (with the WEU), and assisting with the training of the Palestinian police force. No formal use has been made of the third step: employing the WEU to implement an EU mandate.[5]

In fact, the WEU was rather pointedly avoided when the chance arrived to utilize these mechanisms. After the EU met in February 1994 to discuss the protection of Sarajevo, it called for a meeting of the North Atlantic Council (NAC), not the WEU. This may be attributable to the complexity and immediacy of the problem under discussion, but it did nothing to strengthen the CFSP or the commitment to develop a common defense. EU impotence in the former Yugoslavia also brought criticism to the CFSP because these instruments were unable to shape state responses to the conflict. But as former British Foreign Minister Douglas Hurd has stated, "the fact that twelve countries of western Europe have not been able to stop a civil war outside their own border, albeit a civil war supported and abetted from outside, is hardly an argument for bringing the coordination of European foreign policy to an end."[6] Nonetheless, the war in the former Yugoslavia discredited efforts at European security cooperation.

One reason for the EU's inability to devise a CFSP in the former Yugoslavia was the continued priority given to national interests in decisionmaking. Although the CFSP made significant advances over the EPC and was designed to show that the Europeans were serious about intensifying their cooperation on foreign policy and accommodating a new status quo, the Maastricht Treaty preserved intergovernmentalism in foreign affairs by placing it under the auspices of the Council of Ministers and requiring unanimity (unless the Council decides that decisions can be taken by a qualified majority). This goes to the heart of the quality of European security cooperation and the future of the defense pillar. Will foreign and security cooperation remain conceptualized in terms of national interests? Or can a community of interest emerge in the European pillar as new efforts at institutional restructuring are undertaken?

Because of the linkages among European institutions and the interrelationship between the issues of deepening and widening integration, the European Union's Intergovernmental Conference, which began in March 1996, had the potential to answer these questions. The IGC reviewed the goals of the Maastricht Treaty in light of actual developments. Its agenda was limited to institutional reform (deepening and increasing transparency), structural fine-tuning, the future of the CFSP, and with it, the future of the WEU. The two most immediate issues facing the EU—European Monetary Union (EMU) and enlargement to the East—were officially off the table. It is clear that these issues would be affected, however, by the conference outcome. The states of eastern and central Europe anxiously awaited the conclusion of the IGC because they were promised that their applications for membership would then be considered.

The EU's conception of the European pillar can be inferred from the discussions that surrounded the IGC, in which the overriding goal for defense policy, as for all other aspects of reform, was increasing the consistency and efficiency of EU decisionmaking processes. This entails coordinating more closely the CFSP with other foreign policies; defining more clearly the relationship between the EU and WEU, a relationship still characterized by starkly divergent conceptions; and institutionalizing flexibility through a "political solidarity clause" that would assure the support of all members even if actual implementation was left to "coalitions of the willing." Most importantly, it was agreed to include security and defense measures in the treaty that emanated from the IGC, the Amsterdam Treaty. The so-called Petersberg tasks would be formalized in the European pillar. The Petersberg missions were first elaborated in 1992 and provide the most likely arena in which the EU will build its relationship to the WEU. These tasks include peacekeeping and humanitarian missions and remain distinct from the mandate of collective defense. The dual emphasis on flexibility in participation and on the Petersberg tasks suggests an emerging—if limited—role for the European Union in security and defense cooperation that focuses on threats to European stability. Key to implementing these mandates is defining the relationship of the EU to its "defense arm."

THE WESTERN EUROPEAN UNION SINCE 1991

Defining the relationship between the EU and the WEU remains a challenge for both institutions. As noted, the WEU was given a central role in creating the defense identity of the European Union in the Maastricht Treaty, including the "eventual framing of a common defense policy." Although the WEU had been involved in regional security missions in the late 1980s, its way for a more active role was paved by the WEU decisions of 1991 and 1992. In the declaration attached to the Treaty on European Union (TEU), WEU members agreed to Maastricht's conception of the European pillar and outlined three goals: cementing relations with the European Union; defining relations with NATO; and acquiring operational capabilities.[7] At the same time, WEU members pledged to develop a European security identity that was "compatible" with the common defense provided by the Atlantic Alliance.

Determining the fate of the WEU and its relationship to the EU was a central task of the EU's IGC. The main difficulty has been reconciling two competing conceptions of the WEU-EU relationship: one is reflected in the Maastricht Treaty, in which the WEU acts as a bridge between NATO and the EU; the second envisions the synthesis, or even merger, of the two institutions. The status-quo conception implies the continued dominance of NATO and posits the European pillar as a component of the transatlantic relationship. The CFSP would remain in the hands of the EU; the WEU would continue to be based on intergovernmental cooperation; and its ties to the EU would be based upon the latter's request. The option at the other end of the spectrum is the full merger of the WEU with the institutional mechanisms of the European Union. This would imply the strengthening of a truly independent European defense capability. A precision of the EU-WEU relationship continued to be elusive at the 1996–1997 IGC.

Although the WEU has undertaken a series of new missions that have greatly increased thc visibility of the organization in the post-cold-war era, they have been characterized by inefficiency, disorganization, and institutional competition.[8] For this reason, members of the EU and WEU agree on the need for a revision of the strategic mandate of the European pillar, despite disagreement about the nature of the formal relationship between the two. Specifically, EU and WEU members agree that the Europeans ought to be able to conduct the "Petersberg tasks." Meeting in Germany in 1992, WEU members decided that the WEU could go out of area in order to meet new challenges to European security and that the WEU could conduct humanitarian and rescue operations, and peacekeeping missions and crisis management tasks.[9] Although some observers believed this went beyond the organization's treaty provisions, it undoubtedly was intended to help the WEU fulfill its role as the defense arm of the EU and to give it a new lease on life. The EU included the Petersberg tasks in the 1997 Treaty of Amsterdam. This decision is central to the WEU's emerging role, and the WEU is developing the modalities for WEU-led missions for these tasks.[10]

Since Maastricht, WEU members have also sought to increase the WEU's structural capacity for independent analysis and action as it lacked its own operational capabilities. The WEU Council of Ministers, meeting in Lisbon in May 1995, gave the WEU additional institutional form by establishing a politico-military group in support of its council, a Situation Center, and an Intelligence Unit inside the Planning Cell (which itself had become operational in 1993). The WEU continues to refine the list of forces "answerable to WEU," which so far include various national forces as well as multinational units, such as the Eurocorps, the EUROFOR, and the EUROMARFOR.[11] Further, the WEU is acting on a joint French-British initiative on the formation of a "WEU humanitarian task force."

Beyond a lack of operational capabilities, a further stumbling block to WEU development has been the divergent membership of European security organizations. Although all ten of the WEU's members are members of the EU, five members of the EU are outside of the European defense framework. This is further complicated by the lack of overlapping membership with NATO. In addition to WEU full members, there are associate members (non-EU NATO states); observers (EU states that are not members of the WEU); and associate partners (the states of central and eastern Europe).[12] The WEU claims that its wide array of memberships offers it flexibility and inclusivity (now including twenty-eight states), making it a valuable framework for cooperation,[13] and it has also worked to strengthen relations with Russia and Ukraine, which remain outside the WEU. However, because the WEU is at bottom a collective defense organization, these disparate memberships confuse the role of the WEU, muddy the nature of its security guarantee, and complicate relations with eastern European states. The disparity in membership is unlikely to be resolved in the near future, and it has led to a preference for "coalitions of the willing" in the implementation of joint actions. Incongruent membership further acts as a brake on movement beyond the status-quo relationship between the EU and the WEU, as non-WEU members are hesitant to strengthen the EU's defense role.

Finally, the WEU-EU relationship is clouded by the presence of NATO in the equation. In fact, current deliberations of the European pillar rest on the unstated assumption of a continuing U.S. presence in European security. The WEU's function remains overshadowed by NATO's dominance in European security. Although the renewed struggle in the 1990s to define a European Security and Defense Identity has been given more credence with the open support of NATO and the United States, clarifying the division of labor and responsibilities between the two organizations has been difficult. Such clarification must be undertaken if the second pillar is to have substance.

NATO AND EUROPE SINCE 1991

NATO, too, has redefined its mission and its mandate in the post-cold-war era, leading some to assert that it "has changed beyond recognition."[14] In its discussion of "internal adaptation," the Alliance has focused on three sets of issues: military effectiveness, maintaining the transatlantic link, and the development of ESDI.[15]

In its 1991 New Strategic Concept, the North Atlantic Treaty Organization reaffirmed its core task of collective defense. At the same time, NATO recognized a changing security environment in which it had new duties to perform and new roles to play. NATO's broadened conception of security includes not only the political and the military aspects of security (which it has done since the 1967 Harmel Report), but NATO's broad risk conception now also includes economic instability on its borders, terrorism, and the supply of critical resources. Further, the concepts of "cooperative security," conflict prevention, and crisis management have entered into the NATO lexicon. In 1992, after a similar decision had already been taken by the WEU, NATO agreed to conduct U.N. or OSCE peacekeeping missions. In

1994, NATO's mission grew to include the Partnership for Peace, nonproliferation, and, especially important in the current context, the Combined Joint Task Forces (CJTFs) concept in support of a strengthened ESDI. Since 1996, the strengthening of the ESDI has taken center stage in the evolution of the "new NATO," and ESDI is linked explicitly with CJTFs and the Western European Union.

The greatest hurdle to an independent European role, even if limited to the Petersberg tasks (and not collective defense), is resources. In an era of globally shrinking foreign affairs budgets, the pressure is on to reduce costs and avoid duplication of effort. These considerations underlie the creation of Combined Joint Task Forces, the implementation of which remains a central focus of WEU and NATO deliberations. The CJTF concept allows WEU-led operations to utilize NATO assets, including capabilities and headquarters. NATO recognizes: "For any major threat to the Alliance, NATO will take the lead in responding. Yet, it is also possible that some operations, by virtue of their size or location, might be best launched by the WEU with NATO's help. We want to build that additional option—a European-led, WEU-directed operation—into our new structure."[16] According to its proponents, CJTFs have the potential to correct two primary weaknesses of the WEU: access to capabilities and the lack of a command and control structure.[17] Further, it is argued that CJTFs allow the utmost flexibility in meeting new security challenges by enabling the formation of "coalitions of the willing." Although many at first believed this meant that the WEU would have carte blanche over NATO resources, in fact the North Atlantic Council (NAC) will decide on any mission. In effect, the United States has a veto over purely European use of NATO resources.

CJTFs are a recognition that NATO, WEU, and EU will never have identical memberships, preventing a full convergence of their institutional and strategic missions. CJTFs are in this light a pragmatic solution to a practical problem, but they nonetheless relegate WEU to a dependent position vis-à-vis NATO. Although WEU-NATO consultations have increased under the new Security Agreement, and work is being conducted to assure greater transparency and cooperation between the two institutions, this dependency will hinder the development of an independent European defense capability and arguably will prevent the development of a cooperative security framework that encompasses all of the institutions of European security cooperation.

Of course, defining the structure of the European pillar is just one important challenge confronting NATO. Great effort is being invested in enlargement eastward. The creation of the North Atlantic Cooperation Council

(NACC) in 1991 and the Partnership for Peace (PfP) in 1994 underlined the engagement of the West with this issue. An "enhanced PfP," the creation of the Euro-Atlantic Partnership Council (EAPC), and the agreement cementing NATO-Russian relations are all attempts to strengthen the eastward focus of NATO and to reassure Russia. They also serve to eclipse a new role for the WEU in the East.

A look at NATO's transformation would be incomplete without reference to NATO's involvement in the former Yugoslavia. Although NATO was entangled in Bosnia by December 1992 (settling once and for all the debate about the possibility of out-of-area involvement), the United States itself did not become fully engaged in the conflict until a change of heart occured in summer 1995. The December 1995 Dayton Peace Accords, brokered by the United States, resulted in the NATO-led Implementation Force (IFOR), which was replaced in 1997 by the smaller Stabilization Force (SFOR). It is important to note two aspects of NATO's involvement that are portentous for the future of the European pillar. First, the missions throughout this conflict had NATO and WEU working side by side. The organizations cooperated to enforce the embargoes in the Adriatic and on the Danube until the United States unilaterally stopped its enforcement in 1994.[18] Such cooperative NATO-WEU efforts are one subject of the continuing reorganization of the European pillar.

Second, IFOR was viewed by many as a test of PfP and held up as a model for future security cooperation with Russia and Ukraine. Although not a PfP operation per se, the mission included (as does SFOR) thirteen Partners. Of the eleven countries now discussing membership with NATO, nine of them are in Bosnia. (Slovenia and Macedonia understandably are not present.) NATO pledged to continue its deployment in SFOR for one year, but analysts and policymakers alike are convinced that some peacekeeping force will be necessary beyond that time frame. To fill the gap, the WEU's general secretary, Jose Cutileiro, has suggested that the WEU may remain in Bosnia to keep the peace after the withdrawal of NATO and SFOR.[19] Such an assertion of the Petersberg tasks would promote a more active European role in the new security missions of the post-cold-war era, if the United States agrees.

NATIONAL PERSPECTIVES ON THE EUROPEAN PILLAR

In order to evaluate national perspectives on the creation of the European pillar, this section focuses on the discussions that surrounded the IGC. It highlights Great Britain as well as France and Germany because of the pivotal function each has in the process of "deepening" the EU in the security realm. Security policy and the future of the WEU were central to the 1996–1997 IGC discussions, along with transparency, institutional reform, efficiency, and the EU's democratic deficit.

The complexity of these issues and the linkages among them assured that these negotiations would not be easy. The multiple institutions involved further guaranteed that the outcome would be built on the least common denominator. The dichotomy between the CFSP and the WEU; between security and defense; the asymmetry in memberships of the WEU, the EU, and NATO; the overlapping or competing tasks of NATO and the WEU; the desires of central and eastern Europe; and the priorities of member governments prevented both rapid agreement and a fundamental institutional overhaul of the European pillar. In addition, and perhaps more importantly, larger political issues about the shape of European security underlie these technical discussions of institutional reform, issues barely contemplated at Maastricht. These include the nature of the threat in the new security environment, the related question of the types of missions and resources required to meet these challenges, the role of nuclear weapons, and the relationship of the United States and Russia to new European security structures.[20]

Beyond delineating the relationship of these three organizations, the most important institutional question about the European pillar is perhaps the mode of decisionmaking. As noted above, decisions in both CFSP and the WEU are based on the principles of intergovernmentalism and unanimity. Some member governments, most notably the British, do not want to change this. They virulently support the principle of unanimity in the realms of foreign and security policy. Others, such as France, have argued that some form of qualified majority voting is desirable, but only if the role of stronger states (typically defined as Britain, Spain, Italy, Germany, and France) is protected. This would prohibit a coalition of smaller states (which in effect would not do the fighting) from preventing an action supported by the larger states. Some have suggested, therefore, that an EU with a defense component should have a Security Council of sorts and an "opting-out" mechanism for smaller states.[21] This possibility of opting out might provide some flexibility for the "opting in" of nonmember states (through PfP, for example). Finally, a third contingent (including the German government and the European Commission itself) have argued that majority decisionmaking should be broadened to include the security realm, with the important exception of military deployments.

Great Britain

The fundamental principle underlying Great Britain's conception of the European pillar is "Atlanticism." In its prescriptions for the European security architecture, Britain is decidedly "NATO first." The WEU is seen from the British perspective almost completely in terms of burden sharing within the Alliance, as "the means for enhancing the European contribution to NATO's actions."[22] Europe should play a part in enforcing embargoes and in humanitarian, peacekeeping, or rescue missions (always in conjunction with NATO), but collective defense goes beyond Europe's role.

The British government argues that the separate memberships of the EU and WEU require the utmost flexibility and has strongly opposed merging the two organizations. This is due in part to Britain's concern that the divergent memberships of the WEU and NATO would weaken the transatlantic link. At the same time, the British recognize that a mixture of civilian and military components often will be necessary in the new security environment and encourages the cooperation of the WEU and the EU, as well as the implementation of CJTFs. As noted, unanimity remains the key to European decisionmaking as far as the British are concerned, and they are opposed to increasing institutional flexibility to allow for "coalitions of the willing," so strongly supported by other member states. The British argue that unanimity assures the will to act: "We shall not therefore accept a commitment to be constrained by collective decisions which we do not support."[23] True to its intergovernmental bent, Britain favors the creation of a coordination body for European defense, but only if answerable to the Council of Ministers, the intergovernmental decisionmaking body of the EU. Any institution in foreign and security affairs will not be supranational. The British vision of the European pillar is thus decidedly status quo.

France

The French government has been one of the driving forces behind the European pillar. Historically, France's advocacy of the European pillar can be understood as part of its effort to keep Europe free from U.S. influence. In fact, France represents the chief "Europeanist" in the WEU debate.[24] Together with Germany, France has proposed a strengthening of the CFSP and the WEU in many areas. First, France supports the merging of the WEU and the EU. Second, France favors the creation of an *M. Pesc*, an authoritative body or representative to coordinate these policy areas in the EU; and in December 1996, it offered—as it had occasionally in the past—to discuss the nuclear component of a European defense pillar.[25] Jacques Chirac has also expressed his support for flexibility in levels of integration, championing the idea of a multispeed Europe and "coalitions of the willing."[26] It should be noted, however, that flexibility relies on the support of all member states, in both moral and financial terms.

However, there remain signs of ambivalence toward a stronger European pillar, indicating the traditional Gaullist aversion to supranationalism. The French prefer, for example, careful voting schemes to assure "weighted" voting in any revision of the unanimity principle, and they have called for a strengthened role for national parliaments, not the European Parliament. The ambivalence in this realm is exacerbated by the inconsistency shown in French NATO policy. France's decision to step back into NATO's military committee in 1995 is crucial for the momentum behind the European pillar and reflected the surmounting of France's original hesitancy about CJTFs. French demand for NATO's Southern Command in late 1996, however, once again complicated France's relationship with the Alliance and burdened NATO discussions on institutional reform at its 1997 summit, leading France's Socialist prime minister, Lionel Jospin, to table any discussions of France's reintegration into the military command structure of the Alliance.

Germany

Although Germany's Chancellor Kohl, the chief foreign policymaker of the Federal Republic, has moved away from his sweeping endorsement of a "United States of Europe," Bonn remains the chief proponent of a strengthened European Union. Germany has consistently favored increasing the EU's operational capability in the foreign and security policy realms. Bonn's position has been to strengthen the union's role in defense matters, both vis-à-vis alliance commitments and vis-à-vis the member governments of the union. In other words, it wants the European pillar to take on more responsibility for Europe's security and to strengthen its authority over individual member states. Germany's priorities have been closely aligned with those of France on many of these issues, but their conception goes beyond what the French are willing to concede.

The German conception of the European pillar embraces the inclusion of the "Petersberg tasks" in the EU; the creation of coordinating mechanisms in this realm within the EU (a foreign policy secretariat and analysis unit, referred to as *Herr GASP*); a weakening of the requirements of unanimity, except when the issue is the actual deployment of military forces; integration of the WEU in the EU in the "medium term"; and the development of a common policy on weapons procurement and development under the rubric of the new Western European Armaments Organization (WEAO).[27] The German government, unlike the French, calls for increased European-level parliamentary participation in the areas of foreign, security, and defense policies. Importantly, too, Germany is one of the strongest advocates of "flexible integration," that is, allowing countries to go forward at different speeds, a mode of integration proposed by Chancellor Kohl's Christian Democrats (CDU/CSU) as early as 1994.

As one of the "strong states," Germany, like France, is determined to create voting schemes that do not allow a minority of states to prevent the majority from committing themselves to joint action. At the same time, German officials stress that states that disagree with the action will not be forced to participate, although solidarity requires that they support the mission. Germans have emphasized until recently the necessity of EU and NATO enlargement proceeding at roughly the same pace, and some in the governmental coalition have proposed that all EU member countries should join NATO to guarantee "the territorial integrity of EU member states."[28] This proposal neglects the reasons behind the different memberships of the organizations but would facilitate the merger of the EU and the WEU.

At bottom, the Germans argue that an enhanced ESDI strengthens NATO. The WEU is seen as the defense arm of ESDI, and the Germans support giving it operational and command structures to enable it to carry out the Petersberg tasks with or without NATO. A paper by the majority political party explicitly states that collective defense remains in the hands of NATO and suggests that the European Council should be given a mandate to set general guidelines for European defense, and that WEU action should be subject to EU, not NATO, instructions. In the German mind, the purpose of the European pillar is independent action, requiring the revision of the status quo of the European pillar.

CONCLUSIONS: INSTITUTIONS, INTERESTS, AND THE STATUS QUO

The institutional web surrounding the European defense pillar has made its construction difficult and less than transparent. In fact, the changes in the European pillar since the end of the cold war have resulted in a peculiar mix of new and old. Collective defense remains central at the same time as security gets broadened to include "new security" issues. Discussions focus on the *western* European pillar at the same time as Europe opens its doors and institutions to the East. Intergovernmentalism remains at the core of decisionmaking at the same time as cooperative security structures are desired.

Unanimity remains paramount at the same time as professions of faith in deepening the European Union are made. These contradictions help to explain the slow process of constructing a European defense identity. But the fundamental explanation for the halting progress toward independent security cooperation is that the question of the European pillar's purpose has not been resolutely answered.

There are two aspects to this question that continue to haunt Europe. The first is the European pillar's *institutional* purpose. Where should the European pillar be situated within the European security architecture? Will the European pillar supplant or supplement NATO? The second question relates to the pillar's *strategic* purpose in European security cooperation. Is the goal of the European pillar to provide the Europeans with collective defense, or with the means to act more effectively in traditional foreign and security policy, or even in the new tasks of peacekeeping and humanitarian missions? Both of these questions point to the dualism inherent in the current structure of the European pillar that envisions it as the avenue for a European security identity at the same time that it is the "bridge" between the EU and NATO.

Toward which vision are post-cold-war institutional developments leading? "Institutions alone cannot mold common interests or create political will where none exists. But without working institutions that *induce* cooperation, the opportunity for defining and pursuing common policies is seriously impaired."[29] In attempting to construct structures that induce cooperation, the institutions of the European pillar have addressed a number of structural issues.

First, the question of the proper role of security in the processes of European integration had to be answered. Should there emerge a European defense *union* based on supranationalism, interdependence, and a community of interest? Or should the security realm remain embedded in intergovernmental processes that preserve national prerogatives? Second, these institutions have been compelled to redefine their interrelationship. The multiple institutions of the European pillar are elaborating a division of labor that subordinates European efforts to the transatlantic relationship. Third, the EU, WEU, and NATO have been forced to address the complications of divergent institutional memberships in designing security cooperation. The EU's Fifteen, NATO's Sixteen, and the WEU's Ten work against a merger of these institutions or a convergence in their purpose. These institutional constraints have led to an emerging consensus on the role of the European pillar that rests on a continued reliance on NATO and its assets, the Petersberg tasks, and the construction of "coalitions of the willing."

The emphasis on the status quo in the transatlantic relationship and on coalitions of the willing (the buzzword is "flexibility") preserves the sanctity of the national interests of the institutions' member states. Although some progress was made toward majority decisionmaking at the IGC, enshrining an "opting-in" clause for states in security matters means that decisionmaking authority in security policy remains with member states. And with the Europeans' role limited to the Petersberg tasks, the emergence of a multispeed Europe in the realm of defense is a clear possibility, leading to a dual-tier security system in Europe with a real division of labor and multiple levels of inclusion in the European security space.

The preservation of state sovereignty in defense is indicative of the impact of states on European security institutions. What separates the policy priorities of the members of these organizations are precisely the broader questions of purpose. An examination of the European pillar suggests that states are unclear about what they want from a European pillar, and why they want one. Member states have different conceptions of the role of the European pillar and the desirability of moving it beyond the status quo. These differences are most aptly illustrated in the positions of Britain and Germany. The result of such confusion will be a continued reliance on intergovernmentalism and continued confusion over ESDI.

European security cooperation has become an accepted and even integral part of European integration. But its substance remains based on the assumption of a continued U.S. presence in the European security equation. Although doubts about American involvement in Europe may have been eased in the medium term by the U.S. engagement in Bosnia, political and economic pressures are likely to bring it to the fore again. This is why the lack of a larger purpose in the deliberations about Europe's security future is disconcerting. As the European context continues to be transformed, the dualism of the European pillar—as an independent force and as an arm of NATO—will be increasingly difficult to sustain. The preservation of the institutional status quo amid fundamental change in the security environment suggests that the future of the European pillar was not resolved at the latest Intergovernmental Conference.

NOTES

1. David S. Huntington, "A Peacekeeping Role for the Western European Union," in *Preventing Conflict in the Post-Communist World. Mobilizing International and Regional Organizations*, ed. Abram Chayes and Antonia Handler Chayes (Washington, DC: The Brookings Institution, 1996), 429–464, esp. 432.

2. For the text of the Platform, see Alfred Jean Cahen, *The Western European Union and NATO* (London: Brassey's, 1989). On the history of the WEU, see also Clive Archer, *Organizing Europe: The Institutions of Integration* (London: Edward Arnold, 1994), ch. 10.

3. See Douglas Hurd, "Developing the Common Foreign and Security Policy," *International Affairs* 70, no. 3 (1994): 421–428; esp. 425; see also Clive Archer and Fiona Butler, *The European Community: Structure and Process* (New York: St. Martin's Press, 1992), 179.

4. On these joint actions, see Douglas Hurd, "Developing the Common Foreign and Security Policy"; and Jacques Santer, "The European Union's Security and Defense Policy: How to Avoid Missing the 1996 Rendez-vous," *NATO Review* 43, no.6 (November 1995).

5. See Jacques Santer, "The European Union's Security and Defense Policy."

6. Douglas Hurd, "Developing the Common Foreign and Security Policy," 424.

7. For the WEU's assessment of its progress in these areas, see "WEU Contribution to the European Union Intergovernmental Conference of 1996," Press and Information Service of the WEU, 14 November 1995.

8. These missions have included sanctions enforcement on the Adriatic and the Danube; policing functions in Mostar, Bosnia-Herzegovina; and humanitarian aid provision in Rwanda. David S. Huntington, "A Peacekeeping Role for the Western European Union," in *Preventing Conflict in the Post-Communist World. Mobilizing International and Regional Organizations,* 429–464.

9. This made the WEU a more difficult fit for the Federal Republic of Germany, due to its lingering constitutional hesitations over out-of-area involvement.

10. The WEU (also since 1992) can participate in humanitarian or peacekeeping missions under the auspices of the United Nations or the Organization for Security and Cooperation in Europe (OSCE). On these developments, see Willem van Eekelen, "Die Position der WEU in der Europäischen Sicherheitspolitik," 3 December 1993, mimeo.

11. France, Italy, Spain, and Portugal agreed in Lisbon to the formation of these land and sea forces for the southern European region. They are also answerable to NATO. See Jacques Santer, "The European Union's Security and Defense Policy"; and Jose Cutileiro, "WEU's Operational Development and Its Relationship to NATO," *NATO Review* 43, no. 2 (February 1995), web edition. See also the "Lisbon Declaration," WEU Council of Ministers, 15 May 1995, Document #1455.

12. WEU full members are Belgium, France, Germany, Greece, Italy, Luxemburg, Netherlands, Portugal, Spain, and Great Britain. The associate members are Turkey, Iceland, and Norway. Observers are Austria, Denmark, Finland, Ireland, and Sweden. The associate partners are Bulgaria, Czech Republic, Estonia, Latvia, Hungary, Lithuania, Poland, Romania, Slovakia, and Slovenia.

13. This assessment is echoed in David Heathcoat-Amory, "The Next Step for Western European Union," *The World Today* 50, no. 7 (July 1994): 133–136.

14. "The New NATO and the European Security Architecture. Speech by the Secretary General, Javier Solana, in Vienna, 16 January 1997," in *NATO Review*, [www.nato.int/docu/speech/1997/s9701156a.htm].

15. See the NATO communiqués from Berlin and Brussels, 1996.

16. "The New NATO and the European Security Architecture. Speech by the Secretary General, Javier Solana, in Vienna, 16 January 1997," in *NATO Review*, [www.nato.int/docu/speech/1997/s9701156a.htm].

17. David S. Huntington, "A Peacekeeping Role for the Western European Union," in *Preventing Conflict in the Post-Communist World. Mobilizing International and Regional Organizations,* 429–464.

18. Operation Sharp Guard in the Adriatic was the first combined operation between the two organizations.

19. "WEU sucht nach Bewährungsprobe," *Germany-Live*, 4 March 1997, [www.germany-live.de].

20. Technical discussions of European security—or the "Euro-strategic balance"—have always masked these broader political issues. See Wolfram F. Hanrieder, *Germany, America, Europe: Forty Years of German Foreign Policy* (New Haven: Yale University Press, 1989), esp. 1–25.

21. Geoffrey Howe, "Bearing More of the Burden. In Search of a European Foreign and Security Policy," *The World Today* 52, no. 1 (January 1996).

22. "Memorandum on the United Kingdom Government's Approach to the Treatment of European Defence Issues at the 1996 Inter-Governmental Conference," 1 March 1995, [http://www.fco.gov.uk/reference/briefs/defence-igc.htm].

23. "Common Foreign & Security Policy, FCO IGC White Paper," 12 March 1996, [http://www.fco.gov.uk/europe/igc/cfsp].

24. David S. Huntington, "A Peacekeeping Role for the Western European Union," 429–464.

25. "Pesc" is the French acronym for CFSP; GASP is the German. On the nuclear issues, see "France, Germany to Open talks on European Defense," *New York Times*, 25 January 1997, [http://www.nytimes.com]; see also Mark Hibbs, "Tomorrow, a Eurobomb?" *Bulletin of Atomic Scientists* 52, no. 1 (January-February 1996): 16–24.

26. See the French *White Paper on the 1996 Intergovernmental Conference,* vol. 2, [http://europe.eu.int/en/agenda/igc-home/ms-doc/state-fr/pos.htm].

27. "Document: 'Germany's Objectives for the Intergovernmental Conference', March 26, 1996," in the European parliament's *White Paper on the 1996 Intergovernmental Conference*, vol. 2, [http://europe.eu.int/en/agenda/igc-home/ms-doc/state-de/pos.htm].

28. "Discussion Paper on Strengthening the European Union's Ability to Act in the Field of CFSP of 13 June 1995," in the European parliament's *White Paper on the 1996 Intergovernmental Conference*, vol. 2, [http://europe.eu.int/en/agenda/igc-home/ms-doc/state-de/pos.htm].

29. Geoffrey Howe, "Bearing More of the Burden: In Search of a European Foreign and Security Policy," 23–27; esp. 26. Emphasis added.

7

The Organization for Security and Cooperation in Europe: Institutional Reform and Political Reality

RICHARD E. RUPP AND MARY M. MCKENZIE

Perhaps more than any other institution under review in this volume, the Organization for Security and Cooperation in Europe (OSCE) reflects the challenges facing multilateral cooperation in a new and volatile era.[1] Although it remains an incoherent amalgam of process and structure with few means of enforcement at its disposal, the OSCE has nonetheless staked a claim for itself in European security cooperation in the post-cold-war era.

In recent years, the members of the OSCE increasingly have committed themselves to employ the organization to promote security cooperation. At the same time, the OSCE has been denied independent means for pursuing traditional security functions. Is this because the organization has been unable to forge a consensus on the security challenges facing Europe? Are existing institutional mechanisms (many of them residual from the cold war) unable to assure the cooperation of fifty-five disparate member states? Or are the interests of member states so divergent that they cannot collectively accomplish any broader goals? Attempting to answer these questions, this chapter seeks to explain not only the role of the OSCE in today's European security environment but also to account for the process through which its new role has been defined. In other words, we examine how the OSCE is shaping European security cooperation as well as how the organization is being shaped by its member states.[2]

After tracing the OSCE's institutional evolution, we provide an overview of the OSCE's role in fostering security cooperation. In order to gain greater insight into the reforms in the OSCE, we then analyze the policy conceptions and preferences of the organization's major states, focusing on the United States, Russia, and Germany. Next, the chapter dissects the effectiveness of OSCE interventions in the former Soviet Union and the Balkans. Finally, we conclude by showing that the OSCE has a unique and significant role to play in the web of interlocking institutions in post-cold-war Europe.

THE EVOLUTION OF THE OSCE

The OSCE is a product of the era of détente. A result of long-standing Soviet demands for an all-European security conference and the West's desire for conventional arms control, the CSCE preparatory conference began in 1972. The divergent goals of the United States and the Soviet Union reflected two very different conceptions of the CSCE, a dichotomy evident in contemporary discussions about the organization's future. One side wanted the recognition of the permanent inviolability of borders in Europe, and the other wanted to make these borders more porous. One side sought change; the other, the solidification of the status quo.[3]

Nonetheless, the conference resulted in the Helsinki Final Act in 1975—a declaration of intent—that set the parameters for the organization in three so-called issue "baskets": military security; economic, scientific, and environmental concerns; and the human dimension. From the start, the CSCE embodied a conception of security that rested profoundly on its non-military aspects, while recognizing its military and political components. This comprehensive conception of security remains central to OSCE developments and activities and reflects a recognition of security interdependence among European states. Although the founding intent of the United States was for the CSCE to promote conventional arms control, the institution's role in the military-security realm was limited in the beginning to confidence-building measures. Despite the recognized linkage between the political and military aspects of security, discussions of arms would take place in the separate Mutual and Balanced Force Reduction talks (MBFR). In retrospect, instead of being a defect of the CSCE,[4] this decision allowed the CSCE its modest accomplishments before 1989, if the course of the long and failed MBFR negotiations is any guide.

During the cold war, the CSCE consisted primarily of periodic follow-up meetings among its participants. The cold-war ideological divisions within the membership of thirty-five states and the principle of consensus decisionmaking (unanimity voting) stymied the CSCE throughout much of its existence. Often, these forums were characterized by mutual recriminations between East and West, and their chief significance lay in the fact that the CSCE provided the only opportunity for East-West dialogue. However, by the mid-1980s, the cold-war stalemate was ending, and real progress was achieved in these follow-up meetings. Commitments were made on increased economic cooperation and in the human dimension, including the lifting of some restrictions on the press. This process was especially clear at the follow-up meeting in Vienna (1986–1989) and was accelerated by the reforms of Mikhail Gorbachev. During the late 1980s, the CSCE, like the cold-war environment in which it was embedded, was becoming more amenable to compromise and witnessed the agreement on confidence- and security-building measures (CSBMs) in 1986 and the agreement to negotiate the Conventional Armed Forces in Europe Treaty (CFE), signed in 1990.

At the end of the cold war, the CSCE was seen by many as the logical institutional home for collective security in Europe because of its pan-European scope and its broad definition of security. Many leaders, especially in the Soviet Union (and later Russia), but also in the Federal Republic of Germany, lay special emphasis on building the capacities of the CSCE in the traditional security realm. In 1990, CSCE member states held a summit meeting in Paris that served to signify the cold war's end and the emergence of a new era. The euphoria surrounding the Paris summit encapsulated the hopes that accompanied the fall of the Berlin Wall, German unification, and the continuing changes within Warsaw Pact states.

Significant institutional change was begun at this summit to transform the CSCE from an amorphous arrangement among competing states into a pan-European cooperative security institution. The summit produced the "Paris Charter for a New Europe," which contained substantial decisions outlining the direction, goals, and principles that states hoped would guide the organization into the 1990s and the next century. The charter heralded a new age in Europe, and it established an administrative secretariat in Prague, a Conflict Prevention Center (CPC) in Vienna, and an Office for Free Elections in Warsaw (which was later renamed the Office for Democratic Institutions and Human Rights—ODIHR). Further, it created the Council of Foreign Ministers (now the Ministerial Council) and the Committee of Senior Officials (now the Senior Council).

Since Paris, the OSCE has been expanded to include fifty-five states, and additional bodies have been created, including the office of the High Commissioner for National Minorities (HCNM), which is capable of initiating action with no prior mandate; an informal "Troika" modeled after the European Union (EU), with a "Chair-in-Office," capable of appointing special representatives and ad hoc crisis management groups; a standing Permanent Council, which conducts the day-to-day business of the organization; a General Secretariat; an advisory Parliamentary Assembly; and the modest weakening of the consensus principle, allowing for actions by a limited number of states against a member state perceived to be practicing "gross violations" of human rights or fomenting a political crisis. This was invoked twice in 1992, overriding the objections of the former Yugoslav Republic. The capstone to the OSCE's institutions remains the biannual summit of the heads of state and government of the member states. The OSCE is thus characterized by multiple layers and structures, leading many now to call for streamlining the complicated institutional web that has been created since 1990.

Institutional change remained at the forefront of OSCE discussions at the summit meetings of 1994 in Budapest and 1996 in Lisbon. In 1994, many member states had hoped to see significant advances in the structural component of the OSCE in order to somehow make up for its inability to impact the war in the former Yugoslavia. Overshadowed by acrimonious discussions about Bosnia-Herzegovina and by Russia's terse reaction to NATO expansion, the Budapest summit nonetheless continued to refine and rationalize decisionmaking organs and procedures. In addition, the mandates for conflict prevention and crisis management were strengthened.

The Lisbon summit evidenced a renewed enthusiasm for refining the mechanisms of the OSCE and produced a more concrete agenda of institution building that would situate the OSCE alongside the other institutions of European security cooperation. Although the progress toward this "Security Model for Europe" was slower than many had hoped, member states agreed on a declaration that defined the role of the OSCE in European security. The eventual goal is a design for a clear division of labor among the institutions of European security cooperation.

Although significant agreement has been reached on numerous changes to the structure of the OSCE, fundamental differences remain in the conception of its role. The main point of disagreement continues to be how strong to make the OSCE's authority vis-à-vis its member states. Two competing ideas are shaping the OSCE's development. The first fosters collective interests and compromise based on consensus; the second strives to enable the OSCE to play an independent role by weakening the unanimity requirement. Many argue that the OSCE's success—limited though it is—is due precisely to the OSCE's flexibility and reliance on the consensus of all members. This assures both legitimacy and the political will necessary to implement any mandates or missions. In this context, the significant role of the "Chair-in-Office" and the HCNM are singled out, both relatively unstructured and reactive to particular circumstances. The success of the HCNM rests on persuasion, not coercion, an "admittedly unspectacular" method of operation.[5] In fact, it is likely that if coercion stood behind these missions, they would not work because power and interest would be introduced into the equation. Despite the desires of some, especially the Russian government, changes in the underlying principle of consensus remain limited.[6]

THE OSCE AND EUROPEAN SECURITY COOPERATION

In order to understand the evolution of the OSCE, it is important to examine the philosophy of security that underlies its role in European security. Its attempts to remold security cooperation are based on a broad and collective notion of security that encompasses economic stability, human rights, and democratic norms, and thus, security interdependence. In this way, the OSCE's conception of security has fostered rules not only for interstate behavior, but also for the behavior of states toward their own citizens.[7] The degree to which the OSCE should be involved in narrowly defined security matters, on the other hand, has been controversial throughout the organization's lifespan. This debate resulted primarily from different perceptions of the proper role of the United States and NATO in Europe, but it also reflected the two very different views attached to the OSCE: one stressing change, the other emphasizing the preservation of the status quo.[8] With the end of the cold war, would the OSCE become a regional organization of collective security that would encompass all these components?

In defining its security role since the radical transformations of 1989 and 1990, the OSCE has staked a primary claim to arms control and confidence-building measures through its Forum for Security Cooperation (FSC). The OSCE's first success in this realm occurred in 1986 with the conclusion of the first CSBM agreement, followed in 1990 by the Treaty on Conventional Armed Forces in Europe (CFE). Continuing to play a central role in arms control, the OSCE emphasizes not only confidence- and security-building measures but also regional and subregional arms reductions, and the creation of norms to further these efforts in building trust and transparency. For example, member states agreed in 1994 to politically binding commitments regarding their armed forces, including democratic control and preservation of troops' individual rights, in the "Code of Conduct on Politico-Military Aspects of Security."

The real direction for the OSCE in the military-security realm, however, was charted at the Helsinki summit in 1992. The outbreak of war in Europe meant that the OSCE had to come to grips with the question of military power in its considerations of structural reform. In Helsinki, the OSCE became a regional "arrangement" under Chapter VIII of the U.N. Charter, which declares that regional organizations may undertake measures to settle disputes peacefully among their members. The OSCE also decided that it could conduct peacekeeping missions, including overseeing cease-fires, assisting in refugee flows, and disarming warring factions after cease-fires had been negotiated. These measures necessitate the agreement of the concerned states, and the missions must be decided on the basis of consensus within the OSCE. The OSCE stated explicitly that enforcement actions under Article 42 of the U.N. Charter—collective security—are not included in this arrangement.

By initiating the regional arrangement, member states undoubtedly hoped to enhance the status of the OSCE by enabling it to settle disputes peacefully within its region and by tying it to the legal norms of the United Nations. But in fact, this outcome is unlikely precisely because of the decision made on military capabilities, which hands this responsibility to other organizations and states. Instead of creating its own military force, the OSCE would rely on NATO, Western European Union (WEU), and Commonwealth of Independent States (CIS) forces for peacekeeping, although the modalities of such arrangements were far from clear. NATO and the WEU had already declared themselves open to this task; the role of Russia and the CIS has been more problematic, although Russian troops are involved in missions in the former Yugoslavia and the former Soviet Union.

Since Helsinki, OSCE missions under the auspices of the ODIHR and the HCNM have been sent to Bosnia-Herzegovina, Latvia, Ukraine, Estonia, Moldova, Georgia, Tajikistan, Macedonia, Serbia and Montenegro, Chechnya, Croatia, and Albania. These missions have underlined the OSCE's role in "pre military" or "soft" functions, such as conflict prevention and resolution as well as its lack of operational capabilities.[9] The OSCE is also becoming more involved in postconflict rehabilitation and state building, as seen in Bosnia. These tasks are linked to the OSCE's comprehensive evaluation of security, focusing on human rights and the protection of minorities, as well as on the imperatives of economic development for stability.

The incremental nature of the OSCE's accommodations to a rapidly changing European security environment led to the development of a more formal delineation of a security framework for Europe. This resulted in the

"Declaration on a Common and Comprehensive Security Model for the Twenty-first Century" in Lisbon, which emphasizes the linkages between economic growth, social instability, and insecurity.[10] In addition, the declaration stresses the necessity of linking the institutions of European security cooperation together in a complementary manner. Member states of the organization emphasized that the proper and appropriate role for the OSCE lay in its function as an instrument for early warning, conflict prevention, crisis management, and postconflict rehabilitation. Thus, in its arms control efforts, its missions, and its mandates, the OSCE's philosophy revolves around a broad conceptualization of security, institutional linkages, and the creation of norms of state behavior toward each other and toward the citizens of Europe.

STATE INTERESTS AND THE OSCE

The OSCE has come under stinging indictment for "failing" to manage conflicts effectively. Frequently, these criticisms have been leveled by scholars and policymakers from the major powers. Interestingly, as our analysis illustrates, it is the major powers who control the organization and determine its meager budget, staffing, resources, and capabilities. As the authors of a recent Brookings Institution study have remarked, "the OSCE's success is, to a large extent, 'hostage' to the relations and attitudes of the most powerful participating states."[11] The security interests of the OSCE's members have been a determining factor in the structural evolution of the organization during the post-cold-war period. In this section, we examine how the interests of the United States, Russia, and Germany have affected OSCE reforms and structures and defined its role in security cooperation.

The United States and the OSCE

American foreign policymakers have encountered considerable difficulty in articulating an overarching policy to replace the containment strategy that dominated the cold-war years. European governments have repeatedly criticized Washington's vacillating foreign policy and its inability to adapt to changes within the international system, particularly in the Balkans. However, on one important question, U.S. foreign policy has remained largely consistent: that is over NATO's role in European security. Since 1989, Washington has endeavored to shore up support for the NATO alliance and has opposed all efforts to create or enhance competing security organizations. While acknowledging the need to adapt the Atlantic Alliance to shifting post-cold-war politics, both the Bush and Clinton administrations have demonstrated that Washington will harbor no contenders to NATO in European security.

In the aftermath of 1989, the United States joined the other major powers in welcoming the former states of the Soviet Union and eastern Europe into western organizations. Throughout the 1990s, U.S. diplomats have supported the OSCE's democratization efforts, human rights advocacy, and election-monitoring missions. Concurrently, at each summit since 1990, the United States steadfastly has opposed all efforts to transform the OSCE into a formal treaty-based organization with a collective security mandate.[12]

For instance, during the 1992 Helsinki summit, the United States strenuously opposed efforts by the French, Russians, Hungarians, and Austrians that would have resulted in an enhanced security role for the OSCE. While the United States supported institutional reforms to strengthen the OSCE's preventive diplomacy and conflict management missions—such as the creation of the High Commissioner on National Minorities—the American delegation publicly thwarted French efforts to restructure the organization. At one point during the meetings, an American delegate accused a French counterpart of having "a treaty up your sleeve which would put the CSCE on a legal basis."[13]

In response to other nations, the United States called on the OSCE to "develop an entirely new definition of security" but offered little in the way of concrete proposals. American officials have acknowledged that the conflicts in post-cold-war Europe require new approaches, but they have consistently argued that NATO must be the organization through which these conflicts are addressed. Washington does not believe the EU or WEU can replicate NATO's effectiveness and has argued that the OSCE, an organization with over three times the membership of these institutions, would encounter even greater difficulty.[14]

At bottom, Washington's resistance to reform has been based on the belief that any enhanced OSCE security mandate will come at the expense of NATO, and U.S. policymakers perceive any diminution of NATO's role as a threat to the traditional leadership position of the United States in the Alliance. Perhaps the most telling comment by an American official about European security, NATO, the OSCE, and American foreign policy was made in 1995 by then-U.S. Deputy Secretary of State, Richard Holbrooke. The author of the Dayton Peace Accords, Holbrooke effectively closed the door on substantive OSCE reforms by declaring: "In no way can the OSCE be made superior to NATO. Because the functions as well as the structures of the OSCE and NATO are entirely different and shall remain so, OSCE will not become the umbrella organization for European security, nor will it oversee the work of the NATO alliance."[15]

The Soviet Union, Russia, and the OSCE

Since the conception of the OSCE, Moscow and Washington have differed sharply over the organization's mission and structures. These competing outlooks again have become particularly evident since the collapse of the Soviet Union and the reemergence of the Russian nation-state. While the OSCE in many ways contributed to the eventual implosion of the eastern bloc, both the Gorbachev and Yeltsin governments championed the organization as the logical candidate for constructing post-cold-war security arrangements. Moscow logically turned to the OSCE because it was the only security organization that included all of Europe and also included the Soviet Union as an equal partner.

In 1989, with eastern European states scrambling for independence, and as German unification loomed, Gorbachev reached out to the OSCE in hopes that the organization could provide the core for a new pan-European security system. Gorbachev realized that the Warsaw Pact would soon become a relic of the cold war, and he wanted to prevent the eastern Europeans from turning to NATO or to the WEU. A pan-European formula would not only replace the Warsaw Pact, but it would also minimize the role of the Atlantic Alliance. Gorbachev's proposals were coolly received in western capitals, with the notable exception of Bonn. Undeterred by western skepticism, Soviet Foreign Minister Eduard Shevardnadze wrote his OSCE counterparts in May 1990: "The most important architectural element of the future Common European Home is the security system based on all-European cooperation."[16] Shevardnadze avoided specific reference to NATO and the WEU in his communiqué; however, the Soviet goal of eliminating the two organizations was clear, as the communiqué argued that a revamped OSCE could absorb the existing security structures into "European non-aligned structures."

During the first two years of the Yeltsin government, Moscow's foreign policy was characterized by efforts to cooperate with the western powers. By the end of 1993, however, Yeltsin's policy was under intense fire from Russian conservatives and nationalists for placing Moscow in a position subservient to the West. Reacting in part to this criticism, and also to the absence of substantial Western economic assistance, Moscow's foreign policy adopted a more confrontational tone by the end of 1993.

In response to the debate within NATO over enlargement, Moscow firmly stated its opposition to any eastward shift in NATO's focus. Indeed, since 1993, Moscow's primary foreign policy aim—beyond consolidating its influence in the near abroad—has been to scuttle plans for NATO enlargement. As an alternative, Moscow has consistently promoted the OSCE as the only candidate for a revised European security structure. In 1994, Russian Foreign Minister Andrei Kozyrev wrote: "The creation of a unified, non-bloc Europe can best be pursued by upgrading the CSCE into a broader and more universal organization. After all, it was the democratic principles of the 53–member CSCE that won the cold war—not the NATO military machine."[17]

The Yeltsin government has missed few opportunities to call for increasing the scope and responsibilities of the OSCE. At the 1994 OSCE summit in Budapest, Yeltsin startled delegates by declaring, "Europe risks to immerse itself into a 'cold peace.' How to avoid this is a question that we must put to ourselves."[18] During his address, Yeltsin argued that the OSCE should be transformed into a formal treaty-based organization, with the authority and capability to implement peacekeeping missions, a demand repeated in Lisbon in 1996. Yeltsin suggested that a revamped OSCE would be guided by an executive committee of ten member states, a "Security Council" for the OSCE. While the U.S. government rebuffed Yeltsin point for point, Moscow has tangibly demonstrated its commitment to OSCE peacekeeping by permitting the organization to dispatch numerous missions to the territory of the former Soviet Union, and to Russia itself.

As of this writing, Russia remains vehemently opposed to further NATO expansion. However, Moscow has accepted the inevitability of one wave of enlargement and has signaled a willingness to negotiate the rest if granted an appropriate role in the process. The Russians may be recognizing that Washington will not cede traditional NATO responsibilities to the OSCE. Just as important, the West recognizes that Russia needs something in return for NATO expansion to Poland. As invitations were issued to the first wave of new NATO members, a new cooperative agreement, the Founding Act, and a new Euro-Atlantic Partnership Council were also created to reassure Russia that it will have a voice—if not a veto—in European security.

Germany and the OSCE

For the Federal Republic of Germany, the OSCE has a special historical significance, as it had been central to its *Ostpolitik*, providing important opportunities for dialogue and cooperation with eastern European states, especially the German Democratic Republic.[19] In some sense, the German government remains a champion of the OSCE, emphasizing its role in the transformation of security cooperation on the continent. The German government has emphasized that the major promise of the OSCE is that the organization remains the only existing *pan-European* security institution. From Bonn's perspective, the OSCE is an important vehicle for providing stability to eastern and central Europe and the former Soviet Union.

During the debates over German unification and NATO membership throughout 1990, the Kohl-Genscher government's commitment to the organization grew stronger as the concept of a common European home seemed within reach. German enthusiasm for the CSCE in 1990 and 1991 was based on numerous priorities. First, the institution was seen by the German government as a way to embed German unification in all-European processes in order to calm the concerns of its neighbors. Second, the broad conception of security that the CSCE embodied, as well as its inclusiveness, seemed well suited to the changing nature of security and to Germany's foreign policy role. And very importantly, the CSCE was perceived as a way to assure the Soviet Union (and, later, Russia) of its inclusion in the European security framework, while also including the United States. Thus, the German government moved early to institutionalize the OSCE.

Since then, the German government has continued to play a leading role in the transformation of the OSCE. Germany's proposals have aimed at increasing the organization's autonomous capacity to act in all realms, including the development of mechanisms to enforce adherence to OSCE principles. German policymakers view democracy, human rights, and the market economy as the primary responsibilities for the OSCE and believe that the broad definition of security gives the OSCE a unique role to play. Germany's specific priorities have included the creation of OSCE blue and green helmets; the weakening of the consensus decisionmaking principle; the creation of an OSCE parliamentary body; the creation of a steering group—a sort of Security Council; the creation of an arbitration mechanism; increasing the OSCE's role in arms control; and more involvement in postconflict "peace consolidation."[20] By the time of the Lisbon summit in 1996, the German government had shifted its priorities from the creation of new institutions to the fortification of existing ones. Specifically, the Germans continued to advocate the strengthening of the roles of the Chair-in-Office and the Secretary General, and the weakening of the consensus principle in human rights issues.[21] Finally, Bonn continues to emphasize that the OSCE should play an OSCE-first role in the region, whereby conflicts are dealt with in this forum before being brought to the United Nations at the international level. The Germans' chief allies in strengthening the OSCE's capabilities often have been the leaders of central and eastern Europe, and especially Russia.

OSCE IN-COUNTRY MISSIONS

During the 1992 Helsinki summit, member states of the OSCE authorized the organization to engage in preventive diplomacy and conflict prevention. These interventions were grounded in the organization's mandate to promote democratization, monitor human rights violations, and promote the rule of law. According to those that believe institutions can shape state interests and foster security cooperation, these are precisely the types of missions that international organizations can most successfully engage.

In the aftermath of Helsinki, a number of OCSE states, particularly the newer members from the East, began calling on the organization for assistance in a variety of ways, not merely with regard to human rights. To meet these requests, the OSCE devised the concept of long-term missions that would engage the needs of member states in a multifaceted manner. The missions, which were dispatched to the states of the former Soviet bloc and the Balkans, have been active in a range of areas, including security issues, economic restructuring, domestic political reforms, and minority rights. While the OSCE's role in the Dayton Peace Agreement has required the creation of a large mission in Bosnia, the OSCE missions to the former Soviet Union have been of a very limited nature, frequently employing less than a dozen OSCE personnel. Owing in part to the dearth of financial support, the OSCE's long-term missions have been credited with only modest success. In many cases, the impact of the OSCE has been negligible.

Missions to the Former Soviet Union

Between 1975 and 1992, the OSCE's membership increased from thirty-five to fifty-three members. The vast majority of new states were erstwhile republics of the Soviet Union, and they brought to the organization an array of domestic and cross-border conflicts. The OSCE's decision to grant membership to these states was not accompanied by a great and studied debate. Indeed, for some western governments, granting these states membership in the OSCE was a means of stemming their demands for membership in more purposeful western organizations, such as the EU and NATO. In hindsight, the OSCE might have given the region of the former USSR more thought, for in the past five years, it has been in these states that the OSCE has been most active and taxed.

OSCE missions in the Baltic states and Ukraine have focused on political questions, economic reform, and minority rights. In Estonia, the initial OSCE presence monitored the withdrawal of Soviet military forces. With the departure of these forces in 1994, a primary concern of the mission became promoting dialogue among the Estonian government, Moscow, and the ethnic Russian population living in Estonia. Since achieving independence, the Baltic governments have passed laws relating to citizenship, immigration, and language that have been designed to discriminate against ethnic Russians, and Moscow has repeatedly accused the governments in Tallinn and Riga of marginalizing the Russian population within their borders. OSCE missions consistently have striven to ameliorate tensions between the various parties, but with only six individuals representing the organization in Estonia, and four in Latvia, there are obvious limits on the organization's impact.

These missions, while multifaceted, did not operate in states in which armed conflict existed. However, since 1992, the OSCE has dispatched several missions to former Soviet republics plagued by fighting and bloodshed, including the first ones to Armenia and Azerbaijan in 1992. In the years since this initial deployment, the OSCE has sent missions in the FSU to Georgia, Moldova, Tajikistan, and Chechnya. The mandates of these missions have mirrored the responsibilities of the missions in the Baltics. However, in states plagued by armed conflict, the OSCE's tasks are substantially more difficult. In essence, OSCE representatives present themselves as neutral arbiters in the hope that the competing factions will utilize the mission for negotiations and ultimately to broker cease-fires.

With the outbreak of fighting between Chechnya and Moscow in late 1994 (ironically as the Budapest summit was convening), the OSCE, with the agreement of the two parties, created the "OSCE Assistance Group," which dispatched a small delegation to facilitate a cease-fire and broker a permanent peace settlement. The Assistance Group also monitored human rights violations and explored avenues for democratic settlement of the conflict. While both parties, particularly the Russians, encouraged the ongoing OSCE involvement, events in the region were not significantly affected by the Assistance Group. A tenuous peace settlement was concluded in 1996, but the parties were not brought together by the OSCE but rather by events determined on the battlefield and in the streets of Grozny. After the peace settlement, the OSCE certified elections in Chechnya in January 1997 as free and fair. Shortly thereafter, however, the organization was ejected from Chechyna by the newly elected president because the leader of the Assistance Group, Tim Guldimann, had referred to Chechnya as part of the Russian Republic.

The OSCE likely will play a continuing role in the region's conflicts, but as this analysis suggests, its impact will be minimal as long as its purview is not accepted by the involved parties. As with the Baltic missions, restrictions on funding and very limited staffing commitments have placed severe constraints on the OSCE's ability to intervene in regional armed conflicts. (The non-Bosnia missions constitute only 16.5 percent of the 1997 OSCE budget.) Perhaps the organization's chief success story has been the mere fact that its presence has been endorsed by the warring factions and by the Russian government. Indeed, as Diana Chigas argued, the OSCE's greatest achievement in the former Soviet Union has been the fact that for "the first time Russia has accepted an international presence on her territory and international mediation of an internal conflict."[22] At the same time, some view Russia's central role in these missions as a "figleaf for [Russia's] 'neo-imperialist' tendencies."[23]

Missions in the Balkans

The OSCE's involvement in the Balkans illuminates both the organization's limitations and great potential. At the outset of fighting in 1991, the CSCE proved unable to intervene and was effectively barred from any role by Serbia's veto. As the wars in Croatia and Bosnia raged, many observers noted that the CSCE's failure to engage the conflict was causing irreparable damage to the organization. However, four years after fighting commenced, the OSCE emerged as a key player in the Dayton Peace Agreement and the international community's efforts to maintain peace in the region.

In the weeks and months following the Serb military strikes against Slovenia and Croatia in June 1991, the CSCE repeatedly condemned Serb actions and called on Belgrade to refrain from further hostilities. Beyond rhetorical condemnations, it quickly became apparent that the OSCE had no formal mechanisms to compel Serb compliance. Aside from endorsing EU sanctions against Serbia, the OSCE was unable to find a means to engage the crisis constructively. The OSCE's impotence was made manifest when the organization's call for a peace conference was vetoed by Belgrade as the fighting continued into the summer of 1991. The CSCE managed to dispatch small monitoring missions to Kosovo, Sondzak, and Vojvodina in 1992. However, in the aftermath of Serbia's suspension from the organization in 1992, the missions clashed with local Serb authorities, and they were expelled from the region in July 1993.

Between 1991 and 1995, the CSCE stood by as the United Nations, NATO, the EU, and the WEU endeavored to separate the warring parties and secure cease-fires. Consequently, it came as a surprise to many to find the OSCE at the center of the Dayton Peace Talks and the subsequent implementation of the civilian aspects of the Dayton Peace Agreement. The international accords were multidimensional agreements that covered a range of issues including peacekeeping, humanitarian assistance, and nation building. After the agreement was signed in December 1995, Strobe Talbott, the U.S. deputy secretary of state, remarked, "At the very center of this collective effort is the OSCE. That is how it should be."[24]

With a mission of approximately 250 personnel, the OSCE intervention in the Balkans was far larger than any of its previous efforts (it consumes 44% of the 1997 OSCE budget). To date, the OSCE has experienced both success and notable setbacks in its efforts to implement the Dayton Accords. With regard to confidence-building and arms control, Dayton called on the OSCE to oversee negotiations that would lead to the formal exchange of military information and place limitations on military deployments and exercises. More specifically, the Dayton Accords called on the parties to negotiate, under OSCE auspices, "numerical limits on holdings of tanks, artillery, armed combat vehicles, combat aircraft, and attack helicopters." The OSCE experienced considerable progress in these subregional arms control negotiations, which concluded in January 1996 and resulted in the formal exchange of information regarding military resources and installations. Following these agreements, the OSCE brokered understandings in June 1996 that determined limits on the weapons categories noted above. If the parties continue to cooperate, these reductions will have been implemented by October 1997.

Owing to the OSCE's inability to engage the conflict prior to 1995, it is difficult to ascertain why the organization became the international community's primary agent for implementing the civilian components of the Dayton Accords. It may be that the organization's efforts in the former Soviet Union were deemed adequate preparation for the more arduous tasks to be found in the Balkans. Or it may be that the major powers were dubious about the long-term prospects for peace in the Balkans, and preferred that the OSCE, rather than individual states, accept responsibility if the accords failed. This in fact may explain U.S. enthusiasm for the central role of the OSCE in Dayton. In any event, at Dayton, the OSCE agreed to play a key role in consolidating Dayton's peace, with special responsibility for arms control, elections, refugees, and human rights.

In contrast to the OSCE's successful confidence-building and arms control efforts, the organization's role in election monitoring and in facilitating the return of refugees has encountered serious obstacles. In the months preceding the September 14, 1996, elections in Bosnia, the OSCE and other international observers documented repeated efforts to thwart free and fair elections. Indeed, on June 25, the OSCE's Chair-in-Office, Flavio Cotti, publicly confirmed that the actions of all three parties, particularly the Bosnian Serbs, violated the word and spirit of Dayton's law. By failing to permit resettlement of refugees and refusing to register eligible voters, tens of thousands of Bosnian citizens were systematically excluded from the election process. Despite the widespread belief that the elections would not meet Dayton's conditions, voting went forward. While the OSCE warned the major powers of the election's questionable legitimacy, the West, and Washington in particular, was determined to proceed. American policymakers were under considerable pressure to remove U.S. troops expeditiously, and to cancel the elections clearly would have postponed the U.S. timetable. Even though the September 14 elections did not meet the requirements delineated at Dayton, the OSCE certified the election results. Early in 1997, however, the OSCE once again delayed until September 1997 the holding of municipal elections due to concerns about their legitimacy.

The situation in the Balkans, like that in the former Soviet Union, remained tense in mid-1997. In Bosnia, it is not clear whether the Croat-Muslim Federation will hold, nor whether the Bosnian Serb leadership itself will stabilize or relapse into internecine warfare. Sporadic fighting has erupted between Serbs and Muslims, and it remains uncertain if peace can be maintained in the absence of NATO forces. In this environment, the tasks ahead for the OSCE remain daunting and dangerous.

CONCLUSION

The OSCE's evolution from an amorphous "talk shop" to an integral component of European security cooperation has confronted many obstacles, and its future path is by no means certain. Since the Paris summit, the OSCE incrementally has increased its organizational capacity and has met head on many new challenges facing Europe. Maintaining its broad conception of security, the OSCE has attempted to carve out a niche for itself in European security cooperation that does not shy away from engaging in armed conflict. Ironically, what was viewed as a weakness during the cold war is now viewed as the organization's primary strength: its broad conceptualization of security, which rests prominently on the human dimension, the commitments of member states to human rights, and the recognition of security interdependence among nation states.

In the immediate aftermath of the cold war, many believed that a collective security organization could be forged within the CSCE. But the OSCE has rested its sights on more modest goals. Reforms within the OSCE indicate that member states long ago abandoned any hope that the OSCE would evolve into a pan-European collective security system. Rather, institutional developments reveal that member states consistently have sought to create mechanisms that will enable the OSCE to provide an early warning function, prevent conflict, and serve as a neutral third party to disputes among and within its members. Rather than relying upon forceful measures, the OSCE's internal reforms have provided the organization with an array of political vehicles capable of "building trust, opening communication and correcting distortions in perceptions, helping to build mutual understanding of underlying interests, [and] shaping attitudes within relevant governments."[25] The domestic focus of the OSCE's mandate is just as central as its external one when explaining the OSCE's role in security cooperation.

Nonetheless, the OSCE is looked on with less urgency than it was in 1990 and 1991 by its member states. The organization has been condemned for failing to develop effective mechanisms to engage the conflicts that have plagued the Eurasian landscape in recent years. From Bosnia to Chechnya to Albania, the OSCE is consistently cited by those who assert that institutions cannot ameliorate post-cold-war conflicts. It is true that the OSCE has not had great success in managing the more intractable conflicts of its member states, but neither have the United Nations, NATO, or the EU.

We believe that critics of the OSCE hold the organization to unrealistically high expectations. If OSCE effectiveness is measured by its ability to maintain a robust collective security system capable of resolving the armed conflicts of its members, then it is bound to fail. However, if member states agree that the organization's primary mission should be that of a neutral agent, facilitating dialogue and negotiations among competing parties, then the OSCE will make a real contribution toward European security cooperation.

To build an effective organization, the OSCE's members, particularly the organization's major powers, must resolve the ambivalence evident in their policies toward the organization. Despite a consensus on the vital role the organization can play in conflict prevention, amelioration, and peace building, fundamental differences of opinion remain about how strong to make the OSCE vis-à-vis its member states. In order to assure the OSCE's role in

European security cooperation, member states must substantially increase their support for the OSCE, both financially and politically.

The OSCE does not operate in a vacuum, and its evolution has been greatly affected by the reforms within other security organizations, including the EU, the WEU, and NATO. It may be that NATO expansion affords the OSCE an ideal opportunity for enhancing the organization's authority and capabilities. Moscow and NATO are at clear odds over this issue, and the Yeltsin government has made opposition to expansion a central tenet of its foreign policy. NATO states, particularly the United States, are increasingly committed to the organization's eastern enlargement. We believe that a recognition of the centrality of the OSCE to European security cooperation on the part of NATO members could ameliorate many of Moscow's concerns regarding Russia's place in the European security architecture. If NATO governments pledged to increase substantially their financial and political support for the OSCE, and if western publics can be persuaded to increase funding for the OSCE as part of the price of securing Russia's acquiescence to NATO expansion, European security cooperation may very well be advanced.

NOTES

1. The Conference on Security and Cooperation in Europe (CSCE) became the Organization for Security and Cooperation in Europe (OSCE) in 1995. For readability, this chapter uses the concept "OSCE" unless specific CSCE developments are discussed.

2. A primary theoretical debate in international relations has centered on the ability of international institutions to foster cooperation among states. Realists have long been critical of the argument that international organizations can facilitate cooperation among the major powers. For realists, the interests of the major powers determine the role of international organizations in global politics. Although liberal theorists share the view that the role of international organizations is minimal on questions of "high politics," they are more sanguine about the role they can play when issues do not touch upon the immediate security interests of the major powers.

3. Helga Haftendorn argues that there were two contradictory forces unleashed by the CSCE. First, there was the solidifying aspect (recognition of the status quo), and second, a transformational (support for political liberalization within eastern Europe). See Haftendorn, "Nachwort," in *Zwischen Abgrenzung und Verantwortungsgemeinschaft. Zur KSZE-Politik der beiden deutschen Staaten 1984–1989,* ed. Karl E. Birnbaum and Ingo Peters (Baden-Baden: Nomos, 1991), 114–119; see also Clive Archer, *Organizing Europe: The Institutions of Integration* (London: Edward Arnold, 1994), ch. 12.

4. Karl Birnbaum and Ingo Peters, "Die beiden deutschen Staaten auf dem Wiener KSZE-Folgekonferenz," in *Zwischen Abgrenzung*, ed. Karl Birnbaum and Ingo Peters, 71–105.

5. Flavio Cotti, the former Chair-in-Office, used this description of OSCE missions. See Cotti, "The OSCE's Increasing Responsibilities in European Security," *NATO Review* 44, no. 6 (1996): 7–12. Diana Chigas has written that the success of the HCNM turns two traditional beliefs on their heads: first, that organizations need supranational authority in order for them to be successful; and, second, that these organizations need "teeth," or enforcement capabilities. See Diana Chigas, with Elizabeth McClintock and Christophe Kamp, "Preventive Diplomacy and the Organization for Security and Cooperation in Europe," in *Preventing Conflict in the Post-Communist World: Mobilizing International and Regional Organizations*, ed. Abram Chayes and Antonia Handler Chayes (Washington, DC: Brookings Institution, 1996), 25–97.

6. The conflict prevention mechanism, based on consensus-minus-one, has been enacted only twice; the judgments of the Geneva Court on Conciliation and Arbitration (which entered into force in 1994) are not binding; and the Permanent Council does not have the authority of a U.N.-style security council.

7. Flavio Cotti, "The OSCE's Increasing Responsibilities in European Security," 7–12.

8. See note 3, *supra*.

9. Christopher Anstis, "The Conference on Security and Cooperation in Europe (CSCE)," in *Disconcerted Europe: The Search for a New Security Architecture*, ed. Alexander Moens and Christopher Anstis (Boulder, CO: Westview Press, 1994).

10. See *Lisbon Document 1996*, Document S/1/96 (Prague: OSCE, 1996). See also *OSCE Newsletter* 3, no. 12 (December 1996) for the summary of the Lisbon meeting.

11. Diana Chigas, with Elizabeth McClintock and Christophe Kamp, "Preventive Diplomacy and the Organization for Security and Cooperation in Europe," 25–97, esp. 74.

12. Al Gore, "The Role of the OSCE in European Security," *U.S. Department of State Dispatch* 7, no. 50 (9 December 1996).

13. Christopher Anstis, "The Conference on Security and Cooperation in Europe (CSCE)," 89.

14. See Diana Chigas, with Elizabeth McClintock and Christophe Kamp, "Preventive Diplomacy and the Organization for Security and Cooperation in Europe," 73.

15. Richard C. Holbrooke, "Advancing U.S. Interests in Europe," *U.S. Department of State Dispatch* 6, no. 12 (20 March 1995).

16. Shevardnadze as cited in Christopher Anstis, "The Conference on Security and Cooperation in Europe (CSCE)," 79.

17. Kozyrev as cited in Diana Chigas, with Elizabeth McClintock and Christophe Kamp, "Preventive Diplomacy and the Organization for Security and Cooperation in Europe," 94.

18. Boris Yeltsin, "European Securities and Structures," *Vital Speeches* 61, no. 6 (January 1995): 23.

19. See Wolfram F. Hanrieder, *Germany, America, Europe: Forty Years of German Foreign Policy* (New Haven: Yale University Press, 1989), 202–219; and Karl E. Birnbaum and Ingo Peters, "Die beiden deutschen Staaten im KSZE-Prozess," in *Zwischen Abgrenzung*, ed. Karl E. Birnbaum and Ingo Peters.

20. See the speech by Klaus Kinkel on May 17, 1994, in Vienna. *Mitteilung für die Presse 1072/94* (Bonn: Auswärtiges Amt, 1994).

21. "Interview des Bundesministers des Auswärtigen Dr. Klaus Kinkel mit der badischen Zeitung für die Ausgabe vom Samstag, den 30. November 1996 zum OSZE-Gipfel in Lissabon am 2./3.12.96," from the foreign ministry's world wide web homepage at [http:www.auswaertiges-amt.government.de/de/auss_pol/sicherab/R961202.htm].

22. Diana Chigas, with Elizabeth McClintock and Christophe Kamp, "Preventive Diplomacy and the Organization for Security and Cooperation in Europe," 43.

23. Piotr Switalski and Ingrid Tersman, "The Organization for Security and Cooperation in Europe (OSCE)," in *Peacekeeping and the Role of Russia in Eurasia*, ed. Lena Jonson and Clive Archer (Boulder, CO: Westview Press, 1996), 180.

24. Strobe Talbott, "The OSCE in Bosnia," *U.S. Department of State Dispatch*, 6, no. 52 (December 1995).

25. Diana Chigas, with Elizabeth McClintock and Christophe Kamp, "Preventive Diplomacy and the Organization for Security and Cooperation in Europe," 29.

8

Multilateral Security Regimes: The Politics of CFE and CSBMs

GRAEME P. AUTON

On the morning of December 8, 1988, newspapers across the United States featured a photograph of President Ronald Reagan, President-elect George Bush, and Soviet Premier Mikhail Gorbachev standing together on New York's Governor's Island, with overcoats flapping in the chill wind and a wintry Manhattan skyline in the background. It was a uniquely promising, but also troubling, moment in history. The day before, Gorbachev had announced to the U.N. a planned reduction in Soviet military forces and a withdrawal of thousands of Soviet soldiers and tanks from eastern Europe. In just two years, most of those forces would be gone from the western reaches of the Soviet empire, and a divided Germany would be unified. In military terms, what had not been accomplished in fifteen years of mutual and balanced force reduction (MBFR) negotiations would now be simply incidental to larger political changes. In a little over three years, the Soviet Union itself would cease to exist, and the cold war would be over.

These events seem distant from the perspective of the late 1990s, yet the essential architecture of European security and arms control was already well established when Gorbachev made his December 1988 visit to the United States. As Richard Darilek had argued, there were already two well entrenched approaches to the management of European security.[1] The first was a "structural" approach that sought to scale down and otherwise regulate the military structures of participating states. This was the strategy followed in MBFR and the subsequent negotiations on reductions in Conventional Armed Forces in Europe (CFE).[2] The second embodied an "operational" approach to arms control that sought to regulate the activities of armed forces without necessarily reducing them. This was the strategy followed in the Stockholm negotiations of the Conference on Disarmament in Europe (CDE), and the subsequent confidence- and security-building (CSBM) agreements formalized in the Conference of Security and Cooperation in Europe's Vienna Documents of 1992 and 1994 (VD92, VD94).[3] The distinction between these two approaches reflected two corresponding philosophies for managing the East-West security relationship. Within the West, "structural" measures were embraced by Washington, while "operational" measures were more readily promoted by Europeans.[4]

ARMS CONTROL STRATEGIES

The first strategy, focusing on structural measures such as those considered in MBFR and CFE, held that military accommodation in the form of actual force reductions—the paring back of military capabilities—must precede political and operational measures designed to reassure the negotiating parties about each other's intentions. The logic of this was very simple: meaningful political and economic accommodation could not take place as long as there was a high level of military confrontation across the center of Europe, and as long as the negotiating states were not willing to make concrete reductions a litmus test of their desire to move toward a broader kind of East-West normalization. Ultimately, structural measures, as embodied in the CFE Treaty, aimed at reducing the military capabilities of contracting states to the point where offensive military operations would be impossible without substantial political warning time.

The second strategy, focusing on operational measures such as those embodied in CDE and VD92, held that the military status quo reflected underlying political tensions and insecurities, and that it was not possible to arrive at meaningful concrete reductions until the political and perceptual sources of the East-West conflict were addressed through measures designed, over time, to reassure the contracting states about each other's intentions. Advocates of this strategy also sometimes pointed out that qualitative operational measures designed to circumscribe the possibilities for surprise attack or the rapid, unexpected movement of large-scale military forces might be more important for the stability of the East-West relationship than quantitative measures such as force reductions. However, a "subliminal" assumption in European operational arms control—principally confidence- and security-building measures (CSBMs)—was that the East-West divide ought to be *overcome*, eventually eradicated, rather than stabilized and made "safer," and therefore, conceivably more permanent.

The relationship between structural and operational approaches to European security was, and is, a matter of controversy. Structural arms control measures deal with the levels and disposition of military forces themselves, while operational measures deal with confidence-building mechanisms, transparency, crisis management, and efforts to inform states about the intentions—not simply the capabilities—of other states (and coalitions of states). To a certain degree, it is possible to arrive at and implement operational confidence- and security-building measures without substantially affecting the disposition of forces themselves. On the other hand, there is a point beyond which structural measures designed to reduce forces and alter their deposition cannot be avoided if governments are to remain faithful to the spirit and objectives of confidence- and security-building. Not surprisingly, the relationship between structural measures and operational ones can be a source of significant discord between governments. In the pages that follow, we shall look at this and other issues as we look at the background to the CFE Treaty and the CSBMs agreements sponsored by the Organization for Security and Cooperation in Europe (OSCE).

Both strategies, structural and operational, are based on the core assumption that arms control regimes and institutions shape state behavior and reinforce state cooperation, while they at the same time serve critical state interests. This does not mean that institutional dynamics are always determinative in shaping a government's actions, or that governments never revert to competitive "self-help." Rather, it means that international regimes and institutions distill the political objectives of states, and establish their own powerful norms, in a quasi-anarchical environment in which sovereign entities can frequently accomplish more through cooperation and political reassurance than through conflict and distrust.[5] This is true not only for arms control, as such, but also—obviously—for collective security and collective defense regimes.

In proceeding, it is important to bear in mind that arms control and confidence-building measures are more than mere technical measures for managing the military balance. As I have argued elsewhere, arms control is by definition a political undertaking predicated on a political understanding of interstate conflict.[6] Wolfram F. Hanrieder perhaps put it best some years ago, when he wrote that

> . . . arms control inevitably occurs in a political context. The intentions that drive or brake arms control negotiations go beyond avoiding war or stabilizing the military balance. They derive their larger and deeper meaning from political purposes—global, regional, and domestic. In the nuclear age, arms control has become the political sublimation of nuclear weapons that cannot be used, and of rivalries between East and West that are so profound and intractable that they cannot be ameliorated except in regulating the military balance. Arms control has become the "new coin of the realm," which is used by all parties to test the degree of East-West tensions and the limits of political accommodation.[7]

The changes that have transformed the European system in the post-cold-war era have not altered this fundamental truth. Arms control regimes today, as before, are a measure of the political commitment of governments to each other and to their own principles.

CFE

By the mid-1990s, it was often argued in policy circles in Washington that there were three "pillars" supporting the post-cold-war U.S. presence in Europe. The first, and arguably the most important, was NATO. The second was the "bilateral" relationship, or liaison, between the United States and the European Union (EU). The third was the Conventional Armed Forces in Europe (CFE) Treaty, regulating conventional armaments in the Atlantic-to-the-Urals (ATTU) reduction zone, and its politically binding appendage, the CFE-IA Agreement covering military personnel levels in the ATTU area. The importance attached to the CFE regime by the policymaking community in Washington and in European capitals often has been insufficiently appreciated in academic circles, particularly in the United States.

The CFE process, in a direct sense, had three origins: the fifteen-year-old MBFR negotiations, which came to an end on February 2, 1989; the December 11, 1986, Brussels Declaration of NATO's North Atlantic Council, which called for separate negotiations on NATO-Warsaw Pact conventional arms reductions and on confidence- and security-building measures; and Soviet decisions from 1987 to 1988 to negotiate a conventional arms agreement that acknowledged NATO-Warsaw Pact conventional force asymmetries, and included the European part of the Soviet Union in the zone of reduction.[8] CFE negotiations began in Vienna, with twenty-three NATO and Warsaw Pact states, on March 9, 1989. The treaty was signed on November 19, 1990, following expedited talks that focused on the definition of treaty-limited equipment (TLE), subzones for equipment ceilings, and a timetable for reduction and dismantlement. In the end, the CFE Treaty fit the mold of late/post-cold-war arms control and disarmament agreements: actual reduction and destruction, on-site inspection, periodic exchange of detailed information, and the opportunity for "challenge inspections."[9]

Following provisional application, the CFE Treaty entered into force on July 15, 1992, and the forty–month reductions period (during which time all states party to the agreement had to reduce treaty-limited equipment, or TLE, to mandated levels) ended on November 16, 1995. At the beginning of the process, the dissolution of the Soviet Union yielded some incongruities, as eight of the sixteen former Soviet states became parties to the agreement. Many of these incongruities, which delayed entry-into-force of the treaty, were resolved in the Tashkent Agreement of May 15, 1992, in which the participating former Soviet states divided up the Soviet Union's reduction obligations between them.[10]

In broad terms, the obligations spelled out in CFE were apportioned in terms of two "groups of states parties": the North Atlantic Treaty Group and (following the dissolution of the Warsaw Pact) the "Budapest/Tashkent Group." The denomination of treaty obligations in this fashion, rather than purely in terms of separate national ceilings, probably substantiated the criticism that CFE is a cold-war relic unsuited to the conditions of the post-cold-war era.[11] During the summer of 1997, the CFE treaty regime was finally modified to eliminate the "groups of states parties" formula, and obligations were denominated in national terms.

As originally negotiated, the CFE Treaty set equal NATO and "Budapest/Tashkent" ceilings for the Atlantic-to-the-Urals region on armaments essential for large-scale conventional offensive operations. Collectively, the treaty participants agreed that neither group of states parties could have, within the ATTU zone, more than: 20,000 tanks; 20,000 artillery; 30,000 armored combat vehicles (ACVS); 6,800 combat aircraft; and 2,000 attack helicopters. National limits had to be apportioned within these overall ceilings. The treaty also set limits on the number of TLE with active military units (remaining TLE had to be in designated permanent storage sites). Each group of states was limited to the following equipment in active units: 16,500 tanks; 17,000 artillery pieces; and 27,300 armored combat vehicles (ACVS). The treaty further limited equipment that might be held by any one country within the reductions zone to about one-third of the total for all countries in Europe, thus establishing a "sufficiency" rule. These limits were: 13,300 tanks; 13,700 artillery pieces; 20,000 armored combat vehicles (ACVS); 5,150 combat aircraft; and 1,500 attack helicopters. The generosity of these limits was part of the price that had to be paid for Soviet/Russian acquiescence to the agreement's numerical guidelines.

The reduction obligations mandated in the treaty impacted the countries of the former Soviet bloc much more heavily than they did NATO. Consequently, the costs associated with the reduction and destruction of TLE (the specific methods for reduction were spelled out in the Treaty's reductions protocol) impacted the "Budapest/Tashkent" group more heavily than they did the West. Compliance with the treaty was to be assured through intrusive verification measures that included detailed information exchanges, on-site inspections, challenge inspections, and on-site monitoring of destruction.

From the beginning, the CFE Treaty posed problems in its implementation. Russia haggled over the definition of "sufficiency" requirements and attempted to reduce the number of inspections on its territory by deliberately confusing the concepts of "object of verification" (OOV) and "declared site" (at which more than one OOV might be present, thus permitting a prompt follow-on inspection by an inspection team at a declared site). Turkey sought, and received, a CFE "exclusion zone" along its border with Syria and Iraq, arguably not part of the European security architecture. Controversy also swelled over the practice of "cascading": passing newer equipment designated for reduction on to allies, who would in turn meet their own reduction obligation by destroying decidedly older equipment.

The "Flanks" Issue

Perhaps no issue aroused greater controversy, however, than the "flank" restrictions embodied in the CFE Treaty. The Treaty's Article V provided for sublimits to ground TLE (tanks, artillery, and ACVS) in the northern and southern "flank" regions of the former Soviet Union.[12] Following the breakup of the USSR, Moscow began to chafe under the southern flank limitations that still applied to Russia. The Caucasus was now a region of great instability, and, beginning in November 1994, Russian military operations in Chechnya posed an obvious problem for CFE compliance. Russian arguments against the flank limitations were that:

- The CFE Treaty's Article V was originally agreed to in very different circumstances, when the USSR was still intact. Such zone limits were now cold-war artifacts without further utility in the post-cold-war era.

- Limitations that dictated ceilings on the stationing of forces within a country, even if agreed to earlier, were an unwarranted infringement on national sovereignty.
- Massive post-cold-war troop redeployments, under the severe economic constraints confronted by the "new" Russia, demanded flexibility in restationing forces wherever facilities could be made available.
- Instability in the Caucasus and Chechen separatism posed security threats to Russia that Moscow had to be able to address within its full national capacity.[13]

In July 1995, at a meeting in Brussels with NATO governments, Russia demanded an "exclusion zone" in the North Caucasus that—like the Turkish exclusion zone on the Syrian-Iraqi border—would not be subject to CFE limits. At the May 1996 CFE Treaty Review Conference, the matter was provisionally settled, and levels of personnel and equipment were increased for both the northern and southern flank zones.[14] While the Russian case for such a measure in the southern zone was strong, the argument for implementing it in the northern zone was less persuasive and caused some concern in the Baltic states and Scandinavia.

CFE Follow-up

Speculation about the future of CFE has focused on a number of possibilities. Paul Stares and John Steinbruner have argued that "since the goal of cooperative security is to limit forces to levels sufficient for the defense of national territory, the length of border to be defended becomes a logical basis for establishing national force levels."[15] In this formulation, CFE and the CFE-IA manpower accord would be followed by a "force density" agreement that, with appropriate exceptions for special circumstances, would permit each country "a single brigade of standard size and structure for every 100 kilometers of border."[16] Hilmar Linnenkamp, arguing that the CFE Treaty "became an epilogue to the extinct confrontational structure of European relations rather than the hallmark of a new Europe," has proposed national force restructuring on the basis of agreed criteria of "defense dominance."[17] Yet another idea has been to limit the number of a country's military units that could be maintained at active strength.[18] Jennone Walker has questioned the future relevance of structural arms control measures themselves, and has argued that CFE follow-on would most usefully take the form of refined, legally binding CSBMs: "What European conventional arms controllers can do is: (a) help prevent war by accident or miscalculation; (b) prevent internal conflicts from spilling across borders; and (c) by adding steps a country would want to take before launching an attack, increase warning of aggressive intent."[19] Clearly, such goals are more appropriate to a CSBMs regime than to an arms control and disarmament, or arms reductions, agreement.

With respect to existing governmental initiatives, the CFE follow-on formula that has generated the most concern in Washington has been the French proposal for a Pan-European Security Treaty (PEST). Such a treaty would roll CFE into a legally binding version of CSCE/OSCE, thereby diminishing the role of NATO and including formerly neutral and non-aligned (NNA) countries in the limitations regime.[20] Negotiation of the treaty might follow from the "harmonization" component of CSCE/OSCE's Forum for Security Cooperation (FSC) talks, discussed below. When the French idea first surfaced, the outward U.S. response was strongly negative. Within Washington policy circles, however, evaluation of the idea was more guarded—as was also true of the German and British governments.

At the December 1996 OSCE summit in Lisbon, CFE states pledged to undertake negotiations with a view to adapting the treaty to the still-changing security environment in Europe, a task that would not be easy, given rising tensions over NATO's evident decision to extend membership invitations to Poland, the Czech Republic, and Hungary.[21] In 1997, the "groups of states parties" formula was finally dropped, and further reduced force levels under CFE were touted as one inducement to Russia's cooperation in NATO enlargement.[22]

CSBMS

Confidence- and security-building measures (CSBMs) are by definition different from the sort of limitations and reductions, or classical "arms control," measures embodied in CFE (or in INF, START, CWC, etc.). In an international system in which *intentions* are significantly more difficult to gauge than *capabilities*, the purpose of CSBMs is to help reassure governments about the nature of each others' intentions. CSBMs typically include limitations on military maneuvers, advance notification of such maneuvers, exchange of maneuvers, military-to-military contacts, and exchange of information about force structures, weapons acquisitions, and the import or export of military hardware.[23]

The CSCE/OSCE confidence- and security-building measures regime includes all of these. Formulated in the Vienna Documents of 1990, 1992, and 1994, it has its origins in the CSCE's Helsinki Final Act of 1975 and the Stockholm Accord of the Conference of Disarmament in Europe (CDE) of 1986.

CSBM negotiations were mandated by the Madrid CSCE Follow-Up Conference in 1983, and talks took place in Stockholm from 1984 to 1986. The Stockholm document formalized a Conference on Disarmament in Europe that called for notifications, forecasts, and observations of military activities at agreed levels, and provided for on-site inspection to verify compliance. These measures applied to land-based military exercises in the whole of Europe (in the Atlantic-to-the Urals, or ATTU, zone). Consistent with the mandate, the Stockholm agreement's CSBMs were designed to be militarily significant, politically binding, and verifiable.[24]

VD90, VD92, and VD94

The CSCE states agreed during the CSCE's Vienna Review Conference (November 1986 to January 1989) to mandate refinement of the CSBMs regime beyond what was provided in the Stockholm CDE accord. Three sets of negotiations subsequently took place, all in Vienna. The first round (March 1989 to November 1990) produced the Vienna 1990 CSBMs Document (commonly called VD90). This agreement established:

- annual exchange of information on military manpower, equipment, deployments, and budget;
- prior (forty-two days) notification of military activities that involve 13,000 troops or 300 tanks, or 3,000 troops in amphibious or airborne operations;
- annual exchange of calendars of military activities, with large-scale (40,000 troops or more) exercises prohibited unless notified two years in advance;
- mandatory observation of military activities that exceed 17,000 troops for ground operations, 5,000 troops for amphibious or airborne exercises;
- on-site inspection (air and/or ground) to verify compliance with agreed measures;
- evaluation visits to declared active units and formations, with a prescribed evaluation visit quota;

- a mechanism giving signator governments the right to an explanation of unusual or hazardous military activities;
- a communications network for passing information for CFE and CSBMs purposes;
- an annual meeting to review CSBMs data and compliance; and
- improved military-to-military contacts, including mandatory visits to air bases.

The CSCE's Conflict Prevention Center (CPC) was designated as the oversight and implementation body for CSBMs, though the organization's Committee of Senior Officials (CSO) also had a role to play (the CSO was renamed the "Senior Council" at the December 1994 CSCE Budapest summit). The VD90 CSBMs document was adopted at the November 19–21 Paris CSCE summit.[25]

The second set of CSBMs negotiations took place from early 1991 until March 1992, and produced a further refined regime, commonly referred to as the Vienna Document 1992 (or VD92). This agreement enhanced the VD90 by including:

- annual exchange of data on weapon and equipment systems;
- provision for the demonstration of new weapon and equipment types;
- voluntary hosting of visits to dispel concerns about military activities;
- lowered observation thresholds (from 17,000 troops to 13,000 troops or 300 tanks for ground force activities and from 5,000 troops to 3,500 troops for amphibious and airborne operations);
- constraints on the size, frequency, and scheduling of notifiable military activities, and
- the right to include other CSCE states on national CSBMs inspection teams.[26]

The third set of CSBMs refinements was incorporated in the Vienna Document 1994, endorsed at the December 1994 CSCE Budapest Conference, which changed the name of the CSCE to the Organization for Security and Cooperation in Europe (OSCE). VD94 encompassed:

- an enhanced program for military contacts and cooperation (subsequently overtaken in many respects by NATO's Partnership for Peace [PfP]);
- a variety of provisions on defense planning, intended to improve transparency between signator states; and
- a regime for global exchange of military information, including (despite initial U.S. opposition) a naval armaments component.[27]

To begin with, the implementation record of the CSBMs regime was somewhat mixed, with—for example—varied national interpretations of the information exchange requirements. Evaluation visits started in July 1991, and, on the whole, these were executed as intended. During the first year that the accord was in force, the "unusual military activities" mechanism was invoked principally because of events in the former Yugoslavia.[28] It is important to bear in mind that the CSBMs agreement was politically, not legally, binding. The regime worked reasonably well—given the initial intentions underpinning it—and CFE Treaty party governments found the CSCE's CSBMs provisions a useful supplement to the CFE requirements. Nonetheless, there was a continuing concern in the West with maintaining the integrity of the CFE Treaty and with ensuring that CSCE measures did not adversely impact the latter through efforts to "harmonize" the two regimes, a concern that limited the accomplishments of the December 1994 CSCE Budapest summit. The December 1996 OSCE Lisbon summit's commitment to seek "synergy" and cooperation between the OSCE and other multilateral organizations and regimes, notably NATO and CFE (as well as the United Nations and the Council of Europe), did not materially alleviate this concern. The Lisbon Document stood more as an expression of broad intentions than as the expression of any concrete agreement.

Forum for Security Cooperation (FSC)

At the Prague CSCE Council of Ministers meeting (January 30–31, 1992), ministers approved guidelines to strengthen CSCE institutions and better control (or at least monitor) arms transfers. A new "consensus-minus-one" rule was adopted that permitted the CSCE to take political actions against any member country that committed "a clear, gross, and uncorrected" violation of CSCE commitments (essentially eliminating the veto power of a single state). This rule facilitated the suspension of the "rump" Republic of Yugoslavia (Serbia and Montenegro) as an active member of the organization. Perhaps most important, the Prague meeting laid the groundwork for the Helsinki CSCE Follow-Up meeting, which took place March 24 to July 10, 1992.[29]

The Helsinki Follow-Up produced the Helsinki Document, which included the Mandate for a new and comprehensive security dialogue, the Forum for Security Cooperation (FSC).[30] Intended to encompass the broad array of issues faced by CSCE states, the FSC involved all (at the time) fifty-two CSCE member governments, and it began its work in Vienna in September 1992. It is noteworthy that FSC embraced a new, still broader definition of "security."

The Helsinki Mandate (produced by the Helsinki Follow-Up) specified the elements to be addressed in the FSC in a Program for Immediate Action. FSC's work was to proceed in two parallel processes: (1) an enhanced dialogue on military issues, defense conversion, nonproliferation, and regional disputes; and (2) more traditional negotiations on arms control, disarmament, and confidence- and security-building measures. Addressing the need for a new European security architecture, FSC sought to build on existing security regimes in Europe, including the CFE Treaty, the CFE- IA accord, and the Vienna Document on CSBMs.

Mirroring the need for two parallel processes, the FSC agenda was pursued at Vienna in two working groups, whose tasks overlapped substantially. It quickly became evident that some of the FSC agenda items were controversial, and that the United States in particular was disturbed by a potential formulation of FSC that threatened to interfere with what had been accomplished in the CFE Treaty and elsewhere. Controversial aspects of the FSC agenda included:

(1) "Harmonization of Obligations Concerning Arms Control, Disarmament, and Confidence- and Security-Building." Harmonization struck fear into the heart of the Washington policy community, because it potentially entailed bringing CFE and VD92 together into a single overarching regime, which would (in the U.S. view) jeopardize what had been accomplished in the CFE Treaty and might even cast a shadow over the continued utility of NATO. To an uncanny degree, harmonization appeared to be a back door approach to the French Pan-European Security Treaty (PEST) idea. In its most benign interpretation, it entailed bringing the Vienna CSBMs regime up to the same standard of information exchange and inspections that was embodied in CFE. While many European governments (including the French and German) had no particular problem with this, it was viewed as anathema by the Americans. It was also thought to be problematic by governments, not party to the CFE Treaty, the formerly neutral and non-aligned (NNA) governments which did not want the CFE's more demanding provi-

sions (including potential structural limitations) extended to them through the harmonization instrument. Part of the problem with the harmonization component of the agenda was its very vagueness, which appeared—to some—a license to wreak havoc with an evolving European security structure.

(2) "Global Exchange of Military Information." This component of FSC also generated heartburn for the Americans, particularly for the Pentagon. "Global" exchange of information meant exactly that, and Washington was reluctant to assume the responsibility of reporting *global* military commitments and deployments as part of a *European* arms control/CSBMs regime. Complying with such a requirement would, in Washington's view, set an unfortunate precedent (though, in a sense, the Vancouver-to-Vladivostok application zone of the Open Skies Treaty had already set such a precedent). European states potentially party to the agreement were not similarly exercised, since their commitments were not global in scope. Only Russia shared this U.S. dilemma.

(3) "Co-operation in Respect of Nonproliferation." Here again, the United States had significant difficulties. Washington did not want FSC to take up weapons of mass destruction (nuclear/chemical/biological), since these were already being dealt with in other, legally and politically binding, forums (START, INF, CWC, Australia Group, Nuclear Suppliers' Group, etc.). It was argued in the U.S. policy community that FSC could add nothing useful to these other efforts, though it might complicate matters by engaging such a large number of governments with the weapons-of-mass-destruction issue. On the other hand, if FSC were to focus on conventional arms transfers, that, too, would pose a problem for the United States since Washington was not yet willing to sign off on any conventional arms export measures beyond (at the outside) simple information exchange. Once again, most Europeans were far less negative about this part of the agenda.

(4) "Regional Measures." This part of the FSC agenda referred to measures that might be taken in the Balkans, the Caucasus, or northern Europe to regulate regional military balances and provide appropriate regional CSBMs. Opposition to progress in regional measures came primarily from the Scandinavians and Turkey. They were afraid that if the negotiation of regional measures were limited to the countries within each region, the process would by definition exclude the United States, leaving them to deal with Russia without Washington's support. It was also feared that CSCE might, particularly in the Balkans, take on more than it could usefully handle. Obviously, there was a link between the "regional measures" component of the FSC and the "flanks" issue in CFE.

(5) "Code of Conduct on Politico-Military Aspects of Security." This component of the FSC agenda was not fully anticipated in the Helsinki Mandate. It was promoted at the Vienna FSC sessions by some of the formerly "neutral and nonaligned" (NNA) governments, as well as by the United States which saw it was a useful diversion from "harmonization." In the formulation finally adopted at the 1994 Budapest summit, the Code's principal meaningful provisions related to "intrastate norms of behavior with regard to the control and use of military forces in democratic societies."[31] The interstate aspects of the Code did not improve much on the Decalogue of Principles of interstate behavior articulated in the 1975 CSCE Helsinki Final Act. Ultimately, the notion of a Code struck a sensitive note with those governments still unwilling to subject their internal affairs to international monitoring. To a significant degree, NATO's North Atlantic Cooperation Council (NACC) and Partnership for Peace (PfP) accomplished more in this regard.

THE FUTURE

It became clear at the CSCE/OSCE Budapest summit, in December 1994, that the degree of pan-European consensus on the role of the CSBMs regime was, if anything, diminishing, and that this consensus was not likely to be rekindled at OSCE's 1996 Lisbon summit. For one thing, the very purpose of OSCE itself was to an increasing degree viewed differently in Moscow, the capitals of western Europe, and Washington. Despite efforts to depict it in a positive light, the Security Model Declaration agreed to at the December 2–3, 1996, Lisbon summit added little, if anything, new to the commitments that participating states had already made at Paris in 1990, Helsinki in 1992, the Vienna FSC talks (particularly 1992 to 1994), and the 1990, 1992, and 1994 Vienna CSBMs negotiations.[32] The blandness of the Lisbon Document, its reversion to broad declaratory statements and commitments, was a testament to two factors: First, 1996–1997 saw rising tensions in Europe over the issue of NATO enlargement, as well as over the continuing instability of Russia's domestic politics. Second, given these tensions, it is likely that the CSBMs regime had been developed (or "institutionalized") to the extent permitted by the political circumstances. By now, too, it was clear that OSCE and the CSBMs regime to some extent meant different things to different people. The flush of optimism that had publicly defined the process from 1990 to 1994 was now subsiding.

Moscow has seen OSCE as the potential basis for an all-European, legally binding structure, with obligations denominated in national terms, that could supplant "bloc" arrangements such as NATO.[33] In this formulation, OSCE could constrain NATO's development, legitimize the Russian-dominated Commonwealth of Independent States (CIS) as a coequal entity with western security organizations, and perhaps sanction Russia's special responsibilities in the near abroad.[34]

Washington has taken a different tack, calling for relatively minor refinements of the OSCE structure that would not pose a challenge to NATO and would not diminish the integrity of the CFE regime. This is hardly surprising. U.S. policymakers have been skeptical of CSCE/OSCE since the onset of CSCE negotiations in 1972, fearing that the organization encompassed merely "declaratory" measures, and this skepticism was fully evident during the Vienna FSC sessions.

West Europeans (particularly the Germans), on the other hand, have sought a middle road—one that bolsters OSCE and gives it new operational responsibilities (for example, in peacekeeping), but that also maintains the centrality of such cold-war legacies as NATO and CFE. The Europeans have also sought a more durable link between OSCE and other international bodies, notably the United Nations and NATO. It was the desire for such a link that framed the Platform for Cooperative Security in the December 1996 OSCE Lisbon Document, which pledged synergy and cooperation between OSCE and other international bodies. Nonetheless, the Platform—like the Lisbon Document's other components (including the Security Model Declaration and the Framework for Arms Control)—was articulated in only very general terms, indicating, perhaps, the difficulty of obtaining consensus regarding more specific commitments.[35]

At a time when the tenor of European international relations is strained by the issue of NATO enlargement, by potential instability in Russia, and by continuing ethnic conflict in the Balkans, it is perhaps understandable that progress toward linking operational and structural European security measures (and further developing CSBMs) has reached a plateau.[36] In 1997, it is obvious that NATO—with its program for enlargement and the Partnership for Peace—is, along with the European Union (EU), the most dynamic force for determining Europe's security future. Whether the "new" NATO can forge a special, constructive relationship with Russia, and at the same time ensure a continuing role for OSCE, remains to be seen. If everything goes well, Europe will wind up with a multilayered security architecture that incorporates links between the diverse multilateral institutions that have developed over the past half century, including NATO, EU, WEU, OSCE, and the CFE regime. If things do not go well, OSCE's further development may be in question, and CFE's integrity may become precarious. Either way, the continent is poised at the beginning of a new era.

NOTES

1. See Richard F. Darilek, "The Future of Conventional Arms Control in Europe: A Tale of Two Cities: Stockholm, Vienna," *Survival* 24, no. 1 (January-February 1987): 5.

2. See *Treaty on Conventional Armed Forces in Europe* (Paris, 19 November 1990).

3. See *Document of the Stockholm Conference* (Stockholm: CSCE, 19 September 1986); *Vienna Document 1990* (Vienna: CSCE, 17 November 1990); *Vienna Document 1992* (Vienna: CSCE, 4 March 1992).

4. The distinction between "structural" and "operational" measures tracks with the distinction drawn many years earlier by Philip Windsor between "immobiliste" and "revisionist" approaches to the management of East-West détente. See Philip Windsor, *Germany and the Management of Détente* (New York: Praeger, 1971), 165.

5. On the, at times, arid debate between "institutionalists" and "realists," see John J. Mearsheimer, "The False Promise of International Institutions"; Charles R. Glaser, "Realists as Optimists: Cooperation as Self-Help"; and William C. Wohlforth, "Realism and the End of the Cold War"; all in *International Security* 19, no. 3 (Winter 1994/95): 5–129. And Robert O. Keohane and Lisa L. Martin, "The Promise of Institutionalist Theory"; Charles A. Kupchan and Clifford A. Kupchan, "The Promise of Collective Security"; John Gerard Ruggie, "The False Premise of Realism"; Alexander Wendt, "Constructing International Politics"; and John J. Mearsheimer, "A Realist Reply"; all in *International Security* 20, no. 1 (Summer 1995): 39–93.

As all-consuming as the institutionalist-realist debate has been in academic circles, in the policy community the debate is often seen as somewhat specious, with both sides evincing a healthy disregard for how policy is actually made and implemented.

6. See Graeme P. Auton, "The Conceptual Dimensions of Arms Control," in *Arms Control and European Security*, ed. Graeme P. Auton (New York: Praeger, 1989), 5–21.

7. Wolfram F. Hanrieder, *Germany, America, Europe: Forty Years of German Foreign Policy* (New Haven: Yale University Press, 1989), 83–84.

8. See *News and Views from the USSR,* 13 April 1987 (Washington, DC: Soviet Embassy); the 29 May 1987 communiqué of the Warsaw Pact Political Consultative Committee, partially reprinted in *Survival* 24, no. 5 (September-October 1987): 465–466; and Robert D. Blackwill, "Conventional Stability Talks: Specific Approaches to Conventional Arms Control in Europe," *Survival* 30, no. 5 (September-October 1988).

9. The same formula was used in the 1987 INF Treaty, the 1990 START I Treaty, the 1993 START II Treaty, and the 1993 Chemical Weapons Convention.

10. See "Agreement on the Principles of Procedures for Implementing the Treaty on Conventional Armed Forces in Europe," Tashkent Agreement, 15 May 1992.

11. See, for example, Jenonne Walker, *Security and Arms Control in Post-Confrontational Europe* (New York: Oxford University Press, 1994), passim.

12. These flank sublimitations addressed the concerns of Scandinavia and Turkey about Soviet force concentrations in their respective regions.

13. On these arguments, see Dorn Crawford, *Conventional Armed Forces in Europe (CFE): A Review and Update of Key Treaty Elements* (Washington, DC: U.S Arms Control & Disarmament Agency, December 1996), 12.

14. See International Institute for Strategic Studies, *Military Balance 1996/97* (London: IISS, 1996), 37.

15. Paul B. Stares and John D. Steinbruner, "Cooperative Security in the New Europe," in *The New Germany and the New Europe,* ed. Paul B. Stares (Washington, DC: Brookings Institution, 1992), 227.

16. Paul B. Stares and John D. Steinbruner, "Cooperative Security," 228.

17. Defense dominance is defined as "defense sufficiency, crisis stability, and dissuasion stability." See Hilmar Linnenkamp, "The Security Policy of the New Germany," in Paul Stares and John Steinbruner, "Cooperative Security," 113–114.

18. See P. K. Davis, *Central Region Stability in a Deep Cuts Regime* (Santa Monica, CA: Rand Corporation, 1989).

19. See Jennone Walker, *Security and Arms Control.* This is a general theme in Walker's book, but see particularly pp. 26–39.

20. At least two English language versions of the French proposal were circulated in the policy community in late 1991 and early 1992.

21. *Final Document of the OSCE Lisbon Summit* (Lisbon: OSCE, 1996).

22. See Tyler Marshall, "Albright Nudges Russia on NATO Pact," *Los Angeles Times*, (2 May 1997), A4. The first "tranche" of new members includes Poland, the Czech Republic, and Hungary. Moscow, implacably opposed to the Alliance's enlargement, has been offered a formal relationship with NATO, but not membership.

23. While such "operational" measures are theoretically distinct from the "structural" provisions embodied in agreements such as CFE, there is clearly some overlap and interconnection between the two. Implementation of structural measures yields operational confidence-building benefits. By the same token, "operational" measures—even if they do not include reductions and limitations-may have the same effects as structural limitations.

24. See John Borawski, *From the Atlantic to the Urals: Negotiating Arms Control at the Stockholm Conference* (Washington: Pergamon-Brassey's, 1988); and James E. Goodby, "The Stockholm Conference: Negotiating a Cooperative

Security System for Europe," in *U.S.-Soviet Security Cooperation: Achievements, Failures and Lessons*, ed. Alexander L. George, Philip J. Farley, and Alexander Dallin (New York: Oxford University Press, 1988), 144–172.

25. See *Vienna Document 1990 of the Negotiations on Confidence- and Security-building Measures Convened in Accordance with the Relevant Provisions of the Concluding Document of the Vienna Meeting of the Conference on Security and Cooperation in Europe* (Vienna: CSCE, 1990). See also *Charter of Paris for a New Europe* (Paris: CSCE, 1990).

26. See *Vienna Document 1992 of the Negotiations on Confidence- and Security-building Measures Convened in Accordance with the Relevant Provisions of the Concluding Document of the Vienna Meeting of the Conference on Security and Cooperation in Europe* (Vienna: CSCE, 1992).

27. See Victor-Yves Ghebali, "After the Budapest Conference: The Organization for Security and Cooperation in Europe," *NATO Review* 43 no. 2 (March 1995): 26.

28. The first Annual Implementation Meeting (AIM) took place in Vienna, 11–15 November 1991.

29. See *Prague Document of Further Development of CSCE Institutions and Structures* (CSCE: Prague, 1992).

30. See *CSCE Helsinki Document 1992: The Challenges of Change* (CSCE: Helsinki, 1992).

31. Victor-Yves Ghebali, "After the Budapest Conference," 27.

32. See OSCE, *Final Document of the OSCE Lisbon Summit* (Lisbon, 1996); also Giancarlo Aragona, "Lisbon and Beyond: The OSCE in the Emerging European Security Architecture," *NATO Review* 45, no. 2 (March 1997): 7–10.

33. In this respect, the Russian vision has not been all that different from the earlier French idea of a Pan-European Security Treaty.

34. Victor-Yves Ghebali, "After the Budapest Conference," 24.

35. *Final Document of the OSCE Lisbon Summit* (Lisbon, 1996).

36. For a perhaps excessively optimistic view of OSCE's future development, see Flavio Cotti, "The OSCE's Increasing Responsibilities in European Security," *NATO Review* 44, no. 6 (November 1996): 7–12.

9

The Balkan Conflict: The Test Case for European Security Cooperation

RICHARD E. RUPP

On November 21, 1995, after five years of war, the leaders of the former Yugoslavia's Serbs, Muslims, and Croats signed a general peace agreement in Dayton, Ohio. The Dayton Agreement can in large part be credited to the West's use of large-scale aerial bombardment in fall 1995 that compelled the warring parties to the bargaining table. However, the peace plan was not a triumph for western diplomacy. The five years preceding Dayton were characterized by fundamental differences among the major powers, resulting in a series of failed policies that threatened the stability of the Atlantic Alliance and hopes for future multilateral cooperation.

Division among the major powers was mirrored by polarizing debates among realist and neoliberal (institutionalist) scholars of international relations. In the immediate aftermath of the cold war and following the experiences of the 1990–1991 Gulf War, neoliberals heralded the emergence of a markedly new era in global politics. The new period would be characterized by shared security interests among the major powers made possible by altered conditions in the international system. Neoliberals cited a variety of factors in asserting that state interests were converging, including: the growing commitment to democratic principles in states that formerly comprised the Soviet bloc; the general, if sporadic, movement toward free market economies; the belief that unilateral military force was no longer a legitimate means to advance policies; and the view that traditional balance-of-power politics was an outmoded concept.[1] With nations gravitating toward common interests and seeking to coordinate their policies, it was believed that international organizations, particularly collective security organizations, could play a leading role in facilitating peaceful relations among nations in the near future. Beyond identifying conflicts and serving as forums for debate, neoliberals maintained that international organizations could assist in aggregating the interests of their member states. With governments sharing a common understanding of a particular conflict, international organizations would be able to forge consensus on intervention strategies and goals.[2] Neoliberals also argued that in the post-cold-war period, international cooperation among the major powers would be possible in the absence of a hegemon.[3] Charles W. Kegley, Jr., captured the optimism that pervaded much of the literature when he wrote:

> The post-Cold War world no longer has ideological fissures and an unrestrained arms race to preoccupy its attention and encourage a fixation on power politics. . . . The afterglow of the Cold War still flickers, but in its dwindling light are visible the outlines of a potentially new system in which the questions that realism asks (and the answers it provides) may become increasingly less relevant. Instead, increasingly applicable and appropriate may be an image of world politics remarkably consistent with that portrayed by Woodrow Wilson seventy-five years ago.[4]

Realists, too, acknowledged the extraordinary changes in global politics, but very few believed the collapse of the Soviet Union and the end of the cold war had created the conditions necessary for the construction of collective security organizations. For realists, events since 1989, while significant, did not usher in a demonstrably new period in international politics.[5] For realists, the "laws" of anarchy, sovereignty, and relative power calculations had not changed, and would not change in the near future, particularly over questions involving armed conflict. Realists denied a convergence of interests among nations in managing security affairs, and consequently rejected the argument that conditions were present in the international system to facilitate institutionally directed responses to violent disputes among nations.[6] Realists have long argued that the functions of international organizations are primarily and disproportionately determined by the organization's dominant powers. Realists do not believe that international organizations can replace a hegemonic state in facilitating cooperation among governments.[7] Unlike neoliberals, realists deny that international organizations can aggregate the strategies and goals of their member states.

The war in the Balkans provides an excellent opportunity to assess the arguments of realists and neoliberals on questions of security cooperation among the major powers and the impact of international organizations during multilateral interventions. In examining these competing theories, this chapter addresses the following questions: Do states have common interests in stemming humanitarian crises and in responding to acts of aggression? How do the interests of the major powers impact multilateral intervention? Do international organizations serve as forums where the interests of member states are aggregated and the strategies of intervention adopted and implemented? In the absence of a hegemonic state, what is the impact of international organizations in mitigating armed conflict?

The following analysis of the Balkans conflict opens by delineating the interests of the United States and the European powers. An appreciation of the interests of these states is key, for the research will demonstrate that fundamental differences between the United States and Europe led various governments to support competing and contradictory intervention strategies. After the major events of the wars in Croatia and Bosnia are discussed, the theoretical assumptions of realism and neoliberalism are evaluated.

WESTERN INTERESTS IN THE BALKAN CONFLICT

The Balkans have long occupied the major powers. In recent years, policymakers in the West were not oblivious to the central role the Balkans played in this century's European wars, and they recognized that large-scale war in the Balkans, potentially involving the Albanians, Macedonians, Greeks, Bulgarians, and Turks, was a general—if not a direct—threat to their national interests. As war waged between Croatia and Serbia in 1991, and between Serbs and Muslims in 1992, the West was compelled to confront a number of issues, including interstate and intrastate war on Europe's immediate periphery; significant casualties and genocidal murder; brutal human rights violations including systematic rape; vast numbers of refugees; and economic upheaval. The West could agree that all of these issues were of great concern. However, neither Washington nor the European capitals equated these events as direct threats to their vital interests. In the absence of a clear threat, the West was unable to develop a coherent and successful intervention strategy in the Balkans.

George Bush had little difficulty identifying threats to U.S. interests in the Persian Gulf, but was unable to find an equally compelling set of interests in the Balkans.[8] As fighting erupted between Serbia and Croatia during June 1991, Bush and senior U.S. military figures publicly stated that the emerging conflict in the Balkans did not threaten vital U.S. interests. As a State Department official observed during an interview, "Bush comes out victorious from the Gulf where he was able to specify threats to U.S. interests: oil, Israel, and the whole new world order thing. There was nothing comparable in the Balkans during 1991 and 1992."[9] In July 1992, President Bush attended the annual meetings of the Western European Union (WEU) and the Conference on Security and Cooperation in Europe (CSCE) where he stated that while the United States would support humanitarian relief for the region, no U.S. ground forces would join their European counterparts. Arguing that the conflict was primarily a European concern, Bush opposed U.N. intervention and declared that the North Atlantic Treaty Organization (NATO) should not go "out of area."

During his campaign for the presidency in 1992, Bill Clinton criticized the Bush administration's failure to confront Serb aggression. Upon entering the White House, Clinton advocated a policy known as "lift and strike" that would have required lifting the U.N. arms embargo on Bosnian Muslims, and authorizing military air strikes against Serb military positions. While the policy was abandoned in early 1993 because of European opposition, the Clinton White House shared a fundamental concern of the Bush administration, which was the determination not to deploy U.S. troops into the Balkans until a peace settlement had been concluded.

Unlike the United States, the European powers were quick to respond to Serbia's attack on Croatia in 1991. Beyond employing diplomatic and economic measures to bring about an end to hostilities, within the first year of fighting, the British and French deployed 14,000 peacekeeping troops to the region. But this engagement should not be interpreted as a sign that Europe perceived war in the former Yugoslavia as a threat to its vital interests. At no time during the Yugoslavian Conflict were the European governments prepared to intervene with sufficient force to compel a permanent cease-fire. In a July 1992 letter to Lord David Owen, the European Community's chief diplomat in the Balkans, Prime Minister John Major explained that while the British government would participate in diplomatic and peacekeeping efforts to resolve the conflict, a military operation designed to impose a settlement would not be supported. Major wrote: "We are not dealing with an orthodox war, a single enemy, a front line, or clearly identifiable targets. Nor do I detect any support in Parliament or in public opinion for operations which would tie down large numbers of British forces in difficult and dangerous terrain for a long period."[10] The British government maintained that the costs associated with an intervention capable of restoring peace and stability to the region would be intolerably high. British policymakers cited several factors in making the case against large-scale military intervention, including the German experience in the Balkans during World War II, the difficulties in fighting a guerrilla war on Bosnian terrain, and Britain's own ongoing conflict in Northern Ireland. Britain's political leadership reasoned that the conflict in Bosnia was a civil war that would have to play itself out in the region's villages and mountainsides. While the particular views of the European capitals varied,[11] the position of Great Britain was widely shared.

In a compelling study commissioned for the Brookings Institution, Susan Woodward acknowledged that neither Washington nor the European capitals perceived armed conflict in the Balkans as a threat to their vital interests. Aside from this shared perspective, the United States and the European governments were consistently at odds during the war and advocated conflicting intervention strategies. Woodward maintained that the United States largely viewed the crisis as a case of international aggression. Just as Saddam Hussein had crossed internationally recognized borders, Slobodan Milosevic's Serb forces were violating all international norms in their campaign to create a greater Serbia. While the United States was not prepared to employ adequate force to reverse Serb aggression, Washington openly condemned Belgrade and sought to employ measures, short of full-scale military intervention, to punish both Belgrade and the Bosnian Serbs. Washington clearly favored one side in the conflict over another, and it was unable to act as an impartial mediator in settlement negotiations. As Woodward noted, for the United States a cease-fire "was welcome if it was accompanied by a political agreement that reversed [Serb] gains and obtained Serb acceptance of the internationally recognized republics."[12]

The European powers had a markedly different perspective of the conflict. Most European governments viewed the situation in the former Yugoslavia as a civil war in which ethnicity and competing nationalisms were defining factors. Rather than focus on the aggression of one state, the European powers were more inclined to believe that an end to the fighting could only be brought about by a political settlement that was mutually agreeable to Serbs, Croats, and Muslims. It followed that the European governments were prepared to accept the territorial aggrandizement of Serbia and the resulting ethnic partition of Bosnia.

This disagreement between the western powers is central to understanding the pattern of intervention that evolved between 1991 and 1995. By late 1992, the United States was advocating the increased use of peacemaking policies in support of the Muslim Bosnian government.[13] Specifically, the

United States called for the use of air strikes to repel Serb advances on the ground. However, while the United States was willing to employ its aircraft and pilots in action over Bosnia, Washington consistently maintained that no U.S. ground forces would be deployed until a cease-fire and peace agreement were concluded. The European capitals, in contrast, were committed to a traditional peacekeeping intervention, which required impartiality and neutrality on the part of the intervening states. Paris and London were opposed to any U.N. operations that might lead to Serb retaliation against their personnel. In sum:

> The U.S. and the European approaches to the war were . . . in direct conflict. Countries contributing troops to UNPROFOR in Yugoslavia—particularly France and Britain . . . had an interest in preventing decisive military engagement in the war because they had troops on the ground that would be at risk. The result was that . . . [the Europeans] objected, stalled, and weakened each resolution being pressed by the United States that involved the greater use of force.[14]

For the international organizations involved in the Balkans, these contradictory policies inhibited a coherent strategy for intervention. Throughout the war, U.N. and NATO officials were given instructions to implement both peacekeeping and peacemaking. The effect of this confusion will be analyzed below.

CROATIAN-SERBIAN WAR: 1991–1992

American and European diplomacy in the Balkans broke down well before hostilities commenced in 1991.[15] This analysis, however, is limited to western intervention during the armed conflict. Fighting broke out in the Balkans on June 21, 1991, the day following the declarations of independence by the Slovenian and Croatian governments. Combat between Serbia and Slovenia proved to be short lived, but hostilities between Croatia and Serbia continued with great intensity for the next six months.

As news spread that Serb forces had begun military operations against Slovenia and Croatia, the European Community (EC) and CSCE reacted. Representatives from each organization were dispatched to Belgrade and Zagreb, where they urged an immediate cease-fire. Beyond expressing their opposition to armed conflict and offering their good offices for mediation, the EC and the CSCE were not prepared to introduce military units into the conflict. Each body contained security mechanisms, but neither possessed the robust capabilities of the United Nations or NATO. While individual European states maintained independent military forces, multilateral organizations in Europe possessed "no airlift capacity, no independent intelligence collection or surveillance capability, limited combat air force capability, command, and control, and no troops trained for rapid intervention."[16]

While the Bush administration lauded European diplomatic efforts in the summer and fall of 1991, Washington publicly stated that neither U.S. nor NATO ground forces would be considered for military operations in the Balkans. In the absence of U.S. leadership, and an inability on the part of European governments to employ pressure beyond economic and political means, the war continued.

After several months of failed negotiations, the EC turned to the United Nations for assistance in October 1991. The Security Council took two steps toward engaging the conflict. On September 25, 1992, the Security Council adopted Resolution 713, which placed an international arms embargo on all the states of the former Yugoslavia. The Security Council also appointed former U.S. secretary of state, Cyrus Vance, to represent the United Nations in mediation talks between the Serbs and Croats.

Vance's efforts resulted in a cease-fire on November 23, 1991. Two months later, the Security Council created the United Nations Protection Force (UNPROFOR) and agreed to deploy 14,000 peacekeeping troops to the region. A central feature of the Vance Plan was Serb and Croat agreement to a permanent cease-fire and security guarantees for U.N. forces. In presenting the Vance Plan to the Security Council, Secretary-General Boutros Boutros-Ghali acknowledged that the mission's success was predicated "not only on a stable cease-fire but also a clear and unconditional acceptance of the plan by all concerned, with equally clear assurances of their readiness to cooperate in its implementation."[17] With this pledge in hand, the U.N. mission to Croatia was based on traditional peacekeeping guidelines. Specifically, the mission was to oversee the disbanding and withdrawal of all warring parties; supervise local police forces and ensure that basic human rights were protected; and assist international humanitarian agencies in managing the return of refugees.

WAR IN BOSNIA

Many observers regarded the Vance Plan as the beginning of a general peace for the Balkan region. This optimism quickly faded as events unfolded in Bosnia. Following the lead of Croatia and Slovenia, the Bosnian government declared its desire to secede from the Yugoslav Federation in fall 1991; and in late February 1992, the vast majority of Bosnian Muslims and Croats voted for secession. Within weeks of the independence vote, Serb forces began to seize Bosnian territory and expel Muslims and Croats from their homes. On April 6, 1992, Serb forces began shelling Sarajevo, and the Bosnian war commenced with great fury.

As fighting increased during the summer of 1992, it became clear that the Vance Plan was not the beginning of a regional peace process. Indeed, the growing number of civilian casualties reignited western concerns that the entire Balkan peninsula was on the verge of wide-spread conflagration. In June, the United Nations negotiated an agreement among the combatants permitting the deployment of 1,100 peacekeeping troops to the Sarajevo airport. The airport was a vital link in the delivery of humanitarian supplies, and Serb shelling of the facility resulted in regular shutdowns. The Serbs continued their attacks on the airport after the arrival of U.N. troops, and as relief personnel came under fire, additional U.N. troops were deployed. In the face of ongoing attacks by Serb forces, in September 1992 the Security Council formally established the United Nations Protection Force II (UNPROFOR II). The mission's mandate authorized U.N. troops to support the U.N. High Commissioner for Refugees (UNHCR) in its effort to deliver humanitarian supplies and to facilitate a peaceful resolution to the fighting. Throughout the fall, multilateral peacekeeping units began arriving in Bosnia. However, the presence of these troops, including forces from Great Britain and France, did not deter the Serbs from continuing hostile acts. Indeed, beyond attacking Muslim communities, the U.N. mission itself came under attack. Serb failure to comply with the U.N. mission was systematic and overt. Beyond shelling U.N. bases and sniping at peacekeeping troops, the Serbs refused to permit the delivery of food and medical supplies to civilians. Operating under strict U.N. guidelines, peacekeeping troops seldom responded to these provocative acts.

As Serb aggression continued, the United States advocated the use of air strikes against Serb positions. Concurrently, Washington maintained that no U.S. ground forces would be dispatched to the region. This policy was resisted by the Europeans. With thousands of troops in Bosnia operating under traditional U.N. peacekeeping guidelines, the British and French did not want to alter the U.N.'s formal commitment to neutrality. The Europeans reasoned that their troops would become much more susceptible to attack if the Serbs perceived that U.N. forces were actively supporting the cause of Bosnian independence. French diplomats argued that if U.S. planes bombed Serb positions, the Serbs would retaliate against French troops on the ground. The French foreign minister, Alain Juppé declared: "There is a division of tasks that I don't think is acceptable—that of some flying in planes and dropping bombs, and others, especially the French, on the ground."[18] This disagreement was at the core of the western failure in the Balkans.

While NATO would eventually play a key role in the Balkan conflict, the organization was reluctant to become engaged during the early stages. Due to the American government's dominant position within the Atlantic Alliance, the Bush administration opposed NATO participation. A State Department official confided: "If NATO became involved on the ground it would be virtually impossible to prevent the introduction of U.S. forces in Bosnia."[19] However, the initial U.S. opposition to NATO intervention waned as the United Nations and the EC proved unable to manage the conflict. In response to requests made by the United Nations, NATO agreed to deploy warships in the Adriatic to enforce the international arms embargo during fall 1992. As fighting continued into the winter, NATO governments agreed to expand their involvement in the Balkans to include support for "peacekeeping" operations in Bosnia. During the next three years, the NATO "peacekeeping" involvement would include: (1) monitoring the naval blockade in the Adriatic; (2) enforcing the no fly zone; and (3) implementing the U.N. pledge to protect safe zones. NATO involvement was welcomed by the United Nations and the Europeans but the organization's participation was not without controversy. As will be demonstrated below, the United Nations and the Europeans hoped that the NATO commitment would pressure the United States to increase its involvement in the conflict, possibly compelling the United States to introduce ground forces. However, the United States envisioned a more restricted mission for NATO, which was to implement the air strikes that Washington favored.

Disagreement between the United States and the Europeans, and the associated problems involving the United Nations and NATO, can be demonstrated by analyzing UNPROFOR II efforts to establish safe zones in Bosnia. After a year of fighting in which Serb forces had employed the tactics of ethnic cleansing, rape detention centers, and indiscriminate shelling of Bosnian cities, the United Nations responded with the establishment of "safe zones." Safe zones were conceived as a means of guaranteeing the inhabitants of six Bosnian cities (Tuzla, Zepa, Gorazde, Bihac, Srebrenica, and Sarajevo) a ready supply of food and medicine, and the knowledge that their cities would be secure from Serb aggression. In establishing safe zones during April and May 1993, the Security Council authorized UNPROFOR to use force in resisting and preventing ongoing Serb attacks.[20]

In presenting the safe-zone concept to the Security Council, Secretary-General Boutros Boutros-Ghali argued that 34,000 additional U.N. troops would be needed, but stated that 7,600 would be sufficient for a "light option." With the United States continuing to rule out the deployment of its armed forces, the burden of deploying additional troops fell to the Europeans and other U.N. member states. Eventually 3,500 new troops were sent to defend the six safe zones, but the numbers remained insufficient to repel Serb advances. By October 1993, the United Nations was forced to abandon its commitment to Srebrenica, Gorazde, and Bihac. All six U.N. safe zones remained under continuing siege well into 1995.

During summer 1995, Serb forces overran the cities of Srebrenica and Zepa, and several thousand civilians were systematically shot. In response to the Serb attacks, the United Nations authorized NATO to conduct limited air strikes against Serb positions. The Serbs reacted by taking over three-hundred U.N. peacekeepers hostage, which was precisely the response Paris and London had feared since the United States had first advocated the use of air strikes. Events culminated on August 28, when a Serb mortar shell landed in Sarajevo, killing thirty-seven and wounding many more. In response, the western powers abandoned their internal differences over peacekeeping and peacemaking and agreed to a massive bombing campaign on Serb positions throughout Bosnia. During the first two weeks of September, NATO flew 3,400 air sorties over Bosnia attacking a variety of Serb targets including radar, command bunkers, bridges, and ammunition dumps. Bombing did not cease until September 20, when the Serb leadership agreed to terminate hostile actions and participate in peace talks.[21]

THE DAYTON PEACE PROCESS

Following the West's bombing campaign, the presidents of Serbia, Bosnia, and Croatia negotiated an end to the wars in the former Yugoslavia at an American air force base in Dayton, Ohio. After weeks of acrimonious debate, the three presidents signed the Dayton Peace Agreement on December 21, 1995. The agreement included two primary components, one focusing on maintaining the current cease-fire and the role of NATO in guaranteeing that cease-fire; and the second, a comprehensive plan for rebuilding the Bosnian nation-state. The security component of the Dayton Agreement, known as the Implementation Force (IFOR), might best be described as a hybrid between peacekeeping and peacemaking. As in traditional peacekeeping, multilateral forces were to be deployed into a country where a cease-fire had been established, and the combatants had agreed to cooperate with peacekeeping forces. IFOR also contained components that more closely resembled peacemaking operations. First, IFOR was not under direct U.N. authority, as had been the case in previous peacekeeping operations. IFOR was to be administered by NATO, and its forces were under the command of an American general. In past operations, the U.N. deployed limited numbers of lightly armed forces into countries and regions. The American general responsible for IFOR would oversee a command of 60,000 troops, including 32,000 Americans, equipped with heavy armor and supported by U.S. naval and air units. In delegating responsibility to NATO for the implementation of the Dayton security accords, the United Nations agreed to NATO's command and control structure, which permitted NATO commanders wide discretion in the use of force to implement their mission.

Beyond the security components, the Dayton Agreement also featured a complex and multifaceted nation-building framework. Working in close association with the Organization for Security and Cooperation in Europe (OSCE), the United Nations agreed to facilitate refugee relocation, design and administer elections, monitor human rights, and supervise the dispersing of international monies committed to rebuilding Bosnia's war-torn infrastructure.

While NATO has largely succeeded in keeping peace in the region, the nation-building components of Dayton have not faired as well. Two key components of the agreements were the return of refugees and the administration of free and fair elections. By all accounts, few refugees have been permitted to return to their original homes. In September 1996, elections were held throughout Bosnia, however owing to widespread voter fraud, few international observers were satisfied with the results.

As of early 1997, the situation in Bosnia still remains tense. While NATO's presence in Bosnia has been extended through June 1998, many observers believe that fighting will resume once international troops are withdrawn. At present, it is not clear that a Croat-Muslim Federation will hold. In addition, sporadic fighting has erupted between Serbs, Muslims, and Croats. With the parties incapable of political compromise, much of the promised international financial assistance has been suspended.

ASSESSING THE THEORETICAL DEBATE

Interests of the Major Powers

In analyzing the post-cold-war system, realists denied that events had created the necessary conditions for states to view their vital interests in a common light. Realists rejected the neoliberal argument that the emerging system would be one in which international organizations could play a significant role in ameliorating armed conflicts among nations. Examination of the Balkans conflict largely comports with the realist argument. The western governments and international organizations that engaged the conflict did so for a variety of reasons. The wars in the Balkans witnessed human rights violations not perpetrated in Europe since World War II. While limited to the states of the former Yugoslavia, the conflict threatened to spread to other countries in the region, which would further exacerbate mass flows of refugees and economic upheaval. However, western concern for these issues was not translated into a belief that the wars in the Balkans threatened the West's vital security interests.

Had the West chosen to engage the warring parties in the Balkans, adequate military force was available in western Europe and North America to compel a cease-fire at any stage of the conflict:

> As fighting erupted in the Yugoslav Federation, the NATO countries together accounted for two-thirds of the world's gross national product. They had been spending close to $500 billion a year on their armed forces, which, counting those of the United States, numbered close to 4 million at the beginning of 1992. They had overwhelming force at their disposal. In Bosnia, they were opposed only by remnants of the Yugoslav armed forces and by armed local bands of small size.[22]

During the Gulf War, the West dispatched a vast force to the Middle East, and yet, rather miraculously, casualties and loss of resources were extraordinarily light for the allied coalition. However, had the major powers militarily engaged the Balkan combatants, loss of life and physical resources undoubtedly would have been great. This overriding and quite comprehensible factor is insightful when trying to account for the inability of western governments and international organizations to intervene successfully in the Balkans conflict. While it was in the general interest of most nations to see a resolution to the war, no nation viewed the conflict as a direct threat to its national interests, a development that would have caused nations to mobilize and respond.

The four-year war in the Balkans and the West's experience in Somalia have caused many neoliberals to reevaluate the optimism that pervaded so much of the school's writings in the early 1990s. Neoliberals could assert today that their theory should not be condemned in light of the Yugoslavian conflict, because neoliberalism shares the realist belief that the major powers will not cooperate unless their interests coincide. As the major powers held competing views of the Balkan conflict, neoliberalism would not anticipate cooperation. However, if neoliberalism was correct in its assumption that post-cold-war conditions created an environment conducive to shared interests among the major powers, then the Balkans was an excellent test of that assumption. For if these conditions were present, why did the major powers fail to cooperate? During the Balkan conflict, the West was confronted with a war of aggression involving tactics ranging from ethnic cleansing to systematic sexual assault. If the major powers had a common interest in responding to acts of aggression as the neoliberals asserted in the early 1990s, it would be difficult to come up with a better case for action than the 1991–1995 war in the Balkans. The failure of the West to respond effectively to this war casts great doubt over neoliberalism's primary assumption regarding cooperation in the post-cold-war era.

Role of International Organizations

Among realists, John Mearsheimer is a well-known critic of the assertion that international organizations can regulate the relations among nations. Mearsheimer has argued that international organizations simply reflect the interests of the great powers and the distribution of power in the global system. From Mearsheimer's perspective, "institutions are not an important cause of peace. They matter only on the margins . . . and thus hold little promise for promoting stability in the post-Cold War world."[23]

Neoliberals have responded to Mearsheimer's criticism by noting that the theory does not envision international organizations imposing policies on nation-states or possessing the ability to engage successfully every international question or crisis. However, international organizations can facilitate cooperation by providing an ongoing forum where member states exchange information and seek mutually advantageous policy outcomes. In this environment international organizations possess the ability to aggregate the individual preferences of member states and forge common policies and strategies. When successful in promoting consensus, international organizations can be expected to coordinate the resources of states and design and implement strategies to achieve the common goals of various governments.

Three international organizations were actively engaged in the Yugoslavian conflict: the United Nations, the European Union, and NATO. That these organizations served as forums for debate and transmission of information is not in doubt; their archives document that hardly a day passed between 1991 and 1995 without some sort of organizational activity on the

Balkans. The United Nations, NATO, and the EU served as the primary western agents for transmitting hundreds of millions of dollars in humanitarian aid to the region, the deployment of thousands of relief workers and peacekeepers, the identification of war criminals, and diplomatic action designed to end the fighting. In the end, it was NATO that finally brought the warring parties to the bargaining table after unleashing a punishing bombardment upon Serb forces in fall 1995.

Having delineated the contributions of the international organizations, it may seem a contradiction to argue that the international organizations that engaged the Balkans conflict largely failed to ameliorate the fighting; yet that is the consensus of most participants and observers. Throughout the conflict, the United Nations was unable to aggregate the policy preferences of its member states. This analysis has demonstrated the fundamental differences between the United States and Europe over peacekeeping and peacemaking. Divisions became apparent by 1992, and in the following three years the United Nations was unable to forge a coherent intervention policy agreeable to the western powers. Not only was the United Nations unable to aggregate policy preferences, but the organization consistently supported peacekeeping over peacemaking, and repeatedly took steps to thwart the adoption of peacemaking tactics. In this manner, the United Nations became a partisan in an internal debate among its members.

The desire of the United Nations to restrict intervention to peacekeeping was thoroughly understandable. The major powers gave no indication that they were prepared to contribute the forces necessary for either a successful collective security intervention or peacemaking intervention. However, the adherence to the principle of neutrality, and the restrictions placed on U.N. peacekeepers that virtually prevented U.N. troops from acting in self-defense, did considerable harm to the credibility of the organization. For an international organization successfully to engage a conflict, the combatants must have some level of respect for the organization. As events transpired in the Balkans, it became clear that the warring parties held the U.N. mission in contempt. Serb defiance of the United Nations manifested itself in a variety of forms, including violation of cease-fire agreements, preventing the delivery of humanitarian supplies, obstructing the movement of U.N. troops, and directly firing on U.N. personnel. In the effort to bring peace to the Balkans, 204 U.N peacekeepers were killed between 1991 and 1995.

The Presence or Absence of a Hegemonic State

In his 1984 seminal work, Robert Keohane asserted that cooperation was possible among governments in the absence of a hegemonic state. Keohane argued, "Cooperation can under some conditions develop on the basis of complementary interests, and that institutions, broadly defined, affect the patterns of cooperation that emerge."[24] Realists do not share this neoliberal perspective. Realism maintains that the actions taken by organizations are determined by the most powerful state(s) within the organization. For realists, the functions of international organizations can be explained by analyzing the policy preferences of the organizations' dominant state(s).

I have argued elsewhere that had the United States failed to perceive the Iraqi invasion of Kuwait as a threat to its vital interests, no other state would have been willing or able to lead the international community in reversing Iraqi actions.[25] Throughout most of the Balkan conflict, the United States abstained from leading the international community. Without U.S. leadership, it is difficult to envision an international coalition that could have successfully confronted Serb aggression. Since 1991, west European states have pursued a policy of downsizing their armed forces. Washington also scaled back military spending in the post-cold-war years. However, of the major powers, only the United States maintained the airlift and sealift capabilities necessary to maintain two or three hundred thousand troops in the Balkans. James Gow shares this view, arguing that in the Balkan conflict, "because of the U.S.'s crucial role in NATO, as well as the size of its armed forces, no sizeable military intervention with ground forces was conceivable without U.S. involvement."[26]

A great many nations sought to bring peace to the former Yugoslavia between 1991 and 1995; all the major European states, Russia, and many smaller powers were engaged. The United States participated during these years as well but chose not to exercise leadership. However, when the United States chose to lead, events turned. After coordinating and spearheading a massive air attack, U.S. diplomats forged a cease-fire that was respected by the combatants. After pressing negotiations among the warring parties in Dayton, Ohio, U.S. diplomats brokered a comprehensive peace agreement. And after the United States agreed to deploy 32,000 American troops to Bosnia, fighting has ceased in the region for the first time in five years. On the day the Dayton Peace Agreement was signed, President Clinton declared, "Only NATO can do [the] job and the United States, as NATO's leader, must play an essential role in this mission. Without us, the hard-won peace would be lost. The war would resume. The slaughter of innocents would begin again."[27] While Clinton may be rightly criticized for claiming such credit in light of the overall American record, the message is fundamentally compelling.

IN CLOSING

The title of this book, *The Promise and Reality of European Security Cooperation*, was chosen, in part, to reflect the evolution of scholarly opinion since the collapse of the Berlin Wall. At the outset of the 1990s, many international relations specialists argued that the post-cold-war era would be marked by growing multilateral cooperation and the increasing use of international organizations to facilitate peaceful relations among states. The neoliberal contention that the emerging era would be one of international cooperation and solidarity dissipated as events unfolded in the Balkans, Somalia, Rwanda, and Chechnya. As states and international organizations engaged these conflicts, it became apparent that the hurdles confronting multilateral intervention would be difficult to overcome. The optimism of the early 1990s has faded. The continuing conflicts in the world, and the failure of organizations to engage them effectively, have vindicated the writings of many realist scholars.

International organizations themselves were not responsible for the inability of western governments to cooperate during the Balkan conflict. The explanation for this failure resides with the western governments. The major powers who control the United Nations, the European Union, and NATO did not permit these organizations to engage the conflict successfully because their vital interests were not threatened. As Thomas Weiss has observed, in Bosnia "the United Nations provided a convenient theater for the governments to appear to be doing something without really doing anything substantial to thwart aggression, genocide, and the forced movements of people."[28]

While neoliberals will scrutinize the Yugoslavian conflict seeking to uncover lessons in order to enhance the capabilities of international organizations, realists will argue that the wars in the Balkans illustrate the static quality of international politics. So long as the major powers fail to share common interests regarding a particular crisis, international organizations will not play decisive roles in ameliorating large-scale armed conflict among or within nations.

NOTES

1. Stephen Van Evera, "Primed for Peace: Europe after the Cold War," *International Security* 15, no. 3 (Winter 1990–1991).

2. Peter M. Haas, "Do Regimes Matter? Epistemic Communities and Mediterranean Pollution Control," *International Organization* 43, no. 3 (Summer 1989).

3. Robert Keohane, *After Hegemony: Cooperation and Discord in the World Political Economy* (Princeton: Princeton University Press, 1984).

4. Charles W. Kegley, Jr., "The Neoidealist Moment in International Studies? Realist Myths and the New International Realities," *International Studies Quarterly* 37, no. 2 (June 1993): 134.

5. Joseph Grieco, *Cooperation among Nations: Europe, America, and Non-Tariff Barriers to Trade* (Ithaca: Cornell University Press, 1990).

6. Richard Betts, "Systems for Peace or Causes of War? Collective Security, Arms Control, and the New Europe," *International Security* 17, no. 1 (Summer 1992).

7. Bruce Russett, "The Mysterious Case of Vanishing Hegemony; or, Is Mark Twain Really Dead?" *International Organization* 39, no. 2 (Spring 1985).

8. Michael Gordon, "Powell Delivers a Resounding No on Use of Force in Bosnia," *New York Times,* 28 September 1992, A1.

9. Author's confidential interview with U.S. State Department official (1995).

10. Major as cited in David Owen, *Balkan Odyssey* (New York: Harcourt Brace and Company, 1995), 18.

11. Differentiating the individual policies of London, Paris, Bonn, and Rome is beyond the scope of this chapter. For an excellent study, see Lawrence Freedman's, *Military Intervention in European Conflicts* (London: Blackwell Publishers, 1994).

12. Susan Woodward, *Balkan Tragedy: Chaos and Dissolution after the Cold War* (Washington, DC: The Brookings Institution, 1995), 8.

13. "The term peacemaking is used to cover those activities falling between peacekeeping and war-fighting. . . . Unlike pure war-fighting, where the goal is to inflict significant destruction on the adversary, peacemaking is carried out with measurable restraint. Much greater emphasis is placed on limiting the scope of combat . . . and on restoring and creating an environment in which resistance to a peace accord will become marginal and allow peacekeepers to operate." Richard Haass, *Intervention: The Use of American Military Force in the Post-Cold War World* (Washington, DC: The Brookings Institution, 1994), 59.

14. Susan Woodward, *Balkan Tragedy*, 297.

15. Many observers have argued that by failing to intervene forcefully in 1991, as Serb units were devastating Croatian civilian centers, the West missed a key opportunity to engage the conflict and prevent its spread to Bosnia.

16. Jonathan Dean, *Ending Europe's Wars: The Continuing Search for Peace and Security* (New York: The Twentieth Century Fund Press, 1994), 282.

17. Boutros Boutros-Ghali, as cited in Mats Berdal, "United Nations Peacekeeping in the Former Yugoslavia," in *Beyond Traditional Peacekeeping*, ed. Donald C. F. Daniel and Bradd Hayes (New York: St. Martin's Press, 1995), 230.

18. Juppé as cited in David Owen, *Balkan Odyssey* (New York: Harcourt Brace Company, 1995).

19. Author's confidential interview, 1995.

20. Many diplomats within the U.N. Department of Peacekeeping Operations opposed the creation of safe zones because in committing to use force to defend the cities, the United Nations would be violating any pretense of neutrality. As David Owen observed, "To defend [safe zones] was coming close to [becoming] a combatant for most troop-contributing governments, and we knew the mandate for the humanitarian forces had been carefully designed to avoid this very situation." *Balkan Odyssey*, 66.

21. It is important to note that Serb positions in Croatia were also under attack in the latter half of 1995. Throughout the late summer and fall, the Croatian army captured the Croat territory lost to the Serbs in 1991. In the process, 150,000 Serbs were expelled from Croatia. It is now widely known that the Croatian army and Bosnia Muslim army units were supplied by foreign governments, including direct aid from Iran.

22. Jonathan Dean, *Ending Europe's Wars: The Continuing Search for Peace and Security*, 334–335.

23. John Mearsheimer, "The False Promise of International Institutions," *International Security* 19, no. 2 (Winter 1994/95), 7.

24. Robert Keohane, *After Hegemony*, 9.

25. Richard E. Rupp, "Cooperation, International Organizations, and Multilateral Interventions in the Post-Cold War Era: Lessons Learned from the Gulf War, the Balkans, Somalia, and Cambodia." (Ph.D. diss., University of California, Santa Barbara, 1996).

26. James Gow, "Nervous Bunnies—The International Community and the Yugoslav War of Dissolution," in *Military Intervention in European Conflicts*, ed. Lawrence Freedman (London: Blackwell Publisher, 1991), 31–32.

27. Michael Gordon, "Clinton's Words: 'The Promise of Peace,' " *New York Times*, 22 November 1995, A7.

28. Thomas G. Weiss, "On the Brink of a New Era? Humanitarian Interventions, 1991–94," *Beyond Traditional Peacekeeping,* 14.

10

Conclusion: Interests, Institutions, and European Security Cooperation

PETER H. LOEDEL AND MARY M. MCKENZIE

As Europe heads into the twenty-first century, the individual snapshots of European security cooperation captured in the various contributions in this volume remain somewhat blurred. Caught between powerful interest- and institutional-based forces, European security cooperation lingers in a transitionary period. On the one hand, states are having difficulty defining their interests in the new security environment; each state examined has devised slightly different solutions to the security dilemma. On the other hand, institutions are also having difficulty defining their missions; NATO, the EU, the WEU, and the OSCE compete with one another for policy and political influence on the European landscape while seeking to define the character of security challenges facing Europe. Indeed, the promise of developing a coherent European security framework remains unfulfilled. The reality suggests that conflicting interests, institutional competition, and unclear conceptions of security and purpose continue to cloud European security cooperation.

Despite the unclear nature of European security cooperation, it is possible to begin to analyze and evaluate security developments in the post-cold-war era. In order to fully capture the totality of security politics in Europe, we argue that scholars must employ several different cameras with differing lenses and perspectives, each camera providing one critical part of the entire picture. As such, this volume—with its emphasis on different perspectives and related subjects—explains the forces that are shaping European security cooperation in the post-cold-war era by fitting the parts (national interests and institutional developments) into the whole (European security cooperation). The piecing together of such a puzzle is necessary due to the interrelationship of state interests and European security institutions.

Thus, we offer a broader understanding of the events shaping European security cooperation that draws on both interest- and institution-based theoretical perspectives. Reviewing the findings of the contributors and evaluating the debate between interest- and institution-based analyses, we are cautiously optimistic that Europe is developing a complicated layer of interlocking institutional arrangements that may provide the embryonic framework of European security cooperation. However, we do not suggest that a final definition of security cooperation has been conclusively settled upon, or that such interlocking institutional arrangements are a panacea for European security cooperation for the decades to come, especially when they rest on a still-shifting foundation. Indeed, the European security landscape has become increasingly unstable and unpredictable. Events in the Balkans, Albania, and continuing NATO-Russian antagonism over enlargement illustrate a new period of unease.

THE THEORETICAL DEBATE: INTERESTS OR INSTITUTIONS?

This volume demonstrates that the existing theoretical debates between realist and institutional (or neoliberal) scholars will continue as long as the empirical evidence presents a mixed picture. More promising is the development of a framework that incorporates them both.

For realists, events since 1990, while important, did not usher in a demonstrably new period of international politics.[1] The laws of anarchy, sovereignty, and relative power calculations have not changed, and international institutions remain primarily and disproportionately determined by the institutions' dominant powers. Conditions were not, and are not, present in the international system to facilitate institutionally directed responses to violent disputes among nations, and convergence of national interests remains elusive. Moreover, institutions do not aggregate the strategies and goals of their member states; rather, they serve as forums for competition between national priorities. Security interdependence does not exist.

Neoliberal scholars, on the other hand, have argued that the post-cold-war era would be marked by growing multilateral cooperation and the increasing employment of international institutions to facilitate cooperative relations among states. The dawning era of European security cooperation would be characterized by shared security interests. A multiplicity of factors were cited by neoliberals in asserting that state interests were converging: the growing commitment to democratic principles, the general movement toward free markets, the belief that unilateral military force was no longer a legitimate means to advance policy goals. Common interests would prevail, enhanced by the network of multilateral international institutions that would induce international cooperation leading even to the development of cooperative security structures.

In our view, neither approach captures the whole story. European security cooperation cannot be understood with a single stroke from one theoretical brush. In this volume, a much more complicated theoretical picture has emerged.

The chapters by Boilard and Rupp argue persuasively that U.S. interest in European security in general, and U.S. interest in the Balkans more specifically, has been driven by the hard reality of national interests and power politics. First, Boilard critiques U.S. security policy in Europe as afflicted by "double vision." Simultaneously, the United States sees Europe as vital and inconsequential to its interests. Throughout the post-cold-war era, the United States has been searching awkwardly for a redefined role in European security affairs. Recently, though, the Clinton administration has forged a more intelligible policy: NATO restructuring and NATO enlargement. More importantly, the United States has indicated it will continue to lead NATO forcefully in this direction, suggesting that—for the moment—the United States sees that European stability requires U.S. leadership. In this vein, Boilard does not see much chance for a functioning and institutionally independent European security pillar and therefore calls for continued U.S. guidance in structuring European security cooperation.

Rupp presents a compelling realist account of the tragedy of the Balkans. He assesses the arguments of realists and neoliberals on the question of security cooperation among the major powers and the impact of international institutions during multilateral interventions in the former Yugoslavia. For Rupp, the disorder in the Balkans can be easily understood: the war did not threaten the West's vital security interests. As a result, western states did not respond to the crisis and the tragedy that developed. Moreover, while international institutions were actively engaged in the Balkans, Rupp suggests that their "failure" resulted from differences among their member states, not from any sort of inherent inability on the part of institutions. Institutional competition (especially between the U.N. and NATO) may have contributed to Serbian aggression and the West's weakened and damaged reputation, but this competition was due in part to competing interests of member states. Based on the Yugoslav case, Rupp's prognosis is pessimistic: European security cooperation suffered a serious setback with its failure to prevent conflict in Europe. The case for future security interventions, in Europe or elsewhere, will be more difficult to make.

The chapter by Huebner-Monien suggests that Russian security policy also has shifted dramatically from an institution-based policy toward calculations of national interest and power relationships. After the disintegration of the Soviet Union, the Russians appeared intent on pursuing the "good European" option. Multilateralism and institutionalism would guide Russia's policy coherently into the waiting arms of western Europe. An alphabet soup of institutional arrangements—the GATT/WTO, IMF, G-7/8, EU, and the OSCE—tempted the palette of Russian diplomats. Russia, however, soon realized that the old cold-war divisions, mind-sets, and relationships remained. Europe was not quite ready to include the Russians, and the United States apparently saw NATO expansion—against Russian protests—as an appropriate response to instability in eastern and central Europe. In the Russian view, western institutions were not providing the path to peace and prosperity in the post-cold-war era. Rather, the old cold-war structures of European security were merely rearranged around existing U.S.-Russian power calculations of interest in the region. Protestations from U.S. diplomats notwithstanding, one could argue that new geostrategic lines are being drawn between former enemies. With the West set to enlarge, and Russia set to secure its influence in the "near abroad" and Eurasia, the iron curtain may be dropping once again, albeit along the western borders of the old Soviet Union.

Moreover, the chapters by Ladrech and Loedel indicate that the "middle" powers of Europe, France and Germany, have yet to clearly define their security policies or finally determine their interests in Europe. Both countries have struggled to find a new role amid dramatic transformation. Both countries also are torn between competing conceptions of security policy, driven in part by interest-based calculations of national security and institutional variables, especially the requirements of European integration. One can argue that France's conception of security policy and its role in European security cooperation tends toward a more interest-based policy, while German efforts at defining security policy and finding its proper role have been marked by a hesitancy to define national interests and have tended to be driven more by institutional constraints. In both cases, one cannot argue unequivocally that either an interest-based or a fully institution-based model satisfactorily explains their emergent policies.

Specifically, the choices facing the French are quite dramatic: continue to pursue an interest-based policy built on the concepts of grandeur, autonomy, and sovereignty; or pursue a much more institutionally driven and integrated European security option. The options could not be more dramatically drawn—both theoretically and politically. The choice pursued by France is, of course, much more complicated than this dichotomy suggests. As Ladrech aptly illustrates, France has dithered between poles, driven by the powerful domestic continuities of French security policy and the marked changes facing France in Europe—economically, military-strategically, and politically. In the Balkans, France pursued a strongly interest-based policy seeking to assert French historical connections to the region. France's decision partially to initiate nuclear testing in the Pacific, albeit not related to "Europe" per se, also carried on the tradition of autonomy and grandeur. Yet, France's decision to reintegrate into NATO decisionmaking, the offer to "share" its nuclear option with other Europeans, and France's strong push for a more independent WEU force indicate a noticeable change in the contours of French security policy. In each case, institutions of Europe defined the course of French policy. Finally, domestic financial pressures—primarily the result of macroeconomic decisions surrounding the French desire to proceed with European monetary union—have forced the French to rethink defense and armaments spending. In sum, internal and external pressures have constrained the various options available to French policymakers.

For Germany, security policy remains bound by the powerful continuities of a successful cold-war multilateral policy and the demands both within Germany and by some of its partners to play a more "normal" role in European security policy. As the contribution by Loedel emphasized, Germany has not found the policy equilibrium between an interest- or institutional-based policy. Instead, ambiguity, tentativeness and outright confusion characterize the direction of German security policy. Certainly, Germany's attempt to formulate a more "normal" security policy—ostensibly based on a more "interest"-based policy—has not found its mark. Moreover, Germany's attempt to please its partners, from the United States, to France, and including Russia, has led each to wonder in which direction German security policy will lean in the future. This confusion carries over into the institutional preferences of German security policy: will it be NATO, the EU/WEU, or the OSCE that will continue the pattern of German security institutionalization? While NATO appears to be the most recent dominant strain of German security policy, the logic of European integration and the importance of bilateral German-Russian relations suggest that a NATO-first policy might be temporary. Again, theoretically and empirically, Germany presents a commingled container of security policy.

The chapters that elaborated on the institutional components of European security cooperation add a necessary layer of complexity to this picture. They also support the notion that Europe's security institutions are both shaping and being shaped by state behavior. McKenzie's chapter on the European Security and Defense Identity (ESDI) finds that progress toward the construction of an independent European security pillar likely will continue to be halting. The process is characterized by a complex institutional web and by divergent conceptions of purpose. Exacerbating these differences is the structural dualism already inherent in the WEU qua European pillar, envisioning it as the avenue for a European security identity at the same time as the "bridge" between the EU and NATO. The result of such confusion will be a continued reliance on intergovernmentalism and continued confusion over ESDI's proper place in the new European security order. In the short term, this will likely lead to a continued subservience of a purely European security organization to NATO and a continued reliance on intergovernmentalism, compromise, and—at bottom—national interest.

The OSCE, as outlined by Rupp and McKenzie, has played an important role in the post-cold-war security transition in Europe. Although its member states have remained hesitant to endow the organization with operational capabilities in the security realm, they have at the same time agreed to a series of institutional changes that have enabled the OSCE to act (albeit on a small scale) in the conflicts that have emerged in the states of the former Soviet Union and parts of central Europe. These reforms have fallen far short of the desires of the organization's most adamant and ardent supporters, but they have also assured that the OSCE has a significant role to play in conflict prevention, arbitration, and trust building. By virtue of its perceived objectivity and even neutrality, the OSCE can accomplish these tasks far more readily than NATO, an important consideration in addressing the uproar caused by its plans for enlargement. Further, because of its linkage of the international and domestic components of security, the OSCE embodies true security interdependence.

The OSCE's role has been bolstered by the success of arms control regimes under its auspices, although Graeme Auton cautions that these measures may be losing their support as the consensus underlying them in Europe withers away. Developments in NATO as well as the different perceptions of the role of the OSCE among the member states are exerting pressure on these arms control regimes that are so central to European security cooperation. In the current transitional order in Europe, Auton senses an increasing inability of the states involved to reach concrete and meaningful arms control agreements, suggesting that even well-defined and specific goal-oriented institutions are not enough to induce further cooperation on the part of states when interests collide and when uncertainty comes to the fore.

SYNTHESIS: A NEW MODEL?

In the introduction to this volume, we argued, first, that states conceptualize their own understanding of security and seek to provide a level of security commensurate with their perceived national interests. Second, each state's definition of security is not determined in a vacuum and must incorporate existing and possibly new institutional arrangements that can impact state behavior. The explanation of European security cooperation set forth here incorporates both sets of premises and includes both interest- and institution-based variables. We contend that rigid adherence to either a state-level or institutional-level conceptualization of European security cooperation fails to capture the ongoing transition in security policy. While a full "synthesis" of both approaches is impossible,[2] we do not consider it impractical to employ both perspectives in a comprehensive survey of European security cooperation.

Our conceptualization of institutions as both dependent and independent variables further supports the contention that there is no sole legitimate way to explain European security cooperation. As dependent variables, institutional arrangements have resulted from state priorities and interests. In the post-cold-war era, states have felt that security could be enhanced and that they would benefit by restructuring existing institutions (such as the OSCE, the WEU, and of course, NATO) or by constructing new institutional mechanisms (such as the HCNM or CJTFs). Most reforms have sought to enable these institutions to meet the new challenges of European security, although radical change continually has been inhibited by the norms of consensus and intergovernmentalism. Some states have emphasized strengthening particular institutions to serve their interests. For instance, the United States forcefully has pushed for NATO adaptation and enlargement. The Russians, in turn, have resisted NATO adaptation and enlargement—at least on the West's terms—and instead have sought to strengthen the OSCE. The French have tinkered with the notion of NATO, but also have played with both the EU/WEU and the OSCE as security options. The Germans' own search for normalization—including a more interest-based policy—has found instead a confused ambiguity that indicates that Germany has not yet defined its national interests—which may just suit its neighbors.

As independent variables, institutions are important for how they are shaping the security interests of states and how they are fostering European security cooperation. Despite the problems associated with defining new missions and mandates on the part of various security institutions, these institutions were neither weakened nor abandoned. In fact, the institutional arena has determined in large measure the ongoing efforts by all major states to develop a comprehensive framework for European security cooperation. Institutions such as NATO, the EU/WEU, and the OSCE provide the parameters for state action in European security and cultivate specific norms of behavior among member states. They also promulgate a conception of security that demands specific actions. Cooperation then emerges on the basis of shared interests and a recognition of security interdependence. In this way, institutions affect the patterns of cooperation among states.

The OSCE's broad conceptualization of security, with its basis in domestic concerns and conflict prevention, represents the clearest example of this ability of institutions to shape state behavior. Institutionally, it advances state acceptance of the norms of democracy and human rights by promoting unintrusive intervention mechanisms and preserving its objectivity. NATO, on the other hand, continues to emphasize its role in collective defense—despite significant reform—thus promoting a conceptualization of security as "us versus them" or as one that continues to be based on national interests. This has resulted in institutional competition in European security cooperation.

While one might argue that a proliferation of institutions would enhance the potential for cooperation, the reality of the 1990s has shown that institutional competition makes it difficult for various institutions and states to function together. While most successful institutions such as the EU and NATO have developed internal mechanisms to minimize potential divisiveness, there is no such external mechanism performing this crucial function among institutions. Only recently have states focused on clarifying the institutional, political, and functional linkages within the institutional milieu of European security. What is necessary is to further develop clear institutional connections and lines of communication among the OSCE, the EU, the WEU, and NATO.

One way to mitigate against the forces of institutional competition is to legitimize the concept of "interlocking institutions." With the proliferation of institutions, a division of labor is necessary to ensure the compatibility of state interests and institutional roles. Institutions should clearly reflect the responsibilities they carry in the process of European security cooperation. As institutions are rebuilt, it is also imperative that they reflect a clear purpose based on a shared understanding of security among their member states. Only with a forcefully articulated statement of institutional responsibility and purpose and a division of labor can a credible cooperative security framework emerge within which states are comfortable in exercising power and interests. This could result, as Auton suggests, in a multilayered security architecture that incorporates institutional links among diverse multilateral institutions.

In other words, we are suggesting that we need to employ a model that recognizes the interaction between state interests and institutions in order to explain developments in European security cooperation.[3] States will define their interests based on their conception of security and remake security institutions based on these priorities. But it must be recognized at the same time the opportunities such institutional change offers for redefining and even restructuring state interests and behavior. The model we present here emphasizes the dual capacity of institutions as independent and dependent variables. In practice, this means that institutions can serve a vital linkage function between national and collective interests. Much work remains, however, before such a scenario can be fully realized.

CONCLUDING THOUGHTS

We argue that if we are to construct a credible security framework for Europe in the coming years, it is important that we develop an understanding of the dynamic between national interest and security interdependence within the institutional framework of European security. Our hope has been to clarify the complex and underlying connections and relationships that are giving rise to and shaping the efforts of states and institutions in creating a viable security architecture. While the analyses in this volume do not immediately lend themselves to the argument that the best solution or approach to European security cooperation has been found, we believe that we have begun the process of explaining the forces—both interest and institutionally focused—that are shaping European security issues.

Some of the arguments presented in this volume may appear excessively pessimistic about the future of European security cooperation; other arguments suggest that there exists much room for optimism about the future. While much of the European landscape remains unchanged, we live in an era of major historical discontinuities comparable to the transitions of the immediate post-WWII period or even the coming of the modern age in the sixteenth and seventeenth centuries. The only certain thing we can say about the future is that it remains uncertain, to be shaped by human decisions and actions. Wolfram Hanrieder noted, "The emerging state system in Europe and the world at large is a peculiar amalgam of the past and the present, moving toward an uncertain future. It is multidimensional, contradictory, and in transition."[4] Uncertainty breeds creativity and opportunity; it also breeds indecision and confusion.

We believe, however, that conditions exist that are conducive to developing a comprehensive European security framework for the decades to come. The studies in this volume have highlighted new constraints and opportunities for the conduct of foreign policy. Indeed, redesigning the European security architecture amid radical transformation is laden with both opportunities and risks. We trust that decisionmakers will choose wisely, recognizing the consequence of redefining national interests in a changing institutional context. Too much is at stake for Europe and the transatlantic relationship for them to do otherwise.

NOTES

1. These arguments are presented more thoroughly in chapter 9 of this volume by Richard Rupp.

2. Indeed, our mentor Wolfram Hanrieder would have strongly admonished us for suggesting otherwise.

3. In an examination of American foreign policy, John Gerard Ruggie has argued that a more complex theoretical framework is necessary to understand contemporary world politics. He writes: "[O]ur discussion demonstrates the need for contending theoretical approaches in international relations scholarship systematically to engage one another, specifying under which conditions what combinations of factors best account for outcomes in the world of actual international relations. Doing so requires that we abandon the quest for monocausality that is characteristic of so much theoretical work of the past decade." "The Past as Prologue? Interests, Identity, and American Foreign Policy," *International Security* 21, no. 4 (Spring 1997): 89–125; the citation appears on p. 124.

4. Wolfram Hanrieder, *Germany, America, Europe. Forty Years of German Foreign Policy* (New Haven: Yale University Press, 1989), 375.

Selected Bibliography

Adomeit, Hannes. "Russia as a 'Great Power' in World Affairs: Images and Reality." *International Affairs* 71, no. 1 (January 1995): 35–68.

Aragona, Giancarlo. "Lisbon and Beyond: The OSCE in the Emerging European Security Architecture." *NATO Review* 45, no. 2 (March 1997): 7–10.

Arbatov, Alexei. "NATO and Russia." *Security Dialogue* 26, no. 2 (1995): 135–146.

———. "Russia's Foreign Policy Alternatives." *International Security* 18, no. 2 (Fall 1993): 5–43.

Archer, Clive. *Organizing Europe: The Institutions of Integration.* London: Edward Arnold, 1994.

Archer, Clive, and Fiona Butler. *The European Community: Structure and Process.* New York: St. Martin's Press, 1992.

Auton, Graeme P., ed. *Arms Control and European Security.* New York: Praeger, 1989.

Baldwin, David A. "Security Studies and the End of the Cold War." *World Politics* 48 (October 1995): 117–141.

———, ed. *Neorealism and Neoliberalism: The Contemporary Debate.* New York: Columbia University Press, 1993.

Barry, Charles. "NATO's Combined Joint Task Forces in Theory and Practice." *Survival* 38, no. 1 (Spring 1996): 81–97.

Becker, Thorsten. *Schönes Deutschland.* Berlin: Verlag Volk & Welt, 1996.

Bertram, Christoph. *Europe in the Balance: Securing the Peace Won in the Cold War.* Washington, DC: Carnegie Endowment for International Peace, 1995.

Betts, Richard K. "Systems for Peace or Causes of War? Collective Security, Arms Control, and the New Europe." *International Security* 17, no.1 (Summer 1992): 5–43.

Birnbaum, Karl E., and Ingo Peters, eds. *Zwischen Abgrenzung und Verantwortungsgemeinschaft. Zur KSZE-Politik der beiden deutschen Staaten 1984–1989.* Baden-Baden: Nomos, 1991.

Carnovale, Marco, ed. *European Security and International Institutions after the Cold War.* New York: St. Martin's Press, 1995.

Carpenter, Ted Galen. *Beyond NATO: Staying Out of Europe's Wars.* Washington, DC: CATO Institute, 1994.

Chafer, Tony, and Brian Jenkins, eds. *France: From the Cold War to the New World Order.* London: Macmillan, 1996.

Chayes, Abram, and Antonia Handler Chayes, eds. *Preventing Conflict in the Post-Communist World. Mobilizing International and Regional Organizations.* Washington, DC: The Brookings Institution, 1996.

Chernov, Vladislav. "View from Russia. The Expansion of NATO and the Future of the CFE Treaty." *Comparative Strategy* 14 (1995): 87–90.

Clough, Michael. "Grass Roots Policymaking: Say Good-Bye to the 'Wise Men.' " *Foreign Affairs* 73, no. 1 (1994).

Cotti, Flavio. "The OSCE's Increasing Responsibilities in European Security." *NATO Review* 44, no. 6 (1996): 7–12.

Crawford, Beverly, ed. *The Future of European Security.* Berkeley: U.C. Center for German and European Studies, 1992.

Crawford, Dorn. *Conventional Armed Forces in Europe (CFE): A Review and Update of Key Treaty Elements.* Washington, DC: U.S. Arms Control & Disarmament Agency, December 1996.

Crow, Suzanne. "Russian Views on an Eastward Expansion of NATO." *RFE/RL Research Reports* 2, no. 41 (15 October 1993): 21–24.

Daniel, Donald C. F., and Bradd Hayes, eds. *Beyond Traditional Peacekeeping.* New York: St. Martin's Press, 1995.

Darilek, Richard F. "The Future of Conventional Arms Control in Europe: A Tale of Two Cities: Stockholm, Vienna." *Survival* 24, no. 1 (January-February 1987).

Dawisha, Added, and Karen Dawisha, eds. *The Making of Foreign Policy in Russia and the New States of Eurasia.* Armonk, NY: M. E. Sharpe, 1995.

Dean, Jonathan. *Ending Europe's Wars: The Continuing Search for Peace and Security.* New York: The Twentieth Century Fund Press, 1994.

Flynn, Gregory, ed. *Remaking the Hexagon: The New France in the New Europe.* Boulder, CO: Westview Press, 1995.

Freedman, Lawrence. *Military Intervention in European Conflicts.* London: Blackwell Publishers, 1994.

Fukuyama, Francis. "The End of History?" *The National Interest* 16 (1989).

Gaddis, John Lewis. "International Relations Theory and the End of the Cold War." *International Security* 17, no. 3 (Winter 1992).

Geipel, Gary. "Germany and the Burden of Choice." *Current History* 94, no. 595 (November 1995): 375–380.

George, Alexander L., Philip J. Farley, and Alexander Dallin, eds. *U.S.-Soviet Security Cooperation: Achievements, Failures and Lessons.* New York: Oxford University Press, 1988.

Gordon, Philip H. *A Certain Idea of France: French Security Policy and the Gaullist Legacy.* Princeton: Princeton University Press, 1993.

———. *France, Germany, and the Western Alliance.* Boulder, CO: Westview Press, 1995.

Grieco, Joseph. *Cooperation among Nations: Europe, America, and Non-Tariff Barriers to Trade*. Ithaca: Cornell University Press, 1990.

Haas, Ernst. *When Knowledge Is Power: Three Models of Change in International Organizations.* Berkeley: University of California Press, 1990.

Haas, Peter M. "Do Regimes Matter? Epistemic Communities and Mediterranean Pollution Control." *International Organization* 43, no. 3 (Summer 1989).

Haass, Richard. *Intervention: The Use of American Military Force in the Post-Cold War World.* Washington, DC: The Brookings Institution, 1994.

Hanrieder, Wolfram F. "Compatibility and Consensus: A Proposal for the Conceptual Linkage of External and Internal Dimensions of Foreign Policy." *American Political Science Review* 61, no. 4 (1967): 971–982.

———. *Germany, America, Europe: Forty Years of German Foreign Policy.* New Haven: Yale University Press, 1989.

Hibbs, Mark. "Tomorrow, a Eurobomb?" *Bulletin of the Atomic Scientists* 52, no. 1 (January-February 1996): 16–23.

Holbrooke, Richard. "America, a European Power." *Foreign Affairs* 74, no. 2 (1995): 38–51.

Howe, Geoffrey. "Bearing More of the Burden: In Search of a European Foreign and Security Policy." *The World Today* 52, no.1 (January 1996): 23–27.

Hunter, Robert. "Enlargement: Part of a Strategy for Projecting Stability into Central Europe." *NATO Review* (May 1995): 3–8.

Hurd, Douglas. "Developing the Common Foreign and Security Policy." *International Affairs* 70, no. 3 (1994): 421–428.

Jervis, Robert. "The Future of World Politics: Will It Resemble the Past?" *International Security* 16, no. 3 (Winter 1991).

Jonson, Lena, and Clive Archer, eds. *Peacekeeping and the Role of Russia in Eurasia.* Boulder, CO: Westview Press, 1996.

Kahler, Miles, and Werner Feld. *Europe & America: A Return to History*. New York: Council on Foreign Relations Press, 1996.

Katzenstein, Peter J., ed. *The Culture of National Security: Norms and Identity in World Politics*. New York: Columbia University Press, 1996.

———. *Tamed Power: Germany in Europe*. Ithaca: Cornell University Press, 1997.

Kegley, Charles W., Jr. "The Neoidealist Moment in International Studies? Realist Myths and the New International Realities." *International Studies Quarterly* 37, no. 2 (June 1993): 131–146.

Kelleher, Catherine McArdle. *The Future of European Security: An Interim Assessment*. Washington, DC: The Brookings Institution, 1995.

Kennan, George F. *Memoirs 1925–1950*. Boston: Little, Brown, 1967.

[George F. Kennan.] "The Sources of Soviet Conduct." By "X." *Foreign Affairs* 25, no. 4 (1947): 566–576.

Keohane, Robert O. *After Hegemony: Cooperation and Discord in the World Political Economy*. Princeton: Princeton University Press, 1984.

———. *International Institutions and State Power: Essays in International Relations Theory*. Boulder, CO: Westview Press, 1989.

Kozyrev, Andrei. "The Lagging Partnership." *Foreign Affairs* 73, no. 3 (May/June 1994): 59–61.

———. "Partnership or Cold Peace?" *Foreign Policy*, no. 99 (Summer 1995): 3–14.

Kramer, Steven Philip. *Does France Still Count? The French Role in the New Europe*. Westport, CT: Praeger, published with the Center for Strategic and International Studies, 1994.

Kupchan, Charles A., and Clifford Kupchan. "Concerts, Collective Security, and the Future of Europe." *International Security* 16, no. 1 (Summer 1991): 114–161.

Laughland, John. "The Philosophy of 'Europe.' " *The National Interest* 39 (1995).

Lebow, Richard Ned. "The Long Peace, the End of the Cold War, and the Failure of Realism." *International Organization* 48, no. 2 (Spring 1994): 249–277.

Lieven, Anatol. "Russia's Opposition to NATO Expansion." *The World Today* (October 1995): 196–199.

Lipschutz, Ronnie D., ed. *On Security*. New York: Columbia University Press, 1995.

MacFarlane, S. Neil. "Russian Conceptions of Europe." *Post-Soviet Affairs* 10, no. 3 (1994): 234–269.

Mandelbaum, Michael. *The Dawn of Peace in Europe*. Washington, DC: Brookings/Twentieth Century Fund, 1996.

McKenzie, Mary M. "Competing Conceptions of Normality in the Post-Cold War Era: Germany, Europe and Foreign Policy Change." *German Politics and Society* 14, no. 2 (Summer 1996): 1–18.

Mearsheimer, John. "Back to the Future: Instability in Europe after the Cold War." *International Security* 15, no. 1 (Summer 1990): 5–56.

———. "The False Promise of International Institutions." *International Security* 19, no. 2 (Winter 1994/95).

Moens, Alexander, and Christopher Anstis, eds. *Disconcerted Europe: The Search for a New Security Architecture.* Boulder, CO: Westview Press, 1994.

Nye, Joseph S. "The Changing Nature of World Power." *Political Science Quarterly* 105, no. 2 (1990).

Owen, David. *Balkan Odyssey.* New York: Harcourt Brace and Company, 1995.

Risse-Kappen, Thomas. *Cooperation among Democracies: The European Influence on U.S. Foreign Policy.* Princeton: Princeton University Press, 1995.

Ruggie, John Gerard, ed. *Multilateralism Matters. The Theory and Praxis of an Institutional Form.* New York: Columbia Universiy Press, 1993.

Russett, Bruce. "The Mysterious Case of Vanishing Hegemony; or, Is Mark Twain Really Dead?" *International Organization* 39, no. 2 (Spring 1985).

Saikal, Amin, and William Maley, eds. *Russia in Search of Its Future.* Cambridge: Cambridge University Press, 1995.

Sestanovich, Stephen. "Inventing the Soviet National Interest." *The National Interest* (Summer 1990): 3–16.

Shearman, Peter, ed. *Russian Foreign Policy since 1990.* Boulder, CO: Westview Press, 1995.

Sperling, James, and Emil Kirchner. *Recasting the European Order: Security Architectures and Economic Cooperation.* Manchester: Manchester University Press, 1997.

Stares, Paul B., ed. *The New Germany and the New Europe.* Washington, DC: Brookings Institution, 1992.

Steele, Richard. *Temptations of a Superpower.* Cambridge, MA: Harvard University Press, 1995.

Stent, Angela, and Lilia Shevtsova. "Russia's Election: No Turning Back." *Foreign Policy*, no. 103 (Summer 1996): 92–109.

Tonelson, Alan, and Robin Gaster. "Our Interests in Europe." *The Atlantic Monthly* 276, no. 2 (1995).

Van Evera, Stephen. "Primed for Peace: Europe after the Cold War." *International Security* 15, no. 3 (Winter 1990–1991).

Walker, Jenonne. *Security and Arms Control in Post-Confrontational Europe.* New York: Oxford University Press, 1994.

Weidenfeld, Werner. *America and Europe: Is the Break Inevitable*? Washington, DC: The Brookings Institution, 1997.

Weiss, Thomas, ed. *Collective Security in a Changing World.* Boulder, CO: Lynne Rienner Publishers, 1993.

Williams, Nick. "Partnership for Peace: Permanent Fixture or Declining Asset?" *Survival* 38, no. 1 (Spring 1996): 98–110.

Woodward, Susan. *Balkan Tragedy: Chaos and Dissolution after the Cold War.* Washington, DC: The Brookings Institution, 1995.

Wyllie, James H. *European Security in the New Political Environment.* Harlow, Essex: Addison Wesley Longman, 1997.

Index

About the Contributors

MARY M. McKENZIE, Editor, is Assistant Professor in Political Science at Grossmont College. She received her Ph.D. in Political Science from the University of California, Santa Barbara, in 1994. Dr. McKenzie has written several papers and articles dealing with the transatlantic relationship and with German foreign policy, including "Competing Conceptions of Normality in the Post-Cold-War Era: Germany, Europe and Foreign Policy Change," in *German Politics and Society* (1996); and *Germany and the Institutions of Collective Security in Europe* (1994). Dr. McKenzie has held numerous research fellowships, including one in European Peace and Security at the Peace Research Institute Frankfurt in 1993–1994. She is an active member of the German-American Research Group and is currently working on a project on U.S.-European relations.

PETER H. LOEDEL, Editor, is Assistant Professor in Political Science at West Chester University. He received his Ph.D. in Political Science from University of California, Santa Barbara in 1994. Dr. Loedel has written several papers, articles, and chapters on German and European monetary policy. Most recent of these appears in the forthcoming *The Federal Republic at Fifty*, edited by Peter H. Merkl. He is currently working on a manuscript entitled *Deutschmark Politics: Germany in the European and International Monetary System.*

GRAEME P. AUTON is Professor of Government at the University of Redlands. He received his Ph.D. in Political Science from the University of California, Santa Barbara, in 1976. In 1980 he coauthored, with Wolfram F. Hanrieder, *The Foreign Policies of West Germany, France, and Britain,* and since then has published numerous articles and edited one book on European security issues. Dr. Auton has been a NATO Research Fellow and a Ford Fellow in European Society and Western Security at the Center for International Affairs, Harvard University. From 1992 to 1993 he served on the staff of the U.S. Arms Control & Disarmament Agency in Washington and Vienna, with principal responsibilities in the area of European security negotiations.

STEVE D. BOILARD is Assistant Professor of Government at Western Kentucky University. He received his Ph.D. in Political Science from the University of California, Santa Barbara, in 1992. He is the author of *Russia at the 21st Century* and *Reinterpreting Russia.*

ERNST-OTTO CZEMPIEL is Professor of International Relations at the University of Frankfurt and a senior analyst at the Peace Research Institute, Frankfurt, where he served as co-director from 1970 until 1996. Professor Czempiel received his Ph.D. in modern history at the University of Mainz in 1956 and has published extensively in both English and German on global politics, American foreign policy, and international organizations. His works include *Governance without Government: Order and Change in World Politics* and *Global Changes, Theoretical Challenges: Approaches to World Politics for the 1990s* (both with James N. Rosenau), *Are Democracies Peaceful? Not Quite Yet*, and *Die Reform der Vereinten Nationen: Mythen und Mißverständnisse.*

SABINE HUEBNER-MONIEN resides in Germany and is a doctoral candidate in Political Science at the University of California, Santa Barbara. She is completing her dissertation, "Russian and American Foreign Policy after the End of the Cold War: The Case of NATO's Eastward Expansion."

ROBERT LADRECH is Lecturer in European Politics in the Politics Department at Keele University, UK. His research interests are European Union studies, West European party politics, and French politics. His most recent publications include "Partisanship and Party Formation in European

Union Politics," in *Comparative Politics*, and "Political Parties in the European Parliament," in *Political Parties and the European Union*. Dr. Ladrech is co-editor of the forthcoming *A Guide to the Social Democratic Parties of the European Union: 1945 to the Present*.

RICHARD E. RUPP received his Ph.D. in Political Science from the University of California, Santa Barbara, in 1996. His work in this volume reflects his interest in international security issues and the Balkans. Dr. Rupp has spent considerable time in Bulgaria and neighboring countries. His primary research interest is the role of international organizations in post-cold-war multilateral interventions.

ISBN 0-275-95949-X
90000>
EAN
9 780275 959494
HARDCOVER BAR CODE